DEVOLUTION AND
SOCIAL CITIZENSHIP
IN THE UK

Edited by Scott L. Greer

This edition published in Great Britain in 2009 by

The Policy Press
University of Bristol
Fourth Floor
Beacon House
Queen's Road
Bristol BS8 1QU
UK

Tel +44 (0)117 331 4054
Fax +44 (0)117 331 4093
e-mail tpp-info@bristol.ac.uk
www.policypress.org.uk

North American office:
The Policy Press
c/o International Specialized Books Services (ISBS)
920 NE 58th Avenue, Suite 300
Portland, OR 97213-3786, USA
Tel +1 503 287 3093
Fax +1 503 280 8832
e-mail info@isbs.com

British Library Cataloguing in Publication Data
A catalogue record for this book is available from the British Library.

Library of Congress Cataloging-in-Publication Data
A catalog record for this book has been requested.

ISBN 978-1-84742-035-0 paperback
ISBN 978-1-84742-036-7 hardcover

The right of Scott L. Greer to be identified as editor of this work has been asserted by him in accordance with the 1988 Copyright, Designs and Patents Act.

The statements and opinions contained within this publication are solely those of the editor and contributors and not of The University of Bristol or The Policy Press. The University of Bristol and The Policy Press disclaim responsibility for any injury to persons or property resulting from any material published in this publication.

The Policy Press works to counter discrimination on grounds of gender, race, disability, age and sexuality.

Cover design by Qube Design Associates
Front cover: image kindly supplied by www.istockphoto.com
Printed and bound in Great Britain by Hobbs the Printers, Southampton

Contents

List of tables and figures

Tables

Figures

Acknowledgements

This book is based on an Economic and Social Research Council (ESRC) workshop held in Edinburgh under the auspices of the Devolution and Constitutional Change programme. My thanks to the programme and to Charlie Jeffery for supporting the initial meeting, and to Lindsay Adams for organising it. Connie Rockman put together the text and filled in all the various complex gaps that arise when a book is being completed; my sincere thanks. It has been a joy to work with The Policy Press, including Philip de Bary, Leila Ebrahimi, Jessica Hughes and Emily Watt, for their extreme patience as well as help and professionalism.

Finally, as editor, I would like to thank the collaborators. This book has evolved through long conversations with each of them. Some edited books are merely assembled by the editor and some are dictated by the editor, but this one was a product of crucial and collegial interactions, and the contributors' advice, in ways I could never have expected.

Notes on contributors

Richenda Gambles is a lecturer in the Department of Social Policy and Social Work, University of Oxford. Her research interests focus on the gendered dynamics of family, informal care and paid employment. She has published a number of journal articles and book chapters in this area and has recently co-authored with Suzan Lewis and Rhona Rapoport *The myth of work–life balance: The challenge of our time for men, women and societies*, published by Wiley (2006). She is currently completing her PhD at the Open University in 'Parenting discourses and experiences'.

Scott L. Greer is Assistant Professor of Health Management and Policy at the University of Michigan School of Public Health, and Senior Research Fellow at LSE Health. A political scientist, he is author or editor of six books about health, territorial politics, and Western European politics, including a work on devolution and health policy in the UK, *Territorial politics and health policy: UK health policy in comparative perspective* (Manchester University Press, 2004), and *Making European Union health policies: France, Germany, Spain and the UK* (Open University Press, 2009: forthcoming).

Charlie Jeffery is Professor of Politics in the School of Social and Political Studies, University of Edinburgh, and the author and/or editor of many books and articles about devolution and German politics. He directs the ESRC's research programme on Devolution and Constitutional Change. He has recently edited special issues of *Regional and Federal Studies* on territorial finance and *Representation* on the UK's devolved elections.

Michael Keating is Professor of Regional Studies at the European University Institute, Florence, and Professor of Scottish Politics at the University of Aberdeen. He has published widely on urban and regional government, nationalism and devolution in the UK. Among his recent books are *The government of Scotland* (Edinburgh University Press, 2005) and *Scottish social democracy* (Presses interuniversitaires européennes, 2007).

Guy Lodge is Senior Research Fellow at the Institute for Public Policy Research (IPPR) and Head of the Democracy and Power team. He leads the Institute's work on political and constitutional reform and has published widely in this area. He is also a visiting research fellow in the Department of Politics and International Relations, University of Oxford.

Margitta Mätzke received her PhD in Political Science from Northwestern University in 2005. In her dissertation she examined the politics of welfare state inequalities in major German social policy reforms. She now teaches at the University of Göttingen, Germany, and her research interests are in the areas of comparative welfare state research, public policy making in democratic systems and comparative research methods.

Iain McLean is Professor of Politics, University of Oxford, and a fellow of Nuffield College. He has previously held posts at Newcastle and Warwick in the UK, and visiting posts at Stanford, Yale and the Australian National University. He has been both a researcher in, and practitioner of, UK devolution for many years. In the 1970s he was Chair of the Economic Development Committee, Tyne & Wear County Council. He currently serves on the Independent Expert Group advising the Scottish Parliament on devolution finance.

Martin Powell is Professor of Health and Social Policy at the Health Services Management Centre, University of Birmingham. His research interests include citizenship and consumerism, and the principles and history of the British welfare state. He has published in social policy and history journals, and his most recent books are *Understanding the mixed economy of welfare* (The Policy Press, 2007) and *Modernising the welfare state: The Blair legacy* (The Policy Press, 2008).

Katie Schmuecker is Research Fellow at ippr north (Institute for Public Policy Research North), the Newcastle office of IPPR. She specialises in devolution and public policy, governance and regional development. She has published work on the UK devolution settlement and policy divergence and convergence since devolution, co-editing the publication *Devolution in practice 2006: Public policy differences within the UK* (IPPR, 2005) as well as co-authoring two chapters (with John Adams). Other recent publications include 'The end of the union?' (with Guy Lodge) in *Public policy research* (IPPR, 2007), and *Fair shares? Barnett and the politics of public expenditure* (IPPR, 2008) (with Guy Lodge and Iain McLean). Before joining ippr north she worked for the Campaign for Regional Government in the North East of England.

Alan Trench was Senior Research Fellow at the Constitution Unit, University College London between 2001 and 2004, and is now an honorary senior research fellow there. He works on intergovernmental relations, both in the UK and comparatively. A solicitor by profession, he was also specialist adviser to the UK House of Lords Select Committee on the constitution for its inquiry into Devolution: Inter-institutional Relations in the United Kingdom in 2002-03. His publications include the edited volumes *Has devolution made a difference? State of the nations 2001* (Imprint Academic, 2004), *Devolution and power in the United Kingdom* (Manchester University Press, 2007) and *The dynamics of devolution* (Imprint Academic, 2005).

Adam Whitworth is Research Fellow within the Centre for the Analysis of South African Social Policy and Social Disadvantage Research Centre at the University of Oxford. His major research interests are in the areas of poverty and social exclusion, gender, work–family reconciliation, small area statistics, crime and quantitative methodologies. His PhD work focused on lone mothers' experiences of work–family reconciliation in the UK since 1997. His recent and current research includes the development of small area Indices of Multiple Deprivation in the UK and South Africa, as well as evaluations of the National Strategy for Neighbourhood Renewal.

Daniel Wincott holds the Blackwell Law and Society Chair at Cardiff University. Before taking up this position at Cardiff he was Professor of European and Comparative Politics at the University of Birmingham. His research takes an interdisciplinary approach and focuses on European integration, devolution and comparative public policy. He has published widely including articles in such journals as *European Law Journal, Government and Opposition, International Political Science Review, Journal of Common Market Studies, Journal of European Public Policy, Political Quarterly, Political Studies, Public Administration* and *Publius*.

ONE

Introduction: devolution and citizenship rights

Scott L. Greer and Margitta Mätzke

Shared values are the bedrock on which the elements of our nation are built. Our values are given shape and meaning by the institutions that people know and trust, from the NHS to Parliament. (Ministry of Justice, 2007)

'PRESCRIPTIONS FREE FOR EVERYONE: but only if you live in Wales', said the front page of the *Daily Express* on 26 January 2007. 'Anger over double standards in our Health Service' was the topic; 'Critics blame Labour's devolution programme, which handed powers over health from London to Cardiff and Edinburgh', explained the text.

'MEDICAL APARTHEID' said the front page of the *Daily Mail* on 20 October 2006. 'Another life-extending drug joins list of medicines given to Scots but denied the English'. The following story quoted the Conservative health spokesperson: 'either we have a National Health Service or we don't. In fact, it has become a Scottish and a separate English health service.'

'UK's apartheid in medical care' said *The Sun* on 10 January 2008. 'The National Health Service is 60 this year – but don't break out the bubbly and the party poppers just yet. Once the envy of the world, it is now dogged by controversy. Despite a dedicated workforce and record levels of investment, the NHS is unable to guarantee the same level of care for everyone in the UK. Yet this was one of its founding principles when Labour set it up in 1948. A new report blames devolution and claims it has led to four different healthcare systems for England, Scotland, Wales and Northern Ireland.... The break-up has penalised England

most'. A handy guide lists the medicines and services that
are unique to each system, and then gives practical advice
on how to 'BEAT THE SYSTEM', in 'LEGAL experts say
you don't have to live permanently in Scotland to get drugs
banned in England'. It is not clear whether the confusion of
'banned' and 'not funded by the NHS' was a simple mistake
by the paper.

Tabloid headlines are ephemeral. Patches of prose in government
documents with no policy attached have scarcely less shelf life. But
they are signs: signs that politicians, tabloid journalists and others
sense something is happening. What is happening is the evolution of
citizenship rights in the UK, brought on by devolution.

Citizenship talk is everywhere. Much of it is as insubstantial as a
tabloid story, and much of it is much less amusing to read. Some make
efforts to use citizenship as a concept that might change society, whether
through 'citizenship education' in the schools or through lectures
about good behaviour. Some, including Labour governments since
devolution, use it as an argument for the Union. Some add regulatory
content, using citizenship tests and requirements for immigrants to
separate insiders and outsiders. Immigrants who behave in unattractive
ways will, according to the various proposals, be denied citizenship and
its benefits – benefits that are unconditional for those born citizens.
That would give citizenship concrete meaning, at least for those not
born to it.

But citizenship also has a concrete meaning for all its beneficiaries. It
is the set of rights that come with belonging to a political community.
It means rights to participate in the political process, to freedom of
action and expression and to a measure of social rights that citizens
enjoy without regard to their class, colour or creed. And those rights
are changing.

This book argues that territorial politics – the politics and institutions
of devolution, in the case of the UK – influence the citizenship rights
of people in the UK. Citizenship rights are rights to various social
benefits such as healthcare and housing that are distributed equally in an
otherwise unequal society. They are tangibly expressed in public policy
decisions: legislation that creates entitlements, public administration
of health, education, welfare and other bureaucracies, and budgeting
decisions that make social citizenship rights more or less real. The large
literature on devolution makes it clear that the politics and institutions
of devolution shape public administration, legislation, budgeting and
enforceable rights. If money, resources and laws are what make social

citizenship rights real, and devolution shapes the allocation and use of money, resources and laws, then devolution will change the nature of citizenship rights in the UK. The material content of social citizenship, and some of the rhetoric of rights and responsibilities, are now shaped by politics on levels other than the UK – the European Union (EU) and the devolved governments of Northern Ireland, Scotland and Wales.

The *intersection between devolution and citizenship rights* is the topic of this book. The following chapters combine analyses of the changing role of territory with concrete studies of devolution and policy making in the UK. They bring together two literatures and debates that have had only very limited interactions. The literature on citizenship has traditionally paid little attention to territorial politics or concrete social policy, putting much more emphasis on theoretical development, history, identity and migration (Banting, 1999, p 110). The literature on territorial politics tends to do a bit better: those territorial politics works that discuss the welfare state reliably refer to the principal thinker of social citizenship, and indeed the man who coined the term, T.H. Marshall. They will often discuss him for a few pages. But neither literature truly explores the nexus between citizenship rights and territorial politics. This book bridges this gap.

This introduction first discusses the basic concept of citizenship rights, drawing on the famous conceptualisation first put forward by T.H. Marshall, whom Martin Powell, in Chapter Two, identifies as 'one of the least read and understood writers on social policy'. When we talk about social citizenship rights, we are discussing a powerful idea with theoretically interesting lacunae that Chapters Two to Four will explore.

T.H. Marshall and citizenship rights

Many studies of the welfare state nod to Marshall. One of the great thinkers of the welfare state literature and a foundational thinker for the subfield of citizenship studies, he is most famous for a short lecture that he delivered in 1950. In it, he defined three components of citizenship. One component, and the first, is *civil rights* – rights such as free speech, freedom of movement and freedom of assembly. The second, logically and for him chronologically, was *political rights*. Above all, that means suffrage. The third and final kind of citizenship rights, which he judged completed with the passage of Legal Aid just before his speech, was *social citizenship rights*. For him, the three categories came in a sequence – civil rights led to political rights, and political rights, once exercised, brought forth social ones:

> The civil element is composed of the rights necessary for individual freedom – liberty of the person, freedom of speech, thought and faith, the right to own property and to conclude valid contracts, and the right to justice.... By the political element I mean the right to participate in the exercise of political power, as a member of a body invested with political authority or as an elector of the members of such a body.... By the social element I mean the whole range from the right to a modicum of economic welfare and security to the right to share to the full in the social heritage and to live the life of a civilised being according to the standards prevailing in the society. (Marshall, 1950 [1992], p 8)

This Marshall is well known and much cited, including in the literature on territorial politics and the welfare state (for which, see Pierson, 2007). Short references to him do not, however, constitute engagement with the interesting and complex literature that has built up around the topic of citizenship since the 1980s (Somers, 2005), which we cannot hope to review here but which appears throughout this book.

Much of the citizenship literature is critical of Marshall, accusing him of everything from sexism to anglocentrism (Rees, 1996; Breiner, 2006). He stands convicted on many accounts – for example, his essay pays very little attention to women, their very different historical experience of rights or the distinctive gendered effects of rights. And it is a very English story he tells. But his categorisation of citizenship into three kinds of rights has proven useful, and durable, to discussions of both citizenship and the welfare state. Even when its function has been to spark a critique of gaps or exclusions, the starting point has been Marshall.

Criticism of Marshall's conceptualisation of citizenship rights is in part rooted in frustration with T.H. Marshall's seemingly contradictory treatment of inequality in politics and society. But those critiques are in themselves multilayered. Charging him with paying insufficient attention to the gendered effects of rights expresses wariness of the unconditional application of citizenship rights, with not enough consideration of the unequal circumstances in which these rights are meant to operate. Accusing him of anglocentrism, by contrast, amounts to the contrary, to the charge that the three dimensions of citizenship rights are modelled on the mid-20th-century situation in England or Great Britain (which one is not clear). There, equality of all three categories of rights was indeed a central political goal. But the charge of UK-centrism, or anglocentrism, neglects the histories of citizenship rights in other countries and at other times, where 'equal' citizenship status could be reconciled with much greater amounts of social differentiation and unequal treatment.

Marshall's thinking about citizenship revolves around equality. In principle his citizenship rights are defined by equality. They are civil, political or social rights that do not depend on status or income. Yet in practice they operate in a context of social inequality, and they are even compatible with that inequality in (most) other spheres of life.[1] Indeed, part of the distinctiveness and power of Marshall's idea of citizenship rights is that a citizenship right creates equality where otherwise there is none. In the voting booth, rich and poor are equal. Once they step out, that is not the case. This compatibility with inequality is what makes citizenship rights distinctive, and it is Marshall's crucial accomplishment to point this out and explain its consequences in his three categories of citizenship rights. There have been lots of theories of total equality before and since Marshall,[2] but few broad frameworks for the combination of equality and inequality that mark many western democracies.

This also explains why the rhetorical resonance of the idea of a citizenship right is distinctive and powerful. To speak of a citizenship right invites a contrast between the equality of the right and the inequality of most other things. And it is not hard to find people working in the UK's health services, for example, who have not read Marshall but are very proud to provide a service that is equal despite the varying status of the patients. Citizenship rights, for Marshall, are not just compatible with inequality; they are even complementary. He expressed hope that, as Alfred Marshall said, 'progress may ... go on steadily, if slowly, till, by occupation at least, every man is a gentleman' (Marshall, 1950 [1992], p 4). At the same time, however, he insisted that while one must reject qualitative inequalities 'in terms of the essential elements of civilization or culture', which differences of occupation may generate between the gentleman and the labourer, one can accept 'as right and proper a wide range of quantitative or economic inequality' (Marshall, 1950 [1992], p 6). Citizenship rights establish 'a claim to be admitted to a share in the social heritage, which in turn means a claim to be accepted as full members of the society' (Marshall, 1950 [1992], p 6), but they do not establish entitlement to equal treatment or even egalitarian outcomes.

On the contrary, citizenship rights create *islands of equality*, and those who are about to drown in a sea of inequality can clamber onto the islands of equality when ill health or voicelessness might otherwise

5

doom them. The increase in fellow feeling and the dulling of conflict that come from citizenship rights sustain societies otherwise marked by inequality and its consequences. These islands of equality in an otherwise inegalitarian society will therefore remain.

How can we assess this simultaneous, complementary existence of equality and inequality so characteristic, and so powerful about, citizenship rights, and why is the territorial dimension an important and understudied aspect of it? Both inequality and equality have more than one dimension (Mätzke, 2006). Egalitarian policy measures and unequal social and economic conditions can take different forms; these affect groups of people differently, and they employ different means of political intervention. Therefore, the political dynamics of decision making and controversies about citizenship-based equality in principle are also distinctive, and explanations of the politics of citizenship must take account of these typological distinctions. Specifically, two substantive dimensions can be distinguished, which bring to the fore the relevant political aspects of equal rights in unequal contexts.

One dimension distinguishes between different units of reference for egalitarian or 'socially separatist' treatment of people within a given territory. Inequality may take the form of differentiation and unequal treatment within a given group but it may also manifest itself in the boundaries and inclusiveness of the group of people covered by a citizenship right. Students of social rights and welfare state development have often focused more or less exclusively on the structure of entitlement, and conceived of inequality primarily as social differentiation. The territorial dimension highlights the importance of the second dimension, the scope of coverage and the boundaries around the group of people entitled (Ferrera, 2005). The second dimension differentiates between rights and responsibilities as the instruments of political intervention through which citizens encounter state activity. That is, egalitarian or socially differentiated policy can take the form of either granting rights or imposing burdens. To satisfy egalitarian criteria a potential citizenship right would have to be open to all citizens (and maybe some denizens as well), and minimise differentiation and unequal entitlement within that group. Egalitarian citizenship rights on the second dimension would have to distribute responsibilities and rights equally, for example by reducing the options to opt out of public education, pensions or insurance schemes.

Citizenship rights in the UK traditionally fare rather well with regard to the scope of rights and responsibilities, because they are tax-funded rather than based on social insurance schemes, so that access to many services is open to all citizens. Even those who opt out of public services and 'go private' in schools or healthcare pay for local schools and for the NHS, and even those who do not pay much by way of taxes could use the NHS and the public school system as rights of citizenship. The growth in means testing means that many of the well-off are excluded from certain types of benefits, some of which they might conceivably want, but key welfare benefits such as state pensions and the NHS systems remain universal and do not formally distinguish among recipients by status or income (implementation is, as Martin Powell argues in Chapter Nine, a rather different issue). The structure of many publicly granted rights has likewise been egalitarian in the UK. The UK problem is rather, to paraphrase Richard Titmuss, that services for the poor tend to be poor services, so a citizenship right may be so unappealing that citizens opt out (Titmuss, 1968, p 134).

All this may be undergoing profound changes in the wake of devolution or Europeanisation. For each type of inequality, political dynamics and controversies about that potential transformation will be different, but for each type, changing boundaries of the group of citizens that are supposed to share rights and responsibilities will equally deeply affect the perception of equality and 'full membership in the society' (Marshall, 1950 [1992]), that is, citizenship status. Citizenship studies usually divide between 'those who look at the rights of citizens in the "soft inside", and those who focus on national borders and the "excluded hard outside" faced by non-citizens' (Somers, 2008, p 21). But there are other divisions, pressing ones in the contemporary UK, and among them is territory. Therefore paying attention to territory when talking about citizenship rights sheds new light on the politics of equal rights in contemporary, decentralising polities.

Territorial and citizenship politics

If the literature on citizenship rights has typically been silent about territorial politics, the literature on territorial politics that speaks to citizenship has not been much greater. This is despite the fact that social citizenship rights are, among other things, territorial. They are territorial because they come from governments and governments are territorially delineated. Citizenship rights are claims on governments – claims to freedoms or social rights (just as duties are claims by governments). They require what governments command, whether it be laws, money or the resources of the government machine itself (Rose, 1987). Otherwise they are just words on paper. And that means that they might not be met consistently, and that enforcing social citizenship

7

rights takes political action and capable governments. Logically and empirically, this entails that when the distribution of responsibilities between governments changes, the nature of citizenship rights also changes. Devolution changes social citizenship:

- because advocates and citizens are making their claims on a different government (the Scottish rather than UK government, for example), with different politics and party systems;
- because the governments' ability to deliver the resources, laws and money varies with the complexities of the devolution settlement (if a social right requires a law or money to become real, the Scottish and UK governments are better positioned than the Welsh Assembly Government);
- because the governments have different policy processes and administrations, which are likely to enforce, implement and ignore social citizenship rights in different ways;
- and because in many cases, including the UK, these governments did not spring from nothingness. In a multinational state such as the UK, Scotland, Wales and arguably Northern Ireland are nations with as good a claim as any. That means there is dispute; 'defining the sharing community' is an activity that cannot be separated from debating the nature and direction of nationalism (Banting, 2005a).

The result of devolution, and any shift in territorial politics such as Europeanisation, is therefore to bring territorial politics into social citizenship. There is an inexorable slide, from discussion of the changing territorial politics of welfare to the changing nature of citizenship rights.

Indeed, we can restate many of the key issues of devolution in terms of citizenship. First, the basic unit of citizenship – the sharing community – has changed in some, largely unknown, way. To what extent is Scotland or England, rather than the UK, the unit within which we understand citizenship rights? Second, there can no longer be much pretence that there is a simple connection between all three forms of citizenship, because now they adhere to different governments in different ways. Scottish people have different political rights than others because they have three parliaments; Welsh and English people only enjoy two, one of them European and a rather flawed body. Third, this lack of identity spills into social citizenship because it shapes the practical politics of welfare and social policy. Consider a largely subterranean UK–Scottish dispute early in the history of devolution. The Scottish Executive created a right to long-term personal care for older people, a benefit that was means tested in England (see Rachel Simeon, 2003). To do this, they used the (devolved) health budget. The UK Treasury promptly withdrew the means-tested allowances it had paid from the (non-devolved) pensions budget, and there have been occasional squabbles about it ever since. An administrative act shaped by the particular shape of the Scotland Act switched the community responsible for part of the welfare of older people, and created a more distinctive Scottish social citizenship.

Nevertheless, recognition that the comparative territorial politics literature should have something to say to debates about the welfare state, or citizenship rights, has been relatively slow in coming. Traditionally neither the comparative study of the welfare state nor the study of citizenship has been particularly friendly to territorial politics, stateless nations, decentralisation and federalism (Richard Simeon, 2006b). Large multivariate studies of overall welfare spending generally come to negative conclusions about decentralisation (Huber et al, 1993; Crepaz, 1998; Hicks, 1999; Swank, 2001). They have tended to find that federalism or decentralisation produced a lower overall level of welfare spending. Scholars of the welfare state take it as a given that federalism slows welfare state development, and more federalism slows it more (for example, Immergut, 1992; Hacker, 1998; Amenta, 2006, p 18). It even reshapes politics to weaken advocates of the welfare state (Swank, 2001, p 211). Decentralisation therefore joins separation of powers and referenda as barriers to enhanced welfare spending. It appeared, background or foreground, in many histories of welfare state frustration. The upshot was a simple idea: decentralisation, by multiplying veto points, impedes welfare state expansion and possibly interferes with its justice.

So in 1998, the instinct of most experts in comparative welfare states would probably have been to warn that devolution would damage the welfare states and citizenship rights of the UK (Martin Powell and Daniel Wincott discuss this argument in Chapters Two and Three). This would have sat poorly with one of the more obvious attributes of devolved politics: a much greater elite consensus on the value and structure of the welfare state in Scotland and Wales than was seen in England. The legacy of conflict over the welfare state undoubtedly contributed to Scottish and Welsh campaigns for devolution and a nationalist tinge to welfare politics there. While the public opinion data do not suggest particularly higher levels of social democratic feeling in Scotland and Wales relative to England (Jeffery, 2006a, 2006b; and Chapter Five in this book), elite discourse is much more prone to articulate strong communitarian, redistributive, pro-welfare values

(Greer, 2007a). Devolution in the UK – and the development of welfare politics elsewhere – does not look much like a device for lowering welfare standards. In its intent it is, if anything, an effort by Scottish and Welsh elites to quarantine themselves from English policies that change or erode social citizenship rights.

This disconnect between quantitative cross-national work and qualitative evidence has led scholars of territorial politics to engage with welfare state issues. For the territorial politics literature, this is a move beyond a traditional focus on authority migration (Gerber and Kollman, 2004) to examine the ways that territorial politics influence the development of welfare states, and the ways welfare politics become entwined with territorial politics. The result has been a series of edited books and research projects that deal in depth with the relationship between welfare and decentralisation in comparative perspective (McEwen and Moreno, 2005; Obinger et al, 2005; Greer, 2006c; Béland and Lecours, 2008).

They bring their characteristic focus on territorial diversity to this topic. Federalism might be correlated with slower adoption of a welfare state and lower welfare levels, but that aggregate correlation at the level of the state, and even qualitative studies focused on states, does not tell us much. Aggregate correlations are insensitive to multinationalism – the differences between multinational and homogeneous states (Banting and Kymlicka, 2006, p 23). They rule out, or average out, the possibility that some governments can forge ahead of others, developing distinctive and better welfare states that could not be adopted in the larger countries. They also rule out decentralisation in the name of welfare, as seen in Scotland when what Charlie Jeffery refers to as Thatcher's 'contract-breaking' policies spurred a pro-welfare, pro-devolution, Scottish consensus (McEwen, 2002, 2006; McEwen and Parry, 2005; Jeffery, 2006a; Greer, 2007a).

But these cases are precisely what interest students of territorial politics, and they matter. To take a Canadian example, for most of Canadian postwar history there have been rivalries between the provincial and federal welfare states. We are all familiar with the welfare state as nation building; Canadian politics gave us the phrase, and the clear history of, 'province building' as an alternative to state building. The bricks and mortar in competitive province and state building were welfare programmes. And significant competitive divergence meant significantly different levels of social provision, which interacted with any list of Canadian social citizenship rights.

In other words, it means that governments can, effectively, compete for citizens. Citizenship may be seen as a contract in which government and citizens exchange rights and responsibilities. If governments are competing for the loyalty of their citizens, then they might try to extend rights and reap not just credit, but loyalty. This is a far cry from most of the history of citizenship, in which citizens had to struggle to establish claims over the state (Tilly, 1998, p 697; 1999). It is not the norm in most countries. But when there is a live political debate about the appropriate distribution of authority and responsibility between governments, it is not surprising that they would seek the loyalty of voters in the bond known as citizenship. And there is such a debate in the UK right now.

Attentiveness to such issues appears in studies that pay closer attention to the *ways* in which institutions, party systems and other aspects of territorial politics shape welfare politics. Rather than treat decentralisation and federalism as simple variables that we can load into a regression, it views them as interacting components that shape the relationship between state and citizenry. The mission is, if anything, akin to what feminist theorists have done – bring territory into the citizenship debates, because territory, like gender, is necessary to understand the assumptions and real effects of social citizenship. Maurizio Ferrera's magisterial *The boundaries of welfare* marks a breakthrough in this line of analysis, building on T.H. Marshall and the ideas of Albert Hirschman about exit and voice (Ferrera, 2005). It argues that there was a powerful link between the make-up of the welfare state and the rise of the territorial state. The basic architecture of the welfare state depended on serving a limited number of people, and raising funds, *within a territory*. Both Europeanisation and regionalisation – which includes UK devolution – undermine this association of state, polity, welfare state and social citizenship rights. They do it legally, by opening up possibilities for exit, and practically, by destabilising policies that depend on territorial closure (Ong, 2005).

Beyond this specific vein of literature concerned with the interaction of territorial politics, the welfare state and citizenship, there is a much larger literature on territorial politics. The territorial history of citizenship in the UK is yet to be written, and the practical analysis of the territorial components of social citizenship is only starting, but there are raw materials aplenty. Thanks in part to a large Economic and Social Research Council (ESRC) programme on Devolution and Constitutional Change, and Leverhulme Trust-sponsored research, there is now a large body of work on the law, mechanics and politics of devolution. Insofar as intergovernmental relations, EU relations, finance, public administration, public opinion or public policy influence social citizenship rights, we can draw on much research on those topics.

Much of the work is to be synthetic. We know a great deal about devolution and a great deal about citizenship. The problem is to bring them together so that we understand their reciprocal effects.

Devolution and citizenship rights in the UK

Changing territorial politics change citizenship. They change the governments that make citizenship rights real. They change the rules of sharing, of mutual constraint and of policy making. They thereby change the nature and content of citizenship rights. And that means that the often obscure politics and law of devolution and the EU will change social citizenship rights in the UK. The disputants in intergovernmental arguments, furthermore, will invoke social citizenship. They might do so in the language of social citizenship, but they will certainly do so in the language of fairness and nationalism and 'MEDICAL APARTHEID'. It is time to examine the relationship between our theories of citizenship and the practical, changing, territorial politics of the UK.

The chapters in this book do three things. First, they bring some of the insights of citizenship theory together with the literature on territorial politics and the welfare state. And second, they bring a potentially abstract debate to the level of public policy, where budgeting, administrative and legal institutions and decisions make rights real or mere words on paper. Citizenship theory, as Keith Banting noted a few years ago, is not about public policy:

> Much of the literature on citizenship and difference is rooted in political and legal theory, and focuses on the implications of contemporary diversity for democratic theory and conceptions of justice. The political science contribution to this literature has tended to focus on the implications of cultural pluralism for conflict management and the stability of democratic political systems. In general, scholars in these areas have tended to pay relatively little attention to the substance of social policy. (Banting, 1999, p 110)

Despite efforts, the gap has not been filled since. That is what we try to do in this book, and while doing it achieve a third goal: to illuminate and start a debate about the ways changing territorial politics is, theoretically and practically, changing social citizenship in the UK. Devolution matters to social citizenship. Understanding it through that lens makes clear the normative, ideological, constitutional and everyday stakes of sometimes obscure devolution issues.

Theory

The chapters in Part I, by Martin Powell, Daniel Wincott and Richenda Gambles and Adam Whitworth, try to fill the gap between citizenship theory and territorial reality by looking back into the much-cited, and apparently little-read, Marshall. They connect the T.H. Marshall of the citizenship literature to the welfare state that makes social rights real. Marshall is all too often caricatured, or what is discussed is only a narrow slice of a single short lecture. Collectively, the three chapters connect Marshall with broader debates in citizenship theory and territorial politics; identify the questions analysis must answer; and define the social citizenship rights that the rest of the book discusses, in terms of concrete welfare state policies and outcomes. Many takes on Marshall are about identifying difficulties; these chapters are about using him to shed light on what we might say is his core topic: social policy in Britain (or England).

Martin Powell, in Chapter Two, takes on two key points about Marshall that are all too often asserted rather than demonstrated. The first is that Marshall's work is in some simple way about equality. *Citizenship and social class* is *still* innovative, precisely because it is not about equality; it is about the relationship between equality and inequality in the society. The second point is that Marshall described the British welfare state at the time of writing. Powell argues instead that it is possible to identify a Marshallian welfare state (MWS) (Marshall described it to us in some detail, after all) and then place it on a continuum with other models of the welfare state. He argues that the MWS is not the basic welfare state model of contemporary Britain; if anything, the welfare state of Beveridge is a more accurate description. This, in turn, means that many discussions of the welfare state and of Marshall require more or less severe recalibration.

Misunderstood or not, Marshall still has a great deal to say in dialogue with other literatures because his concepts of citizenship give form to an otherwise messy group of ideas about state building, territory, the welfare state and public policy. The connection with literatures on territorial politics and the welfare state comes in the chapter by Daniel Wincott. He discusses the uses of Marshall for territorial politics by identifying the ways in which Marshall helps us analyse contemporary welfare and territorial politics and the ways examining the Marshallian frameworks help us understand the reality of social policy. In the course of relating Marshall's work to those large literatures, he also reworks Marshall by putting emphasis on the independence, complexity and interaction of the three elements of citizenship.

Marshall's story might be English, and debatably British, but it is also one with other well-known theoretical blinders. Territorial politics work that discusses Marshall is prone to pass over them, but they contain traps for the analysis of social citizenship. Here, there is a case that scholars of territorial politics should be learning more from citizenship theorists. There are two abiding topics of citizenship theory, in general and in connection with T.H. Marshall: formal citizenship and migration as well as the status of non-citizens; and gender. Neither has found much echo in work on citizenship and territorial politics.

Failure to discuss formal citizenship and the place of the migrant is not particularly a problem, surprisingly enough, for territorial politics. One of the common denominators of most decentralised states – and emphatically of the UK – is that citizenship, migration and nationality are matters for the state and not decentralised governments. The ability of Scotland or Wales to operate significant formal citizenship policies of their own is nil; they can merely work through programmes to attract or integrate migrants. They get to have an immigration policy, not a citizenship policy. The failure of the UK's devolved regions to make a successful claim on formal citizenship and migration policy is intensely interesting, but for different reasons and for a different book. The only intersection between formal citizenship and 'denizenship' policies, and devolution, is where there is an intersection between EU citizenship and devolved policy, that is discussed in Chapter Ten, which stresses the limited, partial nature of EU citizenship.

On the other hand, excluding gender from analyses of social citizenship is particularly dangerous for those who would integrate it with territorial politics and public policy. The problem is that Marshall's concepts of equality, especially insofar as we take them as descriptors of welfare state realities, are relatively blind to gender. And gender-blind policies can, unsurprisingly, blunder. Chapter Four, by Richenda Gambles and Adam Whitworth, discusses Marshall in light of the citizenship debates about topics such as gender, bringing citizenship debates to the collection while revisiting the 'Marshall' of the literature in the light of the real Marshall and his writings. They highlight the difficulties and complexity of working with his concept of equality in practical and theoretical terms – as well as its political power as an 'aspirational framework'. Above all, they identify the importance of understanding the concrete meaning of social citizenship and its relationship to lived experience. A very attractive standard of citizenship might turn out to mean little in practice, and an island of egalitarian social policy might turn out to be deeply inegalitarian when overlaid with an understanding of how work and caring actually take place.

Practice

The chapters in Part II then go beyond the existing territorial politics literature, with its macroscopic and comparative focus, to identify the ways that territorial politics and citizenship rights interact in the UK today. The first chapter in this section, by Charlie Jeffery, examines public opinion data. Its 'citizen-centred perspective' remedies a curious absence in much citizenship literature – namely, the opinions of citizens. Its conclusion might startle: the 'post-devolution UK lacks the institutional fabric which might continue to frame social rights as most appropriately pursued at a statewide scale. As the UK operates as a series of disconnected political arenas – with signs also that the English are beginning to frame their collective goals in an English territorial frame – it appears likely that the frame of reference for citizens ... will become increasingly divergent'.

Chapter Six, by Michael Keating, reviews the development of policy in England, Scotland and Wales since devolution (he excludes Northern Ireland because its policy development has overwhelmingly been under direct rule by UK junior ministers, a situation about as far from devolution as it is possible to get). He identifies patterns of change in the public services and a 'populist turn' in areas where there were no strong pre-existing policy communities with their own ideas. 'While [the devolved] bodies are functionally restricted', he writes, 'the implications of the new politics are wider, creating new expectations across the political spectrum'. But the 'failure to articulate a coherent Scottish or Welsh conception of social citizenship or indeed a narrative around economic development is in striking contrast to other stateless nations'. He concludes that while true Scottish or Welsh social citizenship may or may not evolve, 'the old British model, captured by Marshall at the moment of its completion, is becoming a thing of the past'. This approach also, implicitly, de-emphasises the mechanics of policy making; policy divergence might change social citizenship, but, as per Keating, it is 'changes in the political superstructure' that are followed by 'slower changes in the infrastructure of policy communities and processes'.

Keating also concludes by highlighting the role of finance and, like Charlie Jeffery, 'interstitial' policies where different governments meet. This is, in a sense, where the rubber hits the road – where we see not only the (in)ability of the devolved administrations, to develop distinctive models, but also where the mechanics of territorial politics are crucial in shaping the future of social citizenship (and where clashes fuelled by arguments about social citizenship could turn to influence the future of devolution).

Alan Trench, in Chapter Seven, on intergovernmental relations, makes the case that an area often thought of as a lawyers' hobby rather than a major political variable is indeed key to the development of social citizenship on the practical and the rhetorical level. Practically, governments cannot develop distinctive social citizenship if it requires policies they cannot make. Welsh social citizenship, for the foreseeable future, will not involve distinctive Welsh pension laws because there can be no such thing. But theoretically, debates about social policy channel and change social citizenship thinking and models of social citizenship. Governments themselves are major participants in the debates through which understandings of citizenship evolve, and the forums in which they meet, the kinds of issues they debate, and the extent to which they shape each other's policies matters. The influence is reciprocal; citizenship, or concepts of fairness, provide much of the fuel for the fires that are increasingly whipped up around financial formulae or representation.

And financial formulae matter, as Iain McLean, Guy Lodge and Katie Schmuecker argue in Chapter Eight. Graduates are taught that all serious policy takes money. No money, no seriousness. Where, then, does the money come from and how is it allocated? Like the UK, they focus on allocation since the money overwhelmingly comes from UK taxes under the reserved control of Westminster. That limits the political rights of citizens to vary their obligations and puts the focus on the extent to which the allocation of funds to the different parts of the UK reflects a coherent concept of equality and whether they deliver it. Their answer is no – current UK financial arrangements work against any shared concept of citizenship because they create inequality for no good reason. While similar levels of funding do not guarantee shared social citizenship, they certainly contribute to governments' ability to achieve it. And while centralised tax collection combined with allocation of spending by formula is of questionable democratic legitimacy, it is both the current UK model and a basic approach that depends for its logic on concepts of shared social citizenship.

Martin Powell, in Chapter Nine, focuses on the meaning of rights when they must be processed through bureaucratic realities. Large social welfare organisations have all the foibles of professions, bureaucracies and the public sector. This means that they often do deliver the 'wrong things'. Neither data nor a good think about public policy suggests that variation can be avoided. Instead, 'more thought is needed on which variations are unacceptable, and how much variation should be tolerated. Given that perfectly uniform services are not possible, how much uniformity can exist before citizenship is undermined?'.

Powell's Chapter Nine focuses on something most chapters mention: the extent to which divergence did not start with devolution. There always was divergence between England, Northern Ireland, Scotland and Wales. And there was always local area divergence within each of them. Devolution might put a clear stamp of democratic political legitimacy on divergence, and strengthen forms of party competition that reward divergence, but it did not create it on the local or the national level.

Finally, Chapter Ten brings the discussion of devolution and citizenship rights together with the much more extensively researched and discussed changes brought to citizenship rights by the development of the EU. The EU creates larger formal changes to citizenship than devolution. Polish citizens can vote in Belfast local elections. Devolution has no such radical formal effect. But the formal citizenship of the EU is a very distinctive and anorexic creature; its power is concentrated in Marshall's civil rights, its contribution to political rights probably negative, and its contribution to social citizenship rights derivative of its focus on certain civil rights. It is as if Marshall's history replayed itself, starting with civil rights and seeing whether, in a different context, they would eventually lead to real political and social ones.

The chapter begins by arguing that only under specific, and sadly narrow, circumstances do regions have the autonomy 'in Europe' to develop distinctive models of society or politics. It does this by tracking the academics and politicians who jointly explored all the possible meanings of a 'Europe of the Regions' during the 1990s, and discovered that most possible meanings of the term ... were meaningless. Regions' relationship with the EU is that of member states, that is, they are regulated and their political possibilities constrained to fit with what the EU allows. They differ from states in that they are weaker; putting aside Belgian and German practices that are grounded in very un–British constitutions, regional governments such as Northern Ireland, Scotland and Wales are essentially lobbies. And while they can be effective lobbyists within their member states, that is not guaranteed (especially when different parties control the devolved and UK governments) and it is not guaranteed that the state will adopt their ideas or achieve what they want. What, then, does the EU do? It has been said to do many things, from triggering races to the bottom to creating an admirable social model that scholars rapidly abbreviated to ESM (for European social model) and began to critique. But the truth is in the middle, and rather bureaucratic: the EU is a regulatory state that cannot stay within its borders. Its effects on social rights come from the 'competency creep' that leads it to regulate the welfare states of the UK in line with its institutional focus on the civil right to movement. To see what the EU does to social citizenship, first, we must accept that it is often harmonising and then examine the effects of its policies on the ability of governments to make social rights work.

It is also worth noting that almost all of the authors in Part II end with clear stances on positions and issues little discussed in standard citizenship theory: Alan Trench, for example, argues for formalisation and mutual respect in intergovernmental relations as a way to improve the quality of debate about the obscure processes that are changing social citizenship rights within the country – and to start reflection 'on what the UK is now for'. McLean, Lodge and Schmuecker delve into the allocation of spending, putting the seriousness in debates about citizenship and social policy. And Michael Keating argues against declarations of UK-wide social rights on the grounds that they would inhibit the development of valuable Scottish or Welsh models. Much of the interest of these arguments is that, because they are rooted in empirical analysis of topics little discussed outside territorial politics, they highlight the consequences of those topics for social citizenship and the values of thinking about them in normative debates about better or worse concepts of social citizenship.

Conclusion

Whether you seek a distinctive Scottish, Welsh or Northern Irish social citizenship or a reinforced British one, then you might find you need a position on taxation and the Barnett formula, declaratory acts about social rights, the EU and intergovernmental dispute resolution. For readers concerned with citizenship theory above all, we hope that this book will convince them of that. For scholars of territorial politics, we hope that this book will convince them that their work has ramifications beyond the study of comparative federalism, policy divergence or other fields – that the common intuition that they are talking about Marshall's social citizenship is true – but that only means that a deeper and more creative engagement with the idea of citizenship, rather than a quick paragraph about three kinds of rights, beckons. And for those who merely care about the component nations of the UK, however many you think they are, we hope this book will convince you of the importance of paying attention to both the institutional, legal and policy details and the high theories that surround one of the most important concepts of western political thought.

Notes

Marshall's language was gendered. Rather than note that in every quotation, we have chosen to opt for readability on the assumption that the age of the work and different reference points he used are visible and discussed enough.

[1] See, for instance, Turner (1992), who expresses some of that wariness about equality in the thinking of Marshall: 'It is not precisely clear from Marshall's theory whether citizenship contradicts the market principle of capitalism by requiring some redistribution of wealth on the basis of need, or whether citizenship merely stands in some relation of tension with capitalism by inhibiting the full impact of the market principle, or whether indeed citizenship actually supports capitalism by integrating the working class into society by some complex means of welfare incorporation' (p 7).

[2] And Esping-Andersen (1990), by turning it into a process of 'decommodification' with no necessary end point, convinced a remarkable number of scholars that Marshall was arguing for a slow transition to socialism rather than a combination of equal citizenship and unequal society.

Part One
T.H. Marshall

TWO

Equality and Marshallian citizenship: why E does not equal MC

Martin Powell

T.H. Marshall is probably one of the leading cited authors in social policy. According to Harris (2004, p 81) Marshall is the most influential and oft-cited work on citizenship published in Britain over the course of the 20th century. Barbalet (1988, Preface) states that today it is almost impossible to pick up a sociology journal that does not contain an article with at least some reference to his work. Heater (1990, p 265) writes that nothing quite so absorbs the attention of scholars and politicians when contemplating the nature of citizenship today as the social rights which adhere to its status, with much of the subsequent literature taking Marshall as its starting-point.

But Marshall may also be one of the least read and understood writers on social policy, and his work has been subject to misleading and partial interpretations (Barbalet, 1988; Lister, 2003; Wincott, 2006; see Rees, 1995, for 'The other T.H. Marshall' and Powell, 2002, for 'The hidden history of social citizenship').

Marshall's own starting point in the (Alfred) Marshall Lectures delivered in Cambridge in 1949 was to consider the question of his namesake of 1873: 'The question is not whether all men will ultimately be equal – that they certainly will not – but whether progress may not go on steadily, if slowly, till, by occupation at least, every man is a gentleman. I hold that it may, and that it will' (in Marshall, 1963, p 69). From there, T.H. Marshall developed his famous three elements of citizenship.

Many arguments link Marshallian citizenship to the welfare state. For example, according to Esping-Andersen (1990, p 21): 'Few can disagree with T.H. Marshall's proposition that social citizenship constitutes the core idea of a welfare state'. In particular, it is often claimed that equality is the core of both T.H. Marshallian citizenship and the welfare state. In simple terms, E=MC and E=PWS, where E is equality, MC is Marshallian citizenship, and PWS is the principles of the welfare state. This may be less profound that Einstein's famous similar equation, but it does underlie much of the discussion about citizenship and the welfare state.

The main aim of this chapter is to argue that E (or at least the way in which E is often considered by social policy writers) does not equal MC (Powell, 2002), and that E does not equal PWS (Powell, 1995a). The first section examines the question of egalitarian social citizenship. It is argued that Marshallian citizenship offers only a limited version of equality of status rather than the more demanding forms of equality favoured by many writers (for example, Le Grand, 1982; Lister, 1990, 2003; Hay, 1996). The second section argues that the welfare state is not primarily based on Marshallian citizenship. Bulmer and Rees (1996, pp 272-3) claim that in the main it was Marshall's prescriptions along with the similar agendas of Tawney, Beveridge, Keynes and others that were given flesh and blood by the postwar Labour government. However, it is argued here that there are significant differences between a Beveridge welfare state (BWS) and a Marshall welfare state (MWS), and it was the less egalitarian BWS rather than the MWS that was implemented, and certainly not as egalitarian as a Titmuss welfare state (TWS), a decommodified Esping-Andersen welfare state (E-AWS) or a basic income welfare state (van Parijs, 1992) (BIWS) or citizen's income welfare state (CIWS).

Egalitarian social citizenship?

Most studies discuss citizenship in terms of equality. For example, Faulks (2000, p 3) writes that modern citizenship is inherently egalitarian. While this is largely the case for civil and political citizenship (for example, 'equality before the law'; 'one person, one vote'), the situation is more complex for social citizenship. Harris (1987, pp 47, 89-90) claims that Marshall seems to distance himself from the philosophy of other citizenship writers by not adopting equality as a key value to be promoted by the welfare state. Marshall explicitly repudiates the pursuit of equality as an objective of social policy. However, as we shall see, Marshall does regard equality as a key objective, but it is a specific version of equality (cf Dwyer, 2004, pp 38-48).

To understand what Marshall really said about equality, it is necessary to consider what types of equality between whom in which services. The first part of this section examines *who* is part of the 'community'. The second part discusses *different types* of equality. The final part focuses on *different services*. These points are then brought together in a section on social rights in the MWS.

Who?

Marshall's famous definition is that 'Citizenship is a status bestowed on those who are full members of a community' (1963, p 87). However, Marshall is never fully clear about defining this 'community'. Harris (2004, p 81) notes that Marshall never mentioned citizenship in the sense of legal nationality even though he was writing at the time of the seminally important British Nationality Act of 1948. Social citizenship cannot simply be equated with holding a passport: the UK passport is not simply a passport to social rights. Some social rights appear to be of denizenship rather than citizenship. Lister (2003, p 49) writes that denizens normally enjoy full social and civil rights. Therefore, from the perspective of socio-economic life chances, once a foreigner has taken up residence, it is the admission to denizenship rather than formal citizenship that really counts, but residence in some cases remains conditional and insecure.

In the Athenian polis, not all were citizens. For example, slaves and women were excluded from citizenship (Heater, 1990). Feminist writers argue that Marshall's analysis focuses on men. For example, his claim that political rights developed in the 19th century is not the case for women. Put another way, 'citizenship' consists of differentiated universalism, with partial or second-class citizenship for some (Lister, 1990, 2003; Lewis, 2004).

The final issue revolves around whether the community is local or national. This will be discussed further in Chapter Nine, and concerns whether citizenship varies across different localities such as local government or across the nations of the UK.

What?

The claim that citizenship can simply be equated with equality is problematic for two reasons. First, social citizenship is not an undifferentiated mass. As Marshall (1963, p 74) states, 'By the social element I mean the whole range from the right to a modicum of economic welfare and security to the right to share to the full in the social heritage and to live the life of a civilized being according to the standards prevailing in the society'. He later argues that 'The most familiar principle in use is not, of course, the scaled price [eg differential pricing used before the NHS] ... but the guaranteed minimum. The state guarantees a minimum supply of certain essential goods and services (such as medical attention and supplies, shelter and education) or a minimum money income available to be spent on essentials – as in the case of Old Age Pensions, insurance benefits and family allowances. Anyone able to exceed the guaranteed minimum out of his own resources is at liberty to do so' (Marshall, 1963, p 105). In other words, Marshall offers a minimal (modicum) and maximal ('share to the full') definition of citizenship. He is not fully clear and consistent (see Marshall, 1970, p 90; and below) on whether services reflect the minimum or the optimum, but it surely defeats the claim that citizenship can simply be equated with equality (Powell, 2002, p 241).

Second, for Marshall, 'equality' was clearly equality of status. He discusses class abatement, class fusion and social integration. While citizenship does diminish inequality, it does not lead to equality of income or equality of condition, but creates 'a universal right to real income which is not proportionate to the market value of the claimant' (1963, p 100).

> The extension of the social services is not primarily a means of equalizing incomes. In some cases it may; in others it may not. The question is relatively unimportant; it belongs to a different department of social policy. What matters is that there is a general enrichment of the concrete substance of civilized life, a general reduction of risk and insecurity, an equalization between the more and the less fortunate at all levels – between the healthy and the sick, the employed and the unemployed, the old and the active, the bachelor and the family of a large family. Equalization is not so much between classes as between individuals within a population which is now treated for this purpose as though it were one class. Equality of status is more important than equality of income. (1963, p 107)

He continues that even when benefits are paid in cash, this class fusion is outwardly expressed in the form of a new common experience, but the extension of services can therefore have 'a profound effect on the qualitative aspects of social differentiation'. He gives examples of 'ex-elementary schoolboy' and 'panel patient'. In other words, Marshall's main objective relates to horizontal rather than vertical redistribution (cf discussion of the Beveridge welfare state below) and in making a national risk pool (cf Harris, 1996; Johnson, 1996). In short, citizenship implies a 'progressive divorce between real and money incomes' which leads to 'the unified civilization which makes social inequalities acceptable.... The advantages obtained by having a larger money income do not disappear, but they are confined to a limited area of consumption' (Marshall, 1963, p 125).

Crosland (1964, p 85) considers that equality of status is more linked to services than benefits. It seems rather doubtful whether the fact that everybody now has an insurance card, and repairs to the local post office, really does much to foster social equality. When we turn to services in kind, however, we find a more direct link with social equality, especially in the spheres of health and education. If the state provides schools and hospitals, teachers and doctors, on a generous scale and of a really high quality, comparable with the best available for private purchase, then the result will indeed not be a greater equality of real incomes, but certainly a greater equality in manners and the texture of social life.

Marquand (1988, p 29) writes that Marshall's formulation caught the aspirations embodied in the welfare strand of the 1940s better than any other. The rich man and the poor man would collect the same pensions from the same post office counter, and sit next to each other in the same doctor's waiting room. They would be no less rich or poor for doing so, but they would be that much more full citizens of one community. The keystone of the system was entitlement that conferred equality of status. Bulmer and Rees (1996, pp 272-3) comment on the 'crucial passage' about equality of status, and point to the dismissive tone about more direct methods of equalisation as 'relatively unimportant'. Thus the equality to be established through social citizenship was above all formal equality of access and entitlement. Roche (1992, pp 19-20) writes that equal citizenship does not involve equality of condition for Marshall as it did for Titmuss and other Left social analysts.

Later writers have discussed this equality of status in terms of civic liberalism (Kaus, 1992), or of 'civic equality' (Prowse, 2000), that instead of trying to equalise monetary outcomes concentrates on increasing the range and significance of areas in which 'money does not count'. Sacks (2000, ch 4) uses the example of Regent's Park as a public space, where we can all go on equal terms. We are all equal citizens. And because we enjoy it and want it to be there, we keep to the rules, usually without having to be told. We keep radios quiet, dogs on a lead, put our litter in the bins, return a passing stranger's smile and otherwise respect people's privacy (one wonders if he has been there lately!).

Nevertheless, this form of equality is concerned more with solidarity, fraternity and integration rather than quantitative equality (Le Grand, 1982) per se. The quantitative forms of equality of the 'Strategy of Equality' (Le Grand, 1982) do not easily map onto Marshall's strategy of citizenship (cf Powell, 1995a, 2002). Barbalet (1988, p 59) argues that it is thus not necessary to demonstrate that the welfare state has failed to redress the balance of class disadvantage (for example, Le Grand, 1982). Such arguments are less relevant to Marshall's analysis than they are to those who insist on a parliamentary route to a classless society.

One can perhaps doubt Marshall's optimism, but not his clarity. Marshall (1981, pp 65-6) is even clearer: equality of persons is compatible with inequality of incomes provided the inequality is not too great. He insists that doctors should regard all their patients, and school teachers all their pupils, as deserving to be treated with the same care, and that all dwellings, however different in size, should be equally convertible by the families that occupy them into homes. 'And that is as near as I can get to a demonstration of what I mean when I speak of a qualitative equality of welfare that can co-exist with a quantitative inequality of income' (1981, pp 65-6). This form of equality may be limited compared with more demanding forms of quantitative equality (Hay, 1996), but represented a major advance at the time that Marshall wrote.

Which?

Marshall does not clearly and consistently recognise the different bases of service provision (universal, insurance, assistance; see below). However, Marshall (1963, pp 101-5) and Crosland (1964, pp 85-6) are clear that citizenship necessarily means universal or free (or 'de-commodified' services; see Powell, 2002). Marshall later reflected that the democratic principle that informs the conduct of affairs of a local Friendly Society can also operate on a large scale. The principle of mutual aid, when applied to a comprehensive scheme of national social insurance, is nothing less than the principle of common citizenship. However, he also claims that the NHS is not given as an insurance benefit, but as a right enjoyed by all citizens. It is a system of mutual aid operated by citizens through Parliament, local government and a host of boards and committees, with the utter rejection of the notion that it is permissible deliberately to offer, in matters of health and welfare, a second-class service for second-class people (Marshall, 1981, pp 71, 79).

Marshall does not appear to recognise the differentiation between local and national services (Chapter Nine, this volume). He appears to conflate 'national' services such as the National Health Service with local or municipal services such as education and housing. His 'national' welfare state of national citizenship consisted partly of local services such as education and housing. Similarly, he does not consistently differentiate between universal, contributory and selective services with their very different bases of entitlement (Lister, 1990; Harris, 1996; Dean, 2002).

Social rights in the MWS

Drawing these points together, Marshall is not fully clear on what constituted 'social rights' (cf Barbalet, 1988). He is fairly clear on a few points, however. First, Marshall (1963, p 108) claims that the guaranteed minimum of public services has been raised to such a height that the term 'minimum' becomes a misnomer. The provided service, not the purchased service, becomes the norm of social welfare. Some people think that, in such circumstances, the independent sector cannot survive for long. If it disappears, the skyscraper will have been converted into a bungalow. However, he continues that benefits in the form of a service have the characteristic that the rights of the citizen cannot be precisely defined. The qualitative element is too great. A modicum of legally enforceable rights may be granted, but what matters to the citizen is the superstructure of legitimate expectations. For example, it may be possible for every citizen who wishes it to be registered with a doctor, but it is much harder to ensure that their ailments will be properly cared for. In the case of housing, the basic right of the individual citizen to have a dwelling at all is minimal. They can claim no more than a roof over their head, and their claim can be met, as we have seen in recent years, by a shakedown in a disused cinema converted into a rest centre (Marshall, 1963, pp 108-9). To adapt Marshall's own phrase, later writers have converted his bungalow into a skyscraper by over-claiming his basic and minimal rights into a more impressive structure (see Rees, 1995; Powell, 2002).

Second, Marshall (1963, p 109) is also clear that individual rights must be subordinated to national plans, with expectations representing details in a design for community living rather than individual claims that must be met in each case when presented. The obligation of the state is towards society as a whole, whose remedy in case of default lies in parliament or a local council, instead of to individual citizens, whose remedy lies in a court of law, or at least in a quasi-judicial tribunal. He later considered that almost any benefit or service that is really designed to satisfy a particular individual need must include an element of discretion. For example, in healthcare, a patient may sue a doctor for gross negligence, but not simply for refusing to prescribe the treatment asked for. But discretion exercised in this way does not make a right inferior in quality to other rights (Marshall, 1981, p 87). In an 'afterthought', Marshall (1981, pp 96-7) sets out a hierarchy of rights and expectations: legally enforceable, discretion, legitimate expectations and generally acceptable standards.

There has been much debate on the issues of whether Marshall's rights were active or passive in two distinct senses. First, Marshall is generally regarded as presenting a liberal as opposed to republican view of citizenship. His citizens are largely passive right bearers rather than active citizens. Finlayson (1994) contrasts the politics of entitlement with the politics of contribution. Marquand (1992, pp 214-16) argues that citizen control through voice remained weak. The pioneers of social citizenship assumed that the institutions and practices of the social citizenship state would be subject to popular control. The surgeon was entitled to operate on the patient because, in the last analysis, the patient controlled the surgeon. As the 1970s wore on, that assumption was increasingly called into question. Voice was not playing the enhanced role assigned to it. The institutions of social citizenship were not effectively subject to popular control, or not, at any rate, in a fashion which the supposed citizens themselves – the patients in the doctor's waiting room, the parents outside the school playground, the crowd waiting to approach the DHSS (Department of Health and Social Security) counter – considered satisfactory.

At the point where the shoe pinched, at the point where ordinary members of the public brushed up against the institutions which were supposed to be acting in their names, the social citizenship state did not feel like a citizenship state at all. All too often, it felt more like a ramshackle, on the whole benevolent, but often remote and high-handed despotism. Marshall, Crosland and the rest had been dangerously over-optimistic: they had tried to build the top floor of citizenship before the first floor was in place. For the pioneers of social citizenship were wrong in supposing that political citizenship had already been achieved. In the most profound sense, Britain's (or, at least, England's) was not really a civic culture. The British were not, and never had been, citizens of a state with the rights and duties that go with citizenship; they were subjects of a monarch, with a subject culture that had little or no place for active and participatory citizenship. The case for non-statist, decentralist, participatory forms of public intervention was rarely made, and still more rarely heard. Exit won the argument, in short, because the culture provided too little space for voice. Social citizenship faltered because political citizenship was lacking.

Second, the role of rights and responsibilities in citizenship has been extensively debated. Many authors claim that Marshall wrote little or nothing about duties. Roche (1992, p 30) claims that while the dominant Marshall paradigm clearly places great emphasis on social rights, it is wrong to portray Marshall as having no conception of duties. 'However, the various versions of duty that it undoubtedly has are typically either unspoken, relatively muted or under-emphasised in relation to its emphasis on the new social rights of individuals in the postwar welfare state' (Roche, 1992, p 30). While it is the case that Marshall wrote more about rights than responsibilities, the latter appear at a number of places (see Janowitz, 1980; Janoski, 1998). 'If citizenship is invoked in defence of rights, the corresponding duties of citizenship cannot be ignored' (Roche, 1992, p 117). Similarly, according to Marshall (1981, p 92), 'Every right to receive involves an obligation to give'. Moreover, the duty whose discharge is most obviously and immediately necessary for the fulfilment of the right is the duty to pay taxes and insurance contributions. Since these are compulsory, no act of will is involved, and no keen sentiment of loyalty. Education and military service are also compulsory. The other duties are vague, and are included in the general obligation to live the life of a good citizen, giving such service as can promote the welfare of the community. Of paramount importance is the duty to work, but the essential duty is not to have a job and hold it, since that is relatively simple in conditions of full employment, but to put one's heart and soul into one's job and to work hard (Marshall, 1981, pp 122-4). Marshall, then, gives few clues to his views on conditionality in periods of high unemployment.

On the one hand, King and Wickham-Jones (1999, p 257) argue that the idea that benefit entitlement should be unconditional was at the core of Marshallian social rights of citizenship. This fits with the view of Dahrendorf (1996, p 33):

> Citizenship is a social contract, generally valid for all members; work is a private contract.... For when the general rights of citizenship are made dependent on people entering into private relations of employment, these lose their private and fundamentally voluntary character. In an indirect, but compelling manner, labour becomes forced labour. It is imperative that the obligations of citizenship are themselves general and public as it were.

He allows paying taxes and conscription, and perhaps community service, although such service, whether military or civilian, is of course also 'forced labour'. But it is strictly circumscribed and in all respects a part of the public domain in which citizens exist. Compulsory voting is a dubious interpretation of citizenship rights. In principle the rights of citizenship are not conditional, but categorical. What citizenship offers does not depend on the readiness of people to pay a price in the private domain. Citizenship cannot be marketed.

On the other hand, some writers are more ready to embrace certain aspects of conditionality (for example, White, 2003; see Deacon, 2002). The 'third way' of New Labour asserts that rights and responsibilities should be linked (Dean, 1999; Powell, 1999). Plant (1991, p 61) points out that civil and political rights are not generally conditional (although prisoners in the UK had traditionally been disenfranchised), and is not clear why one sort should be unconditional and the other conditional. Many citizens consider that rights should be 'earned' and should be 'conditional, and that other citizens should not have "something for nothing"' (see the views in Dwyer, 2000, ch 5). As Pinker (1971, pp 141-2) puts it, 'the idea of holding authentic claims by virtue of citizenship remains largely an intellectual conceit of the social scientist and the socialist. For the majority the idea of participant citizenship in distributive processes outside the market place has very little meaning. Consequently most applicants for social services remain paupers at heart'.

The equal welfare state?

The translation of Marshallian citizenship (MC) into the Marshall welfare state (MWS) presents further problems such as the definition of social rights and the conflation of different bases of entitlements. Faulks (2000, p 63) writes that 'social rights include income support, state-funded education and public health'. Crouch (2003, pp 5-7) claims that the list of items included in what we can call 'citizenship services' has varied across societies and over time, but usually includes education, health, care and financial support in old age and to cover loss of earnings through unemployment, ill health or injury. However, these typically include a mix of universal, insurance and selective services. Marquand (1988, pp 29-30) points out that entitlements had different bases, embodying conflicting views of how the social rights of citizenship arose. The right to medical care sprang from citizenship pure and simple, all eligible and paid for from general taxation, similarly family allowances. Elsewhere, entitlement rested on the fiction of social insurance. Benefits earned entitlements. Citizenship was not a sufficient basis for entitlement: the basis was individualistic not communal, whereas the opposite was the case in the NHS.

As Moran (1991, p 35) stresses, 'pure' citizenship services are rare: rights to social citizenship have two distinguishing features; they are 'universal' entitlements, claimable under impersonal eligibility rules by all people called citizens; and the quality of entitlements bear no relation to an individual's income or wealth. 'Healthcare citizenship' might thus be summarily defined as the right to healthcare for all citizens free at the point of treatment. However, 'no Western country offers this right' (Moran, 1991, p 35). National practices are in some ways more generous, and in some ways less generous. It is common for instance, to extend entitlements well beyond the category of political citizens (for example, to foreign residents and to minors). The scope and conditions of eligiblity are circumscribed through professional judgement, the range of services vary (for example, some systems exclude homeopathy) and even core or essential services are never completely free. In short, 'rights' are limited and problematic (Barbalet, 1988; Dwyer, 2004). Roche (1992, p 30) contrasts Marshall's generally rights-dominated conception of social citizenship with Beveridge's emphasis on social insurance and work duties. Marquand (1988, p 29) argues that Beveridge and his followers insisted on trying to square the communal notion of social citizenship with individualistic values that ran counter to it.

Marshall on a continuum

Titmuss (1974, pp 30-1) set out three models of welfare provision: residual, industrial achievement performance and institutional redistributive (see Figure 2.1). The first sees two main channels for meeting needs – the market and the family. Only when these break down should social welfare institutions come into play and then only temporarily. Its theoretical model is the Poor Law and the Institute of Economic Affairs (IEA). It is based on an individualised actuarial model and private insurance, and on selective, stigmatising and second-class, poor services for poor people (Titmuss, 1974, p 120). The second (also termed the 'Handmaiden model') incorporates a significant set role for social welfare institutions. Social needs should be met on the basis of merit, work performance and productivity. The third provides universalist services outside the market on the principle of need, based on social equality and redistribution. This is based on a 'gift relationship' and on altruistic providers (see Deacon, 2002; Le Grand, 2003). Titmuss also noted that social services are not a single system of welfare with a single objective, but a number of systems – social, fiscal and occupational welfare – with a number of objectives, some in harmony, some in conflict, with each other (Titmuss, 1974, p 137).

Figure 2.1: Welfare states and the Titmuss model

Residual ---------- Industrial achievement performance ---------- Institutional redistributive   (Titmuss Model)
-------------------------- BWS -------------------------------------- MWS ---------- E-AWS; BIWS/CIWS; TWS   (Welfare States)

Placed very roughly in terms of Titmuss's model, BWS is the least egalitarian and closest to the residual model. Beveridge supported earned entitlements rather than rights. Finlayson (1994, pp 261-2) writes that belief in the contributory principle permeated the Beveridge report, which was first and foremost a plan of insurance of giving in return for contributions benefits up to subsistence level, as of right, and without a means test, so that individuals may build freely on it. Social security must be achieved by cooperation between the state and the individual. The state should offer security for service and contribution. Beveridge retained his opposition to the Santa Claus states, preferring the social service state to the welfare state. In many respects, Beveridge embodied one of the central tenets of the New Liberalism of the first decade of the century: that the active state encouraged, rather than impeded, the active citizen, and that the citizenship of entitlement would be a spur to the citizenship of contribution by voluntary means. Benefits in return for contributions, rather than free allowances from the state, are what the people of Britain desire was perhaps the key sentiment in the whole of the Beveridge report, and the one most often quoted by contemporary commentators (Finlayson, 1994, p 419). Crosland (1964, p 81) considers that the Beveridge report gave the most complete and explicit statement of the philosophy of the national minimum.

The decommodification, basic income (BI), citizen's income (CI) and Titmuss versions are closest to the institutional redistributive model. Faulks (2000, p 119) links BI and decommodification. According to Esping-Andersen (1990, p 21), 'the outstanding criterion of social rights must be the degree to which they permit people to make their living standards independently of pure market forces'. CI seems the policy most likely to achieve a decommodification of social rights. While there are different versions of BI/CI, few social rights and no welfare states are fully unconditional (Pierson, 2001; Kleinman, 2002).

Marshall, Beveridge and equality

MWS sits somewhere between these, based on universal (rather than contributory or selective) services but with weak (rather than strong) egalitarianism. As we saw earlier, many writers have over-claimed the egalitarian aspects of Marshall's thesis. However, while an MWS is probably less egalitarian than a Titmuss or Tawney welfare state (TTWS), it would probably be more egalitarian than the BWS. While there may be some differences between the degree of class abatement between Marshall and Beveridge, the BWS was, in many ways, a limited and conservative plan based on a system of social insurance, and on contributors rather than citizens, to secure the national minimum (Hewitt and Powell, 1998).

Harris (2004, pp 82-3) points out that Marshall's account of social rights is open to question, since it may be argued that at least in formal terms, the Poor Laws, both old and new, were more deeply rooted in an absolute right to public relief than were many aspects of the welfare state, the latter being dependent on contractual rights and participation in the labour market rather than on the fundamental status of citizenship. Harris (1996, pp 124-5) pointed out that contributory insurance could never be 'universal'. It might be argued (and indeed was argued by many 19th-century radicals from Cobbett to Keir Hardie) that – contrary to its reputation for stigma, discretion and selectivity – the English Poor Law had been available for several centuries as a system of relief rooted not in contribution and contract but in mere membership of the community. Despite all the long catalogue of attempts to limit that entitlement – by civic disabilities, less eligibility, settlement laws and the workhouse – poor relief was, in the last resort, available to all who needed it as a matter of citizen right. An armchair political theorist who analysed the two systems, not as historic institutions but as abstract legal and normative structures, might conclude that, contrary to popular parlance, it was the Poor Law that carried connotations of universality, communitarianism and citizenship, while it was social insurance that entailed exclusion, differentiation and limited contractual rights. How then did it come about that the story of the welfare state in the 1940s came to be constructed by both academics and practitioners of policy in a way almost exactly opposite to that which pure theory might imply? Harris later adds that the findings of the Nuffield College Reconstruction Survey seemed to confirm Beveridge's belief that 'benefits in return for contributions, rather than free allowances from the State, is what the people of Britain desire', and that Beveridge in 1930 had specifically linked the theme of contributory insurance to the advance of civic freedom, whereas non-contributory public assistance was associated with a semi-feudal dependence and servility. In other words, contribution based on employment was both the sign and substance of full citizenship, as public service based on property had been in ages long gone by (Harris, 1996, pp 130, 134).

Twine (1994, p 95) argues that welfare provisions that involve means testing, stigmatisation and discretion, or contribution records, present key difficulties for the concept of citizenship and the development of social rights. Only child benefit meets the citizenship criteria as it does not depend on labour market participation nor is it means tested. He concludes that Beveridge's subsistence benefits, to be supplemented by voluntary insurance, were not designed to provide the basis for the social rights of citizenship (Harris, 1996, pp 110-11). Similarly, Faulks (2000, p 117) states that means-tested benefits have been seen by many recipients not as rights of citizenship but as state handouts. 'The link between citizenship and the welfare state that emerged after 1945 was comparatively a weak one.' In short, 'contract' is not 'citizenship' (Lister 1990, 2003; Dwyer, 2000, 2004; Dean, 2002).

Many writers have over-claimed in their argument that equality is one of the main objectives of the welfare state (for example, Le Grand, 1982). There are good reasons to accept a 'soft' rather than a 'hard' version of Marshall's social citizenship thesis, and of the equal welfare state thesis (Powell, 1995a; Powell and Hewitt, 1998). Cash benefits are based on earned entitlements, underpinned by means-tested benefits, pitched at subsistence levels, and intended to address the problem of absolute rather than relative poverty (Powell and Hewitt, 2002, pp 34-7). It follows that services rather than benefits are more likely to contribute to the equal welfare state thesis (cf Crosland, 1964). However, even here it is unclear whether equality is the only or the most important rationale for services (for example, Le Grand et al, 1992; Barr, 2004). Service objectives are often vague, multiple and conflicting. Even single objectives are problematic. There are many different types of equality (Le Grand, 1982; Powell, 1995a; Powell and Exworthy, 2003). It is claimed that equity is an important objective for health care (Powell, 1997; Powell and Exworthy, 2003). However, 'equity' is a multidimensional criterion, and varies between dimensions and groups (Powell and Exworthy, 2003). For example, the 'what' question of equity ranges from equality of inputs to equality of outcomes, and from equality of input to equality of input for equal need (Le Grand, 1982; Powell, 1997; Boyne et al, 2003). Similarly, the 'who' question may focus on social class, geography, race or gender. Combining these dimensions, Powell and Exworthy (2003) produce an equality matrix of *N* different cells. They claim that NHS policies on equality have tended to be vague and are often inconsistent. However, they have tended to suggest a 'weak' version of equality such as equal entitlements rather than a 'strong' version such as equal outcomes.

Finally, the welfare state tends to be in line with T.H. Marshall's argument that individual 'rights' are not enforceable. While citizens are entitled to be registered with a GP, it is the professional rather than the patient who decides on treatment. While citizens are entitled to visit the GP, they leave their rights at the surgery door, with the professional or 'street-level bureaucrat' (Lipsky, 1980) deciding on treatment on the basis of clinical judgement. The Secretary of State is responsible for providing a 'comprehensive' health service, and the courts have largely decided against individual and enforceable rights to treatment even for life-saving drugs (for example, Brazier, 1993; Woodhouse, 1998). Brazier (1993, pp 56-7) writes that although patients enjoy a cluster of legally enforceable rights, it is extremely dubious whether there is in the UK any legally enforceable right to healthcare on demand. The right to healthcare on the basis of clinical need in the 'Patient's Charter' is 'pure rhetoric'. She adds that rights are collective rather than individual rights. The courts will intervene to protect individual interest in the collective right only in the most exceptional sand restricted circumstances. (However, it is surprising that there have not been cases against the Secretary of State for his or her failure to provide a comprehensive general dental service.) Again and again the English courts have in effect declared that the 'doctor knows best'. The courts take refuge in professional opinion, in effect leaving doctors holding the baby (although some recent decisions have supported patients) (Brazier, 1993, pp 60, 69-70). In short, at least in terms of matters of treatment, patients are clients rather than citizens or consumers.

Conclusion

This chapter has attempted to disentangle the links often made between conventional definitions of equality and Marshallian citizenship. We do not have equal rights to state welfare because there are few 'rights' and they are not based on conventional understandings of equality. This is based on two main claims. First, Marshallian citizenship is not based on conventional definitions of equality. Marshallian citizenship is based on equality of status, and this provides the foundation for inequality of condition: 'citizenship has itself become, in certain respects, the architect of legitimate social inequality' (Marshall, 1963, p 73). Moreover, 'rights' are not simply unconditional and individually enforceable. Second, even if Marshallian citizenship could be equated with equal rights, the British welfare state tends to be based on a less egalitarian Beveridge welfare state (BWS), consisting of earned entitlements underpinned by means-tested assistance rather than citizenship rights per se. In short: E does not equal MC, and E does not equal PWS.

THREE

Citizenship in space and time: observations on T.H. Marshall's *Citizenship and social class*

Daniel Wincott

One of Marshall's most memorable maxims casts citizenship as a 'status extended to all those who are full members of the community' (1950 [1992], p 18, also p 6). The key reference here – to community – remains somewhat obscure (it is worth noting that Marshall sometimes seems to use it interchangeably with 'society'); it has attracted surprisingly little detailed analysis. I focus on Marshall's depiction of equality as a defining feature of democratic community membership, that is, of citizenship. Marshall treats 'equality' as a social-political construction, that is, as the product of norms emerging from social interaction as well as explicit political negotiation. As a consequence, we find Marshall arguing from an explicitly egalitarian perspective that citizenship endorses 'legitimate inequalities', underscoring once more the paradoxical quality of his analysis. And he consistently finds a significant role for social meaning and perceptions when analysing its 'spatial' – that is territorial-geographical and membership – dimensions. That begs an important question about how we make sense of changes in citizenship, and its social meaning, over time. This issue is of some political significance, as part of the attraction of citizenship discourses – and particularly the sense of inviolability that attaches to citizenship 'rights' – is as a resource for those seeking to resist welfare retrenchment. To the extent that these rights are rooted in a social consensus they may be more vulnerable to change than advocates and analysts of citizenship seem to believe. The UK is playing this out now, with arguments about devolution, citizenship and the fate of the welfare state constantly edging closer together.

Territory

Territorial politics provides a partially hidden subtext to Marshall's analysis. Only rarely does it break the surface of his narrative, but it is a key theme running through and animating his account. On one of the rare moments when it does come into view, Marshall depicts the politics of citizenship as a process of nationalisation. The crucial passage runs as follows: 'the citizenship whose history I wish to trace is, by definition, national. Its evolution involved a double process of fusion and of separation. The fusion was geographical, the separation functional' (1950 [1992], p 9). Marshall's vision of nationalisation was, in fact, essentially a process of delocalisation. In effect, he contrasts earlier, functionally integrated, but locally specific, bundles of benefits and duties with national citizenship that may be functionally differentiated, but is, he implies, geographically uniform.

The theme of geographical integration chimes sweetly with the dominant strand in postwar British political discourse, especially that of the Labour Party, which saw centralised state power as a crucial instrument for the establishment of democratic socialism. Vernon Bogdanor is a prominent scholarly exponent of this argument. He asserts that a fundamental principle which 'lay at the very heart of the Welfare State' was that the allocation of welfare 'benefits and burdens ... should depend upon need and not on geography' (Bogdanor, 2001, pp 152-3). Devolution, he has argued, 'negates' the 'need not geography' 'philosophy', hence it 'marks the end of' the welfare state and a key 'strand ... of ... social democracy' (Bogdanor, 2001, p 154; see also Wincott, 2006, particularly for the 'negation' reference). Having survived (we must presume) the crisis-ridden 1970s and Thatcherite predations of the 1980s, the British welfare state seems to have met its demise with a whimper, not a bang. It was killed off as an inadvertent by-product of constitutional change promulgated by the Labour Party.

The British welfare state is saturated with an imagery of national integration and territorial equality that, on closer viewing, is revealed as profoundly ambiguous. This ambiguity turns out to have important implications for our understanding of the place of the UK welfare state for − and of Marshall's analysis of social citizenship in − wider comparative analyses as well as for scholarship on the territorial dimension of (social) politics in the UK. The ambiguity is easiest to identify in relation to the UK's character as a multinational state.

There are, of course, important respects in which the imagery of the nation and the ideal of territorial equality were crucial − the welfare state was an important factor that bound the nations of the UK together in the period after the Second World War − and it may still serve some such role today (McEwen, 2002). The symbols of the postwar welfare state were saturated with images of integration and unity. Writing at the end of the 1940s Marshall must have found it easy to take national integration for granted. Many policy responsibilities, from the Poor Laws to health services, had recently been stripped away from local government. The idea of the nation was central to the symbolic representation of the institutions that replaced them – National Insurance, National Assistance and the National Health Service. Taking enterprises into public ownership came to be known as *nationalisation* (and the resulting organisations given such names as British Coal, British Rail, British Steel and latterly British Leyland), the new health system was the *National* Health Service. This iconography of the national was matched by higher levels of self-identification as British and pride in Britishness than we have seen in subsequent generations (Heath, 2005). To be fair, during the inter-war period new (multi)national institutions tended to be given the sobriquet 'British', which also signified a kind of integration. But even such examples as the BBC became much more comprehensive in their coverage of the UK territory after the Second World War – and particular events such as the widely viewed television transmission of the coronation of Elizabeth II (Elizabeth I of Scotland) served both to usher in the television age and to cement the integrative function of such (multi)national institutions.

Although some social functions – like social assistance and insurance – were integrated on a UK-wide basis during this period, others were not. Distinct education systems were maintained in Scotland and Northern Ireland. Scotland had separate legislation to that which created the 'National' Health Service in England and Wales. Contemporary political actors occasionally talked of a distinct Scottish health service even in the 1940s and 1950s, an issue that has spawned a certain amount of debate among historians. Social provision was certainly delocalising – being removed from local authorities – during this period, and there may be a sense in which it was 'nationalising' on a British, or UK-wide, basis (although the definition of a metric against which this claim could be measured would be fiendishly complicated). Nevertheless, it is clear that the construction of the welfare state as a 'national' feature of Britain, was an artefact of social and political discourse – the mood of the times – at least as much as, and probably more than, it was inscribed in or driven forward by the structure and content of public policies.

Moreover, the 'nation' to which commentators make reference is an infamously slippery concept in the context of the UK: not only is there no collective noun for the citizens/subjects of this state (UKanian?) but the question of how far the nation taps into British identities as compared to Welsh, Scottish or English ones is notoriously complex and contested. In particular, the territorial scale of community and political authority to which Marshall makes reference is much less clear-cut than is usually recognised. In fact, Marshall presents an analysis of English, not British, 'historical development' in *Citizenship and social class* (as Bottomore acknowledges, 1992, p 65; see also Wincott, 2006, for a discussion of this point). Yet such is the tenacity of the discourse and iconography of national integration and territorial equality, that distinguished scholars do not merely point to the 'real' consequences of these ideas as ties that helped to bind the UK together, but they continue to treat Marshall's work as if it provided a substantial analysis of social rights entrenched in public policies as a factor for the integration of British citizens into the multinational UK (welfare) state (see Roche, 2002, p 70; Gamble, 2003, pp 50-1; Obinger et al, 2005, p 3).

The picture may be still more complex. It might be possible to dismiss the peculiarities of roughly 10% of the UK population as oddities of the 'Celtic fringes': if the story holds true for the English majority, perhaps we should not be overly concerned. And yet, even as concerns England, there may be a sense in which Marshall's analysis reinforces a particular, rather metropolitan and elitist, perspective, although his account may not itself explicitly espouse it. The manner and form in which political power was centralised at Westminster and in Whitehall during the postwar period has frequently deployed the imagery of the 'village' (Heclo and Wildavsky, 1981; Moran, 2003; also compare with Bulpitt, 1983). In fact, centralisation of power in the national metropole often served as a means of insulating key decisions from public pressure, in a manner that left geographical variation in public service position in the periphery occluded from the centre, and largely 'illegible' from any point of view.

Certain actors did, of course, seek to use central power for the purposes of territorial equalisation, at least on some occasions. But even when we focus on these moments, they reveal as much about the limited and late character of such efforts at distributing public services on the basis of 'need not geography'. For example, the first attempt to provide hospital services on the basis of a comprehensive analysis of the spread of needs across territory did not take place until the 1962 Hospital Plan – the only attempt to do so during the welfare state's so-called 'golden age' (Greer, 2004, pp 35-6). Moreover, the efficient exploitation of this plan by the Scottish Office arguably meant that rather than reducing the territorial unevenness of such services it increased the divergence in hospital service provision between Scotland and the rest of the UK. But the evidence is that in 1973, more than 10 years on from the plan, and just as the 'golden age' was drawing to an end, 'the spread of [NHS] provision around the national average was about 50 per cent, and this degree of variance *was precisely the same*' as in 1948 when the service was created (Sharpe, 1982, p 155; emphasis added). Analysis of the 'nationalisation' of 'English Britain', then, can easily slip into an Anglocentric point of view – indeed the clubby perspective of the London/Oxbridge elite – as if this provided an accurate history of England/Britain as a whole. For all that the Westminster system concentrates power, it proved incapable of delivering 'egalitarian social citizenship where need replaced geography as the basis of provision', across the nations of the UK or even within England itself (as I have argued at length; see Wincott, 2006, p 181; see also Mitchell, 2006).

The peculiar character of nationalisation and centralisation in the UK also raises important questions about the place of this state in a broader comparative context. *Citizenship and social class* has often been criticised for its 'culture-bound' quality, for being part of a British tradition of social administration that allegedly emphasised 'unique British historical development' (see Flora and Heidenheimer, 1981, p 21). The sequential and purportedly evolutionary image of citizenship developing from civil through political to social rights has been particularly heavily criticised in this way (for a discussion see Janoski and Gran, 2002, p 37). Ferrera also criticises Marshall's neglect of 'external' questions of how citizens relate to non-citizens, relative to the three 'internal' dimensions of citizenship. In fact, this seems a somewhat otiose criticism. Marshall did not present his essay as a comparative analysis: Stein Rokkan has argued that Marshall recognised that the order of the 'three-step sequence' he proposed 'was primarily based on the history of institutional change in Britain' (Kuhnle and Rokkan, 1979, p 508).

Nevertheless, Marshall's analysis has served as an inspiration for key comparative analysts of nation building, from Bendix (1964) and Rokkan (for example, Kuhnle and Rokkan, 1979) to Ferrera (2005). In other words, Marshall's (albeit somewhat submerged and gnomic) preoccupation with the *nationalising* dynamic of citizenship may point towards a general tendency of western (European) political development). In the context of a (perhaps rather obscure) biographical essay on Marshall, Rokkan argues that the 'class-state, class-nation polarity' structured citizenship rights. Moreover, the 'history of the[ir] extension ... result[ed ... from] a sequence of counter-strategies in the struggle to maintain territorial-national unity in the face of the increasing bitterness of class conflicts under capitalism' (Kuhnle and Rokkan, 1979, p 509; see also Flora and Alber, 1981, p 40).

This aspect – the welfare state as a nation-building project – is currently gaining greater scholarly attention, especially from an explicitly Rokkanian perspective: 'Welfare rights, legitimised through the electoral channel gave a fundamental contribution for nationalizing the citizenry and accentuating territorial identities' (Ferrera, 2004, p 102). Interrogation of either *Citizenship and social class* or the subsequent comparative literature (for silences and ambiguities as much as substantive claims) reveals that this socio-political struggle is over the meaning or interpretation of public policies as much as their content and scope. It also suggests that 'unity' is always at stake or in play, never decisively achieved; we should expect general tendencies to be challenged by counter-tendencies.

Flora and Heidenheimer (1981) rightly claim 'that intensive study of the British case is not the optimal way of starting to grasp the general characteristics of welfare state development', insisting that they 'deviate from Marshall's Britain-centered conceptualization' (1981, p 21). Perhaps they do so to distance themselves from the sequential development of citizenship he proposed and from his argument that the welfare state depended on austerity. Ironically, however, if his nationalisation subtext has a general relevance, the British case may have a peculiar fit with it. Whether or not it is typical, Flora and Heidenheimer themselves suggest that in Britain a national solidarity generated by the Second World War triggered the rapid expansion of welfare provision in the 1940s: 'the war created a national solidarity that formed the foundation for the new institutions' and this solidarity 'at the same time' was also 'strengthened by it' (1981, p 20). To the extent that welfare feedback strengthened national solidarity, it did so through a general sense that these institutions increased (social) security for the mass population and perhaps because people believed they delivered services and benefits on the basis of territorial equality, but not because public policies actually achieved the latter idea (or were even designed to do so). Of course, no state will have 'achieved' territorial equality in full; and many states – including federations – may have set explicit limits to their aspirations in this direction. It is this juxtaposition of a powerful 'need not geography' ideal or ideology associated with the British welfare state with its relatively feeble practical efforts in this direction, reflecting the structures and priorities of the political village of Whitehall and Westminster (Bulpitt, 1983; Moran, 2003), that is particularly striking.

The territorial scale of community and political authority to which Marshall makes reference in the British case is much less clear-cut than is usually recognised. For all that the nation is sometimes treated as a primordial political identity, the ambiguity in Marshall illustrates that the role of social policy in constructing a national citizenship in Britain is 'territorial-political', caught up in the play of symbols as much as institutionalised in egalitarian patterns of public policy. As a result it may be relatively fragile or vulnerable, especially if compared with the robust quality that many analysts, following Pierson (1994) attribute to social rights of citizenship in the welfare state. I will return to these issues in the conclusion, when I turn to the implications of current debates about devolution for contemporary citizenship in the UK. But these issues of territorial politics also begin to raise questions about membership, which is the subject of the next section.

Citizenship and membership

We have just seen both that social policy has played a key role in the national-democratic integration of modern European states *and* that this role was rather more complex than is usually understood. As a result, the focus fell on the political processes by which differences (as well as similarities) were negotiated. Even if we were to ignore the central (and ambiguous) role of nationalisation, we can still find this kind of social and/or political ambiguity; the politics of difference would still play a significant part in Marshall.

So, even when we turn to topics that *are* central preoccupations of *Citizenship and social class*, it has a somewhat elliptical and elusive quality; almost self-consciously so in Marshall's explicit embrace of the paradoxical quality of the 'contemporary social system' – the 'stew' from which 'human society can make a square meal' (Marshall, 1950 [1992], pp 43, 49). Indeed, these features, to which we will return in the next section, contribute to the essay's richness, depth and texture, the qualities that draw readers nearly 50 years after its original publication, as a generative text for 'citizenship studies' (which now amounts to an interdisciplinary academic field with, since the late 1990s, its own specialist journal – see Isin and Turner, 2002; Somers, 2005, p 461). In fact, Marshall's core concepts are deeply inscribed with (productive) tensions.

While Marshall may later have expressed concern about the negative impact of social on civil rights, Somers reveals why it is difficult to attach a simple liberal tag to *Citizenship and social class*. Keith Faulks exemplifies this tendency when he declares that 'the social liberalism of Marshall should be considered a step forward' for a limited reason: it envisages that citizenship 'can offset some ... negative aspects of market inequalities' (2000, p 63). Labelling it as liberal is to pass up the opportunity to delve more deeply into Marshall's analysis. If tensions between civil, political and social rights have received a good deal of attention, Somers points to an even more fundamental source of creative friction within Marshall's analysis: his marriage of *citizenship* and *rights*. These two concepts, she argues, 'have different and deeply conflicting ontological meanings rooted in their different genealogical and conceptual *sites*' (2005, p 441; emphasis in original): citizenship draws on republicanism, while rights evoke liberalism. Part of the recent allure of 'citizenship' both in public debate and the burgeoning scholarly literature may flow from a wish to marry republican emphasis on the political, to liberal claims about the inviolability of rights.

Yet, Somers continues, for all that republicanism and liberalism differ on which side of the public and private divide they valorise, *both* reflect and reproduce 'the long-prevailing dominance of the[se] binary depictions of the social universe' (2005, p 447). Mirroring one another in this way, Somers argues, both republicanism and liberalism erase any distinct space for 'the social'. Yet, she continues, by bringing citizenship and rights together, Marshall begins to create space for 'the social' and hence to free citizenship from the horns of the 'public–private' dilemma. His 'social' conception (or, in Brubaker's [1992] terms, 'sociologization') of citizenship offers 'a fully-fledged *causally* dynamic institution extending from property to law to political participation to social policy' and implies a 'triadic conceptual landscape' (with a distinct space for 'the social') (Somers, 2005, pp 442, 453, 441). This is, for example, an important implication of Marshall couching his conception of citizenship in terms of 'full membership of the *community*', rather than of the state (1950 [1992], pp 6, 18; emphasis added). Consequently, Somers suggests, it provides useful analytic resources to address the 'troubles' of citizenship.

Marshall linked citizenship to community through a conception of equality, following his famous remark on 'full membership' with the argument that 'All who possess the status [of citizenship] are equal with respect to the rights and duties with which the status is endowed' (1950 [1992], p 18). Clearly, Marshall was concerned to juxtapose class (inequality) to (the equality of) citizenship: after all, this is the headline theme of *Citizenship and social class*. But there is much more to the essay than this banner. If we focus on equality – a core issue in *Citizenship and social class* – Marshall seems to understand this concept as neither fixed nor exclusively rooted in welfare provision, instead emphasising its socio-political and negotiated quality. Paradoxically, these features of Marshall's egalitarianism are fundamentally linked to (and best illustrated by an analysis of) his argument that 'citizenship is itself becoming the architect of social inequality' (1950 [1992], p 36). That is, his conception of citizenship was itself a complex mix of egalitarianism with acceptance of – even arguments for – inequality. In general, then,

Marshall was interested in the *forms* and *levels* of inequality that were acceptable within – and for him perhaps even necessary elements of – citizenship itself in mass democratic capitalist society. Although care must be taken not to read Marshall out of his time, these aspects of his account share some of the features of the 'postmodern citizenship' whose champions are generally critical of *Citizenship and social class* for its liberalism and national-statism. The purpose of this section is to illustrate this aspect of Marshall's analysis in some detail, as well as pointing to similar issues in Esping-Andersen's more recent (1990), and highly influential, expansive use of Marshall.

The discussion of wages illustrates these issues. Marshall's repudiation of (purely) market-based remuneration *is* partly based on his expectation that the alternative to it will be more equal. Nevertheless, a 'fair wage' 'includes the notion of ... stratified, not uniform, status' (1950 [1992], p 42). Marshall hints that legitimate inequality in remuneration results from the sense that some groups deserve more. This point is sufficiently important to justify a lengthy quotation from the original text:

> What *ought* a medical specialist or a dentist to earn, we ask? Would twice the salary of a university professor be about right, or is that not enough?... The claim is not merely for a basic living wage with such variations above that level as can be extracted by each grade from the conditions in the market at the moment. The claims of status are to a hierarchical wage structure, each level of which represents a social right and not merely a market value. Collective bargaining must involve, even in its elementary forms, the classification of workers into groups, or grades, within which minor occupational differences are ignored.... As the area of negotiation spreads, the assimilation of groups necessarily follows on the assimilation of individuals, until the stratification of the whole population of workers is, as far as possible, standardised. Only then can general principles of social justice be formulated. (1950 [1992], p 42)

Although today this discussion of wage determination may sound somewhat quaint, that is not my main point here. Instead, I want to emphasise that the determination of status is conceived as a *social* and *political* process – negotiation or contest – in which some groups ultimately recognise that they *deserve less* than others.

The objection might be raised that I have abstracted only one example of 'legitimate inequality' from Marshall's otherwise basically egalitarian position. Such a claim is unsustainable. Not only is wage determination a vital part of any argument concerning (in)equality, but Marshall offers the same broad line of argument in other policy areas. In relation to housing policy, Marshall distinguishes the proper (welfare state) role of town planners from that of the 'speculative builder, merely responding to a commercial demand' (1950 [1992], p 36). He also argues that they should not:

> ... build working class neighbourhoods and middle-class neighbourhoods, but they do propose to build working-class houses and middle-class houses. Their aim is not a classless society, but a society in which class differences are legitimate in terms of social justice, and in which therefore, the classes cooperate more than at present for the common benefit of all. When a planning authority decides that it needs a larger middle-class element in its town (as it very often does) ... [it] makes designs to meet its needs and fit its standards.... It must reinterpret the demand in harmony with its total plan and then give it the sanction of its authority as the responsible organ of a community of citizens. The middle-class man can then say, not 'I will come if you pay the price I feel strong enough to demand', but 'If you want me as a citizen, you must give me the status which is due as of right to the kind of citizen I am'. (1950 [1992], p 36)

Similarly in relation to education, Marshall states:

> If it were possible for the school system to treat the pupil entirely as an end in himself, and to regard education as giving him something whose value he could enjoy to the full whatever his station in after-life, then it might be possible to mould the education plan to the shape demanded by individual needs, regardless of any other considerations. But, as we know, education today is closely linked to occupation, and one, at least, of the values the pupil expects to get from it is a qualification for employment at an appropriate level. Unless great changes take place, it seems likely that the educational plan will be adjusted to occupational demand. The proportion between Grammar, Technical and Modern Secondary Schools cannot well be fixed without reference to the proportion between jobs of corresponding grades. And a balance between the two systems may have to be

sought in justice to the pupil himself. For if a boy who is
given a Grammar School education can then get nothing
but a Modern School job, he will cherish a grievance and
feel that he has been cheated. It is highly desirable that this
attitude should change, so that a boy in such circumstances
will be grateful for his education and not resentful at his
job. But to accomplish such a change is not an easy task.
(1950 [1992], pp 37-8)

Similar issues ramify through influential recent current scholarship
that makes use of Marshall. Today it is difficult to read *Citizenship
and social class* without interpreting it through the lens of *The three
worlds of welfare capitalism* (Esping-Andersen, 1990), a work which has
a pervasive scholarly influence, setting the terms in which we think
about the welfare state. Strikingly, Esping-Andersen uses social rights of
citizenship as discriminating criteria to determine when a state qualifies
as a welfare state (and ceases to so qualify). To do so, however, he finds
it necessary to introduce a further concept – decommodification – that
is not present in Marshall. Two points need to be made here. First, on
a strict definition, Esping-Andersen notes that very few states actually
qualify as welfare states, and even those that do so 'are, in practice, of
very recent date' (Esping-Andersen, 1990, p 23). Yet Esping-Andersen
continues to call all the countries he investigates 'welfare states' (albeit,
famously, taking three distinct configurations). The analysis oscillates
between a strictly egalitarian 'social citizenship', which relegates most
western countries from the welfare state league, and a less discriminating
concept, within which various citizenship configurations generate
distinct patterns of social stratification. Maintaining these mutually
contradictory conceptions allows Esping-Andersen to sustain the
notion that the welfare state is the central feature of contemporary
political economy (see Wincott, 2001, for a critical discussion). Arguably,
by retaining both the idea that social citizenship is essentially egalitarian
and that it produces (three worlds of) social stratification, Esping-
Andersen has helped to occlude the complexity, ambiguity and political
quality of 'equal citizenship' in Marshall.

Second, Esping-Andersen's conceptualisation of decommodification
may also be more complex than it appears at face value. 'A minimal
definition', he writes, 'must entail that citizens can freely, and without
potential loss of job, income, or general welfare, opt out of work when
they themselves consider it necessary.... These conditions, it is worth
noting, are those usually enjoyed by academics, civil servants, and
higher-echelon white-collar employees' (1990, p 23). But this definition

may not mean that individuals can 'opt out of work' permanently – the relationship between employment and commodification is more complex. Kalecki (1943) has described a full employment paradox (that full employment decommodifies work), which suggests that commodification concerns the quality of social relations in work. Moreover, Esping-Andersen argues that 'the most salient characteristic of the social democratic [that is, the most 'decommodifying'] regime is its fusion of welfare and work. It is at once genuinely committed to a full-employment guarantee, and entirely dependent on its attainment' (1990, p 28).

So, a close reading of Marshall's own essay and of its subsequent deployment in more recent influential texts suggests that even within territorially bounded states, the egalitarianism of citizenship is rather less complete, and more of a political construction than is generally recognised. If legitimate inequality is socio-politically 'negotiated', what happens when some groups in society do not accept that a given pattern of stratification *is*, in fact, legitimate? Moreover, as society changes – and with it social expectations alter – large numbers of people (perhaps even the overall 'climate of opinion') might also change. For example, if neoliberal ideas and values came to pervade a society in such a way that even 'losers' in the market accepted that the system as a whole (and their position within it) was legitimate, leading to significant welfare retrenchment, does Marshall's theory provide a theoretical basis on which we could object to it? Is there a vantage point from which we can judge legitimate from illegitimate inequalities? Is political mediation enough? My reading of this aspect of Marshall alters – and may weaken – the potential to use of this theory to defend the welfare state against retrenchment (but see King and Waldron, 1988, for an elegant deployment of Marshall in defence of the welfare state – compare with Klausen's 1995 discussion of the use of Marshall in 'social rights advocacy'). Marshall himself believed the UK became an 'affluent society' some time in the 1950s or 1960s, ceasing to be a welfare state as it did so (cited in Flora and Heidenheimer, 1981, p 20). Taken together, the political construction of citizenship in territorial and membership spaces begs questions about how it changes over time.

Time: the changing contours of citizenship

The account so far suggests that we are consistently finding that social meaning and perceptions matter when we examine the meaning of territory and membership in citizenship. But that begs an important question. How do we make sense of changes in citizenship over time as its social meaning alters? This issue is of some political significance, as part of the attraction of talking about citizenship, and the sense of inviolability that attaches to citizenship 'rights' is as a resource for those resisting welfare state retrenchment. To the extent that rights are rooted in a social consensus, they may be more vulnerable to change than the advocates and the analysts of citizenship seem to believe. At the same time, changing expectations and perceptions of legitimacy may expand the scope of citizenship in ways these same advocates and analysts are more inclined to endorse. Similarly, the 'welfare state itself' is often treated in an ahistorical fashion, as if its scope and meaning has not changed since it was fully and finally set at some moment in the past. This section considers these 'temporal' aspects of social citizenship.

Even a cursory perusal of the text indicates that if Marshall thought that citizenship had an essential quality, it was dynamism not timelessness. Marshall's conception of citizenship is best understood as a combination of interacting elements, as Michael Lister has argued recently (2005). Lister's argument draws attention to the manner in which a change to one aspect (whether civil, political, social, or some other) has immediate consequences for the overall character of citizenship. Dynamism is clearly a feature of the developmental process that Marshall traces from civil through political to social rights; but the achievement of 'social citizenship' does not bring it to an end. Instead, after arguing that there 'is no universal principle that determines what [the] rights and duties [of citizenship] shall be', in a piece of cod–Hegelianism, Marshall argues that 'societies in which citizenship is a developing institution create an image of an ideal citizenship against which achievement can be measured and towards which aspiration can be directed' (1950 [1992], p 18). Two implications of this position need to be drawn out.

First, a citizenship 'ideal' is not absolute; each is created by (particular) societies or communities. So, presumably, the ideal itself (as well as the means of achieving it) may be subject to social change. We have just seen that Marshall can be read as constructing citizenship in terms of equality, even while citizenship itself recognises, reproduces and even generates inequalities. We cannot expect that these political constructions of citizenship will remain stable. What was once accepted as a legitimate inequality may come to be seen as unacceptable, even odious. Equally, previously widely accepted signs of similarity may be repudiated in the name of recognising and respecting difference (often, in the process, uncovering oppressive features of earlier putative uniformity). That is, the 'ideal' of citizenship may have changed since Marshall wrote, as, for example, gender roles change, as do perceptions of personal and intimate relationships and societies have become more multicultural (Orloff, 1993; Faulks, 2000). Ken Plummer's fascinating discussion of citizenship and intimate relationships is exemplary in his claims that '"intimate citizenship" will not be like the citizenship of old' (2001, p 251). Yet, Plummer's reasons for regarding intimate citizenship as new seem familiar, at least in some respects. Its novelty results from the need 'to recognise the constant skirmish of (a) insider with outsider, (b) of traditional tribalism struggling against multicultural diversities, (c) of the need for dialogues across these seemingly impossible differences, and (d) of the need to try to establish – against all the fragmentations of post-modern social theory – some emerging sense of a "differentiated universalism"' (2001, p 251). Marshall neither addressed multiculturalism nor used the language of insiders and outsiders, although citizenship might be seen as overcoming tribal qualities of 'class' and could be translated into the latter terminology relatively easily. I believe that Marshall was indeed struggling with something like 'differentiated universalism', which begs questions about the depth of his egalitarianism, and that it is helpful to read *Citizenship and social class*, if not as an effort at dialogue, certainly as an attempt to articulate politically such a position across what earlier appeared as 'seemingly impossible differences' (Plummer, 2001, p 251).

Secondly, Marshall's argument that a 'society' creates its citizenship ideal suggests an organically unified conception of 'the social'. Relatedly, *Citizenship and social class* has been sharply criticised for downplaying the role of 'struggle in the formation of citizenship' (Tilly, 1995, p 12). It does offer a somewhat 'bloodless' account (in the Hall and Taylor [1996] sense), within which very few 'actors' appear. But Marshall also emphasised the tensions and contradictions, social 'paradoxes', within citizenship and between this status and social class. These paradoxes, he argues, 'are not the invention of muddled brains; they are inherent in our contemporary social system' (1950 [1992], p 43). While Marshall seems to believe that paradoxes ultimately require resolution, he suggests it can take quite a long time to get to the ultimatum: 'society can make a square meal out of a stew of paradox without getting indigestion – at least for quite a long time' (1950 [1992], p 49). Equally he argues that 'a little common sense can often move a mountain of paradox in the world of action, though logic may be unable to surmount it in the world of thought' (1950 [1992], p 43). While the bloodless quality of Marshall's essay may reflect a Fabian-style paternalistic elitism, in the light of the emphasis he placed on paradox it may also reflect his political purpose: downplaying explicit 'struggles' and identifying relatively few actors allowed him to present his position as consensually 'commonsensical'.

The interaction between changing gender roles and citizenship is a key example of changing citizenship ideals. Feminists have attacked Marshall's masculine bias (see especially Pateman on 'The patriarchal welfare state', 1988 [2000]). *Citizenship and social class* had very little to say about women, beyond noting that 'the status of women, or at least of married women, was in some important respects peculiar' – a backhanded recognition that many of his arguments applied to men, not adults in general (1950 [1992], p 12). From a feminist perspective, Marshall illustrates the manner in which inequalities may (appear to) be accepted as legitimate (at least partly) on the basis of the weak position of those (women) who suffer as a result. Subsequently, gender egalitarianism has gradually moved towards *normative* status, albeit in a spatially and temporally uneven manner, while remaining both incomplete and contested (including by anti-feminist forces of various sorts). In other words, the increasingly normative status of gender equality does not reflect a complete social consensus.

At the same time, many changes in public policies that alter the terms of citizenship, partly in the light of changes in gender roles, seem to occur in a gradual, almost subterranean, manner. These changes may be linked to pervasive (almost ethereal) but nonetheless far from uniform or universal alterations in the climate of opinion. Social and political analysts seem poorly equipped to make sense of changes of this sort. In the case of social policy, attempts to grasp these changes have come to revolve around the notion of 'new social risks' (Bonoli, 2005, 2007). Here, scholarly analysts place particular emphasis on changing patterns of domestic life, gendered employment and demography, while noting the relative weakness of specific social mobilisations as a cause of these changes. The relevant literature emerged during the 1990s, at least partly in an attempt to make sense of changes in social policy that could not easily be encompassed within the conventional periodisations of welfare history. The latter tended to treat the welfare state 'after the golden age' as crumbling or at best bolstered by important forces of inertia and were poorly placed to grasp apparently novel social policies.

And yet the claim that these social risks and policies were 'new' is seriously misleading in at least two significant ways. First, many of the concerns discussed under the rubric of new risks echo the preoccupations of much earlier, pre-'golden age' social policy and debates. Secondly, and more significant for my current concerns, both the relevant 'current' social trends and the policies through which states have sought to address them have rather earlier roots than is usually recognised. Socio-demographic trends related to changing gender roles and population ageing are key here. These trends date back at least to the 1960s (Alber, 1995; Morgan, 2001) – and some argue that the gender changes are rooted in the 1950s (Becker, 1981). A general rise in demand for 'care' is related to these changes, which also tend to reduce the amount of care supplied informally and unpaid within households. Moreover, careful analyses focused on the dynamics of care provision (particularly for those not of 'working age') suggest that in most western states the public role in the provision of social (care) services has tended to grow in the period since the 1960s (albeit in a fitful and uneven manner): through the last years of the 'golden age', into phases usually understood as crisis-ridden and retrenchment-prone, as well as since 'new social risks' have been recognised. Nordic social policy – and particularly the Swedish welfare state – which has come to be seen as the apotheosis of 'golden age' welfarism, arguably developed some of its most expansive and distinctive features from the late 1960s, precisely in the area of (purportedly universal) care services. In other words, rather than identifying new social risks with a new phase of welfare development, we understand the rhythms of social policy-making better if they are conceived as layered over one another, perhaps sometimes even interwoven.

If its citizenship 'ideals' can change, it remains striking that analysts and advocates continue to articulate some claims in terms of *citizenship*, rather than human, rights. This suggests that even as its substance or ideal changes, some 'citizenly' quality remains. The continued attraction of citizenship can be puzzling, particularly when an effort is also being made to detach it from any relationship to a state or territory (see, for example, Faulks, 2000). In cases where it remains unclear why rights should attach to individuals as citizens rather than as humans, I am tempted to conclude that some link to political authority or the mutual ties of a specific community retain a role, or continue to exert some appeal within the analysis. This temptation is all the stronger because the dilemmas and tensions that attach to citizenship in these contexts are not wholly novel products of globalisation, postmodern citizenship, multiculturalism or intimate citizenship, but can, in some form, be detected in Marshall.

Conclusion

The major argument running through this chapter is that citizenship has been as much a matter of social or political construction – of meanings and symbols whose use and significance can be subject to considerable change – as it has of substantive and inviolable rights entrenched in public policies. *Citizenship and social class* can seem strangely 'bloodless' (Hall and Taylor, 1996), as disembodied collectivities (societies, abstract communities), rather than 'flesh and blood' actors, often seem to be 'doing' things. It is, however, easy to amplify the role of social actors, to write it back into Marshall's account. Equally, these 'disembodied' collectivities may stand in for intersubjective understandings – the social or political construction of citizenship. They may also reflect Marshall's own political agenda – the particular form of citizenship he was advocating, which was 'constructed' in terms of equality and national integration. Yet we have seen that Marshall's construction of equality included explicit elements of 'legitimate inequalities' within citizenship, while his remarks on national integration were fragmentary, but certainly did not include the whole territory of the UK state. Moreover, *pace* Bogdanor, major territorial variations continued to exist both within British society and in public policy throughout the purported 'golden age' of its welfare state. But if Bogdanor is wrong in terms of policy substance, he may have been right in political spirit: within Britain major territorial policy variations long coexisted with a general sense of common and broadly equal social citizenship. Like Sidney Low's view of the 'tacit understandings' that animate – even 'constitute' – the English constitution, 'the understandings' that served to bind together what we might call the British territorial constitution 'themselves are not always understood' (1904, p 12). (And, as Bogdanor has himself argued in another context, this suggests that 'the "understandings" themselves are not fixed, but change through time' [1987, p 457].) So a partial misreading of Marshall seems to have served as a legitimising reference for a 'tacit understanding', or productive myth, that citizenship and the welfare state involved a strong commitment to territorial egalitarianism.

Why should this 'tacit understanding' have changed? The shift began in Scotland, where it probably focused primarily on a perception of general retrenchment, reneging on the citizenship deal – albeit one driven by English politicians and unwanted in Scotland – as much as a specific sense that Scotland was being treated differently (worse than) England. (Although the symbolic role of the Poll Tax, and perception that is was being trialled in Scotland before being rolled out for England, might point towards a sense of different treatment being politically significant even here.) If devolution began to address the Scottish legitimacy problem, its unintended consequence was (eventually) to draw English attention to the territorial dimension of British territorial politics. Yet the politicians responsible for devolution seem to have devoted very little time to its design. Because, during its period of 'bedding down', devolution provoked few problems, little or no effort was devoted to the construction of a new political discourse for Britain's changed territorial constitution: 'let sleeping dogs lie' seems to have been the ethos. For example, the new constitution requires reconsideration of the arcane public spending allocation system across the UK's nations, but Downing Street and the Treasury have been equally reluctant to provoke a public debate on the 'Barnett formula'. If Labour wanted devolution to strengthen the Union in the long term, it needs to emphasise policies that symbolise and embody shared UK values. And where policies differ, the rationale for divergence must be more widely understood.

Another issue sits alongside that of commonality and diversity in the territorial provision of public policies, and even in the political discourses that animate these specific themes. It is the absence of any sustained attempt to articulate a comprehensive social purpose for public – particularly welfare – policies. Neither Brown nor Blair has (yet) sought to develop a coherent, integrative political narrative around the major, often UK-wide, efforts they have made in some aspects of social policy. As much as the problematic quality of the UK's post-devolution territorial politics, this failure also reflects a general reluctance to draw attention to the scale of redistribution they have achieved. Geoff Mulgan, until recently a close adviser to the former Prime Minister Tony Blair, has been disarmingly frank on this point, noting that the Labour leadership judged 'over a number of years' that they should avoid 'talking too much about redistribution' (Mulgan, 2005). The rationale he provides for this position is also revealing: emphasising redistribution calls it to the attention of middle-class swing voters and 'you therefore undermine your support'. Equally, Labour assumed the beneficiaries of its redistribution would reward the government for it, a view that Mulgan now accepts was misplaced (2005). *Citizenship and social class* discloses that the social and political construction of social rights attached to citizenship was crucial in the 1940s and 1950s; particularly in the context of devolution, the same is true today.

FOUR

Social citizenship and the question of gender: the suitability and possibilities of a Marshallian framework

Richenda Gambles and Adam Whitworth

> Citizenship is a status bestowed on those who are full members of a community. All who possess the status are equal with respect to the rights and duties with which the status is endowed. There is no universal principle that determines what those rights and duties shall be, but societies in which citizenship is a developing institution create an image of an ideal citizenship against which achievement can be measured and towards which aspiration can be directed. (Marshall, 1950 [1992], p 18)

In this chapter, we reflect on T.H. Marshall's theory from a gender perspective and explore the extent to which a gendered analysis of welfare provisions challenges the 'universal' and 'inclusive' claims of Marshall's account of citizenship. In doing so we aim to consider the suitability, problems and possibilities of a Marshallian approach to citizenship from a gender perspective. We begin by considering women's relationship with welfare: how women's entitlement to social rights has been compromised because of their gender and the ways in which this creates their paradoxical inclusion and exclusion from citizenship. We then discuss some of the policy dilemmas that arise when trying to enhance the inclusiveness of citizenship experiences from a gender perspective. We end by considering whether Marshall's conceptualisation of citizenship serves as a useful benchmark for measuring achievement and whether it offers an aspirational or enabling device – as Marshall indicates in the extract above – once the question of gender is raised.

Marshall's citizenship framework, the postwar welfare state and gender

For Marshall, citizenship offers qualifying members of a nation a certain type of equality in the context of inherent economic inequalities of the capitalist system (Barbalet, 1988). Citizenship – through the equally shared entitlement to civil, political and social rights – ensures that all stand equally with respect to the formal status of citizenship, and entitlements to welfare benefits offer all citizens the right to a socially acceptable minimum standard of living. Marshall's work has been tremendously influential on the political reality of welfare claims in the UK and beyond, yet as Christopher Pierson (1998, p 34) summarises: 'who counts as a citizen, whether citizenship is gender-specific, what is to count as a citizen's entitlement and under what circumstances welfare rights will be granted and by whom, continue to be daily concerns of political life'. Reflecting here on citizenship with respect to gender we first reflect on women's compromised relationship with citizenship in terms of welfare entitlements and then go on to discuss how women have simultaneously been both included and excluded as citizens.

The gendered nature of social rights to welfare entitlements in historical perspective

A historical account of the gradual evolution of citizenship rights, according to Marshall's chronology, is deeply flawed as soon as gender is introduced. In a discussion of the gendered nature of citizenship, Ruth Lister (2003, p 4) argues that 'behind the cloak of gender-neutrality … there lurks in much of the literature, a definitely white, male citizen and it is his interests and concerns that have traditionally dictated the agenda'. For example, women have long had a compromised relationship with civil rights. When men were entitled to own their own property women were not; when men were offered the right to bodily integrity and protection through the courts and criminal justice system, women could be beaten by their husbands (see James, 1992). In terms of political rights, women have also had a compromised experience as they were granted the vote and right to stand for elected office much later than men. With compromised – and unresolved – experiences of the 'forerunning' civil and political rights, women's compromised experiences of social rights seem somewhat inevitable.

While Marshall's theory of citizenship takes in the evolution of a whole set of civil, political and social rights we focus here on the *social rights of citizenship*. Social rights, according to Marshall, include 'the whole range from the right to a modicum of economic welfare and security to the right to share to the full in the social heritage and to live the civilised life according to the standards prevailing in society' (Marshall, 1950 [1992], p 8). Marshall argued that these rights emerged with the development of the comprehensive, cradle-to-grave protection offered through the postwar welfare state (Glennerster, 1995; Timmins, 2001). But while Marshall's theory rests on universal and inclusive entitlement to these social rights, the universality of his theory has been questioned in a range of areas (see Bottomore, in Marshall and Bottomore, 1992, and Dwyer, 2004, for useful overviews).

The Beveridgean welfare model – on which Marshall based his universal citizenship theory – has been described as a 'male breadwinner' model (Lewis, 1992) in which households are assumed to comprise of a two-adult heterosexual couple where the male is in paid work and responsible for providing the household's finances while the female is responsible for the household's unpaid housework and care activities in the private sphere, freeing the now unencumbered male from such tasks and enabling him to dedicate himself solely to the public activity of paid work. In a now infamous passage, Beveridge asserted that 'the great majority of women must be regarded as occupied on work which is vital though unpaid, without which their husbands could not do their paid work and without which the nation could not continue' (cited by Pateman, 1988, p 139). For Beveridge – and within welfare policies designed around his 1942 report – marriage was viewed as women's main occupation and only intermittent spells in paid work were expected from them. Despite the fact that this model of male earner–female carer has at no point been a particularly accurate representation of reality (Lewis, 1991; Davidoff et al, 1999; Tosh, 1999; Carabine, 2004; Fink, 2004; Gambles et al, 2006), this model remains the basis by which individuals are assumed to behave and the foundations for the way in which citizenship rights are 'earned'. Here we see that different activities were (and continue to be) expected of men and women, with implications for both women's and men's experience of citizenship. So to what extent does this compromise women's experience of citizenship?

While Beveridge gave verbal recognition to the 'vital' importance of women's contribution through unpaid work, this recognition did not translate into women's equal entitlement to welfare provisions. In an influential essay, Carole Pateman (1988) highlights that as paid employment became the 'key to citizenship' (1988, p 239) – with many social provisions linked to levels of national insurance and tax contributions taken from the pay packet – married women who made mothering or other forms of care work and housework their main contribution were (and continue to be) entitled to many welfare benefits only indirectly through their husbands' paid employment-based contributions. Although the welfare state offers women a social assistance minimum in the absence of a wage-earning male partner, without sufficient direct tax and national insurance contributions this social assistance minimum is lower than many men would typically be entitled to through their entitlement to employment-based social insurance (and potentially also occupational) provision. As a result, while men make up the majority of claimants of employment-related contributory benefits, women accessing benefits in their own right make up the majority of claimants of the meagre and more stigmatising non-contributory means-tested benefits (Lister, 1994). Moreover, such gendered outcomes were not an oversight – they were ascribed into the model. Men, or so the logic went, needed financial guarantees in times of hardship as they had the primary responsibility for the household's financial provision through the 'family wage'. The majority of women, who would prioritise homemaking activities, did not require similar levels of direct support: social security had only a secondary role for married women because of the security offered by men in marriage (Pascall, 1986, p 8). Thus the assumption of a rigid sexual division of labour, in which women freely undertook domestic responsibilities and men took responsibility for bringing home and benevolently sharing their 'family wage', was reinforced through welfare provisions.

Although Beveridge justified these social security logics through a conceptualisation of marriage as a rather harmonious and freely giving partnership, these assumptions have proved problematic for women. As neatly summarised by Gillian Pascall:

> ... nowhere does [Marshall] analyse the problematic relationship between citizenship and dependency in the family as he does between citizenship and social class. The status of married women as dependents belongs, in terms of Marshall's analysis, to a feudal era, in that status is ascribed rather than achieved. Such ascribed positions are the very fabric which citizenship rights – in Marshall's analysis – are replacing. (Pascall, 1986, p 9)

Thus, one of the central problems of Marshall's citizenship theory from a gendered perspective is his failure to problematise relationships of family dependence and how this affects entitlement and access to social rights. Assumptions that financial resources are redistributed equitably within households are unfounded and there is much research showing how the assumptions of equal sharing and income pooling within the model are not borne out in reality (Pahl, 1989; Lundberg et al, 1997; Goode et al, 1998). With men dominating household income earning, research shows how on aggregate women have weaker access to supposedly household resources, and may also experience power relations of dependency as a result of these gendered household roles (Pahl, 1989; Daly, 1992; Daly and Rake, 2003). Moreover, with women more likely to lack an independent income source they are more vulnerable to poverty if the marriage or partnership breaks down (Hobson, 1990; Lister, 1994, 2003; Daly and Rake, 2003), and can as a consequence lack exit power from potentially abusive or unhappy relationships (Hobson, 1990; Orloff, 1993). In this sense, it becomes increasingly apparent that concrete experience of Marshall's citizenship – being awarded economic and social welfare to live the life according to the standard prevailing – has differed markedly according to whether one is male or female, with women often finding themselves as indirect or second-class citizens (Pascall, 1986; Pateman, 1988; Vogel, 1991, 1994; Lister, 1994).

Simultaneous exclusion and inclusion from citizenship

While Marshall's work is usually linked immediately to the provision of rights, his emphasis on the need for citizens to fulfil their citizenship obligations in order to access these rights should not be neglected (White, 2000). Therefore, it is also important to consider the activities or obligations expected of men and women as part of the citizenship contract alongside a discussion of social rights. The citizenship contract – what one must do (citizenship obligations) in order to gain access to different types of welfare benefits (social rights[1]) – is central to questions about the universal nature of the concept, and the terms of the citizenship contract has been a key area of debate and contestation for women. Historically, the activities that have been considered 'legitimate' and sufficiently worthy to warrant the realisation of citizenship rights have been built around the activities of soldiering, paid work and childbirth and caring for young children. Each of these reflects different routes to achieving social rights: the 'citizen-warrior', the 'citizen-worker' and the 'citizen-carer'. In most nations the postwar period has seen the demise of the citizen-warrior as an important route to social rights, leaving the citizen-worker and the citizen-carer as the two remaining ideal types of citizenship (Pateman, 1992). For

Marshall, paid work was seen as the key citizenship obligation. In an age of the male breadwinner model – in which men were expected to be active in paid work and women were expected to primarily take on an unpaid caring role within the home – paid work was assumed to relate predominantly to men. As has been discussed above, in Marshall's account and in the postwar male breadwinner welfare state on which Marshall's theories were based, it is the model of the male citizen-worker rather than the female citizen-carer around whom many social rights are constructed.

Writing of the paradoxes and contradictions of the welfare state for women's citizenship, Pateman (1988) argues, however, that the very factors that serve to exclude many women from full citizenship – their primary role as mothers, carers and housewives that has constrained their ability to participate as soldiers or paid workers – also simultaneously serve to include them. For Pateman, herein lies the paradox: 'How could women, dependents of men, whose legitimate "work" is held to be located in the private sphere, be citizens of the welfare state? What could, or did, women contribute? The paradoxical answer is that women contributed – welfare!' (Pateman, 1988, p 137). Here, Pateman draws attention to the way in which women are the major providers of welfare. At the time of Marshall's writing women were the major providers of 'private' welfare provision in the home (as well as voluntary activity in the community). Yet they were excluded from the same level of entitlements to welfare benefits accorded to men because they failed to fulfil the core responsibility expected of a citizen, the activity at the peak of the hierarchy of citizenship obligations – to participate and contribute through paid work. Thus women, because of assumptions that they will be primary caregivers but the lack of entitlement this offers for individual welfare rights, have a compromised, contradictory – and second-class – relationship with citizenship, both included and excluded at the same time. This second-class relationship that women have with citizenship is overlooked by Marshall.

Marshall's lack of attention to the gendered nature of citizenship becomes particularly problematic when considering recent shifts in family and labour market experiences. Since the time of Marshall's writing there has been a decline in marriage rates, a rise in divorce rates and, consequently, an increase in 'non-traditional' household types, particularly lone parents; there has also been rising male unemployment and declining male wage rates, shifts which have undermined the assumption that men would and could provide economically for the household via a 'family wage'. Connected to both these sets of changes, as well as feminist demands for greater 'equality', there have been rapidly increasing rates of female labour market participation. This begs the question: is women's increasing engagement with paid work evidence that they are increasingly enjoying the same standards and rewards of citizenship enjoyed by men? The evidence suggests not. Because of assumptions and realities that women take on the majority of private welfare work – an activity women have been expected and obliged to do throughout history – they suffer a compromised relationship with paid employment (the activity guaranteeing the most generous social rights). Many women find they are concentrated in low-pay work when compared with men. This is because they tend to dominate lower-paid public sector welfare work, they are clustered at the lower end of the wage hierarchy, and because many women work in part-time employment as a result of the demands of their continued responsibilities for providing family care in the home (Blau et al, 2002; Daly and Rake, 2003; Gornick and Meyers, 2003). Earning low wages means some women do not qualify for contributions-based welfare entitlements (Lister, 1994) and evidence consistently shows that women are more vulnerable than men to poverty throughout the whole of their life course (Rake, 1999; Ginn et al, 2001). Additionally, and crucially for any modern gendered analysis of citizenship, women who work full time may have greater access to economic independence and individually earned welfare rights, yet continuing expectations that women are primarily responsible for family care mean they often experience a 'dual burden' of combining paid work alongside obligations in the home (Hochschild, 1989; Hewitt, 1993). Indeed, some have even argued that working women tend to experience a 'triple burden' as they seek not only to physically combine work and care – with all the stresses and strains which that brings – but that it is women rather than men who also tend to be faced with the difficult task of continuously questioning whether the care that is being provided to the family (and particularly to children) is 'good enough' (Hochschild, 1997; Williams, 2004).

Policy dilemmas: making citizenship of the welfare state sensitive to gender

How, then, have gender theorists responded to this changing context of family and labour market experiences and sought to fully include women as citizens? Herein lies a central dilemma for gendered citizenship: a dichotomy and apparent Hobson's choice between whether women are to be fully included as citizens on the basis of their historical dominance of unpaid caring roles or via greater inclusion in paid employment. This age-old dilemma, often referred to as Wollstonecraft's dilemma because of the contradictions and tensions found within the writing of Mary Wollstonecraft's *A vindication of the rights of women*, published in 1792 (1978 [1792]), centres on whether women should be included as full citizens on the basis of their 'difference' from men (that is, unpaid care role) or on the basis of their 'sameness' to men (that is, through paid employment) (Pateman, 1988; Lister, 1994, 2003; Fraser, 1997). So how might these different strands play out in policy, and what are the problems with the two approaches to women's citizenship?

Nancy Fraser (1997) sets out two 'ideal' models that map onto the approaches of sameness and of difference. The first, reflecting a sameness approach, is called a 'universal breadwinner' model and is concerned with ensuring women can participate as men currently do: as full-time and fully active members of the paid labour market. If a universal breadwinner approach is desired, policies required to make this a reality include those that remove the 'burden' of care. By ensuring that care services catering for the needs of young children, dependent adults and frail older people are available, women will be freed up to concentrate fully on paid work. The second, reflecting a difference approach, is called a 'caregiver parity' model and is concerned with offering financial remuneration and security for those who spend time engaged in care activities. The logic here is that care is a necessary part of life and valuable to those being directly cared for as well as society more generally. It is an important life activity and failing to offer support and recognition of the value of care may result in carers being particularly vulnerable to poverty and/or a lack of time and interest in providing care potentially leading to suboptimal levels of care being delivered (see Folbre and Nelson, 2000; Knijn, 2000; Williams, 2001). If a caregiver parity model is desired, policies required include a range of family and care-related leave, generous cash benefits for time taken out of the labour market to care and the development of flexible and quality part-time work that offers the same standard of welfare entitlements as for those in full-time paid work. The rationale here is that women can move in and out of paid work depending on their circumstances in a way that supports their changing needs and does not compromise their experience of citizenship rights to welfare.

Fraser finds, however, that both models are problematic. The universal breadwinner model requires women to adapt to a male worker norm. It ignores the fact that some people might want more active involvement in family care activities, perhaps seeing this as 'the proper thing to do' or a duty-bound yet important 'labour of love' (Finch and Groves, 1983; Williams, 2004). Moreover, care can never be fully commodified: even if care services are comprehensive and fully available, there will be times when services cannot provide everything. Moreover, the time and energy invested in existing and evolving emotional bonds and attachments are overlooked in the universal breadwinner model. This means that, in practice, many women struggle to combine paid work alongside family responsibilities and can be perceived as less committed or competent employees (see Rapoport et al, 2002; Gambles et al, 2006). The second caregiver parity model, in contrast, offers women greater support and recognition of their caring roles. Yet it reinforces socially constructed assumptions about gender differences between men and women and these differences can be used to justify inferior access to welfare provisions, as well as workplace inequalities and marginalisation. The problem, Fraser contends, is that neither model requires men to change. Women continue to be positioned as the 'other' citizen that has to fit in against the standard male 'norm'.

It is possible to see elements of both these models within recent policy developments across most of the developed world. The growing number and extension of family care-related leave policies as well as rights for parents with children under a certain age to request flexible working conditions, taken overwhelmingly by women rather than men (DTI, 2005), suggest aspects of the caregiver parity model. Yet the more dominating overarching direction has been towards a universal breadwinner model. The numbers of women participating in paid work have been increasing consistently since the postwar period with increasing expectations that men and women will both be in paid employment (Lewis, 2001). This masks how women have a compromised relationship with paid employment and so continues to bring problems for women's experience of citizenship. The relationship between gender and differential access to employment-based social rights persists and, indeed, it can be argued that women's position is potentially weaker as welfare provisions are increasingly made on inaccurate assumptions that all men and women are self-sufficient and fully and equally able to participate in paid work (Lewis, S., 2001; Lewis, J., 2002).

Most feminist scholars would agree that the universal breadwinner model of welfare, work, family and citizenship lacks adequate consideration of care responsibilities and the gendered experiences of paid work and care (Knijn, 2000; Lewis, S., 2001; Lewis, J., 2002; Williams, 2004). The question of how to sensitise the underlying assumptions and terms of citizenship (and the welfare state structures that link with these) to gender, continues to nag.

Moving beyond the sameness–difference dichotomy: possibilities for a citizen-worker-carer

Pateman (1988) argues that in the context of a welfare state that privileges and prioritises the experiences of men over the experiences of women, and thus the experiences of paid work according to a male norm or 'ideal' over the experiences of care, it is difficult to move forward in ways that do not compromise women's citizenship. Treating women as different from men – as primary caregivers – offers them lesser entitlements and access to welfare provision in comparison with men. Yet treating them the same as men – as adult workers – also offers only a lesser experience of citizenship as many women lack the time or resources to operate in paid work like men do currently and when in work women tend to remain responsible for unpaid or informal care, both physically and emotionally. We return to Fraser's observation: neither approach requires men to change. Women have to act as citizens in relation to a male standard: either like them through a citizenship approach of sameness, or differently from them through a citizenship approach of difference. So, like a number of scholars who are increasingly calling for a recognition of the gendered assumptions governing men, men's daily lives and notions of citizenship that evoke the socially constructed experiences of a privileged white male breadwinner (see for example Hearn, 1998; Connell, 2001), Fraser develops a third model that decentres men and notions of masculinity within citizenship assumptions and images of the 'ideal' citizen. Fraser argues:

> The key to achieving gender equity … is to make women's current life-patterns the norm for everyone. Women often combine breadwinning and caregiving, albeit with great difficulty and strain. A postindustrial welfare state must ensure that men do the same, while redesigning institutions so as to eliminate the difficulty and strain. (Fraser, 1997, p 61)

Thus, to achieve experiences of citizenship that are fully inclusive of both men and women, it is necessary to work from the assumption that both men and women will have both paid work and care responsibilities to fulfill. The model she develops, called a 'universal caregiver' model (similar to the dual-earner/dual-carer model discussed by Crompton, 1999; Gornick and Meyers, 2003), would be reflected in a set of changes that would free up time and energy for both men and women to participate in a range of paid and unpaid activities, including reduced paid working hours, widely available leaves and entitlements to a range of support services for care needs and activities. The universal caregiver approach focuses attention on gender relations and a more equitable sharing of activities between women and men. This model envisages change not only in state welfare policies but in the structure and culture of workplace organisations, as well as within assumptions and practices within the family and society more generally, so that those with care responsibilities are not seen as 'unusual' but rather the norm.

Although it has been suggested that men and women exercise increasing choice in terms of the ways they approach work–family reconciliation challenges (see Hakim, 1996, 2000), evidence consistently shows that men and women are differently constrained by gendered norm assumptions that play out and interact between policy, workplace, family and 'personal' levels (see Crompton and Harris, 1998; Perrons, 2003; Mooney, 2004; Williams, 2004; Gambles et al, 2006). As a consequence, a universal caregiver model needs not only to promote flexible working legislation, the provision of care services or policies to encourage (or coerce) paternal care leave (although these are all likely to be important elements within a bigger package of changes), but also to be sensitive to evolving gender relationships between men and women and the various barriers and tensions that arise as shifts in policy and practice are attempted (see Gambles et al, 2007).

Conclusion

So what about Marshall in all of this? In this concluding section, we draw together the discussion so far and reflect on the extent to which Marshall's account of citizenship is a suitable framework for thinking about citizenship – and in particular the social rights of citizenship – from a gendered perspective.

As this chapter has begun to illustrate, there are many feminist scholars who do not see Marshall's account as sufficiently sensitive to a gendered perspective for it to hold any useful promise or purpose to be used for gendered analyses. We have outlined many of the key tensions and problems in relation to social rights in particular, and overcoming these obstacles to the use of Marshall's account in a gendered analysis would take considerable political and social will, effort and thought. We recognise that there are serious tensions within the account centring on the differential obligations expected of men and women and the unequal access these activities bring for welfare entitlement. Yet we feel that Marshall's framework remains useful for gendered studies of social policy and that it can serve both as a useful benchmark for measuring women's citizenship and as an aspirational device for more gender-sensitive citizenship.

To begin this line of thought, it is necessary to briefly return to Marshall's original account and to clarify a distinction that he makes between the status and the practice of citizenship. Marshall famously defines each of these elements as follows:

> The civil element is composed of the rights necessary for individual freedom–liberty of the person, freedom of speech, thought and faith, the right to own property and to conclude valid contracts, and the right to justice.... By the political element I mean the right to participate in the exercise of political power, as a member of a body invested with political authority or as an elector of the members of such a body.... By the social element I mean the whole range from the right to a modicum of economic welfare and security to the right to share to the full in the social heritage and to live the life of a civilised being according to the standards prevailing in the society. (Marshall, 1950 [1992], p 8)

While entitlement to these rights brings with it the formal status of citizenship, these rights for Marshall also represent a means of achieving the end of 'full membership of a community' (Marshall, 1950 [1992], p 6). There is, therefore, a distinction within Marshall's work between the status and the practice of citizenship, a distinction common within the citizenship literature (Lister, 2003, p 92). The status of citizenship refers to the formal package of rights and obligations possessed by a legal citizen, typically in a nation-state, and is a more legalistic approach to the notion of citizenship. Denial of the full complement of rights (and obligations) of citizenship can be argued to represent a denial of the full status of citizenship. The practice of citizenship, in contrast, reflects a more sociological approach. It refers to the individual's participation in activities deemed to be pivotal or customary for the life of citizens in order that they, in Marshall's terms, are able to 'share to the full in the social heritage and to live the life of a civilised being', and the activities and resources required to achieve this citizenship in practice will vary over time and place and between different accounts.

Marshall does, however, provide some signposts as to what he has in mind as relevant for the life of a fully included citizen in practice, and his view of these relevant dimensions is broad and qualitative. He says that citizenship can be understood as moving 'away from a quantitative assessment of standards of living in terms of goods consumed and services enjoyed towards a qualitative assessment of life as a whole in terms of the essential elements in civilisation or culture' (Marshall, 1950 [1992], p 6). Marshall's emphasis on the breadth and qualitative richness of life suggests the need to support the realisation of a wide variety of life projects and activities that can include experiences of caregiving and receiving. He says that it is equality between people across broad life dimensions that is relevant to citizenship, not merely with regards to the political right to vote, the social right to education or a minimum of income from the state. He states that '[W]hat matters is that there is a general enrichment of the concrete substance of life, a general reduction of risk and insecurity, an equalisation between the more and the less fortunate at all levels' (Marshall, 1950 [1992], p 33).

King and Waldron claim that 'for Marshall, citizenship seems to be about expanding and enriching society's notion of equality by extending its scope through civil, political and social rights. The development of universal rights of citizenship has pushed forward the meaning of equality by broadening the scope of its application' (1988, p 205). The authors state further that 'citizenship remains a dynamic process likely to expand into other areas in the future' (1988, pp 423–4). Marshall presents a progressive account of an ever-increasing equality along two dimensions: first, to an ever-increasing number of people and, second, to broader dimensions of life. He claims that nations develop an ideal of citizenship towards which they progress, commenting that: '[T]he urge forward along the path thus plotted is an urge towards a fuller measure of equality, an enrichment of the stuff of which the status is made and an increase in the number of those on whom the status is bestowed' (Marshall, 1950 [1992], p 18).

It can be argued, therefore, that citizenship practice for Marshall relates to all aspects of life, and the role of the rights and obligations of citizenship status is to support equality in citizenship practice across the various dimensions of life as a whole, including experiences of giving and receiving care. To return to where we began in this chapter, in Marshall's own words, '[T]here is no universal principle that determines what those rights and duties shall be, but societies in which citizenship is a developing institution create an image of ideal citizenship against which achievement can be measured and towards which aspiration can be directed' (Marshall, 1950 [1992], p 18). Despite all of the problems, concerns and tensions within Marshall's original account, therefore, we would argue that this idea of what Marshallian citizenship can be is a potentially powerful message which leaves his framework with significant promise for gender scholars. It has also been noted that while gender is a significant dimension of social difference it is not necessarily the only or the most significant dimension of difference: indeed compelling cases for rethinking universal gendered and universal welfare claims have been put forward by those exploring 'difference' from 'race' as well as from gender and class dimensions (see, for example, Bhavnani, 2001; Lewis, 2003). It is for these scholars – in dialogue with each other and the wider academy community – and societies as a whole to make a sufficiently powerful case that Fraser's vision of a citizen-worker-carer, or beyond, or some entirely different gendered vision, ought to be the interests and aims defining the nature and extent of society's and – in policy terms – government's dominant image of an ideal citizenship practice. Attention to gender and debates about equality and difference open up and feed into wider debates about what makes for and who counts as a citizen in potentially useful and enriching ways. In this respect, Marshall's account has much possibility. But only when gender – alongside other interacting dimensions of social 'difference' – becomes a central part of our thinking around citizenship will Marshall's framework of citizenship be suitable for such a task.

Note
[1] Although indeed citizens must also fulfil certain obligations (for example, abiding by the law) in order to retain their civil and political rights.

Part Two
Territorial politics and citizenship rights

FIVE

Devolution, public attitudes and social citizenship

Charlie Jeffery

One of the most enduring debates about decentralised forms of government has been the tension between equity and diversity. Postwar conceptions of the welfare state have stressed the principle of state-wide equality of citizens' rights of access to public services. But federal, regional and devolved forms of government enable territorially differentiated packages of public services. And decentralised government has become significantly more widespread and more powerful over the last 30 years (Marks et al, 2008). The scope for tension between the equity goals of the welfare state and the diversity of outcomes that decentralised government brings has grown.

This chapter explores this tension in the case of the UK a decade or so on from the introduction of devolved government in Scotland, Wales and Northern Ireland. Its focus is twofold. It explores how ordinary citizens negotiate the additional opportunities for political participation that devolution has brought; and it asks whether devolution has prompted any rethinking of the appropriate territorial scale – devolved or UK-wide – at which citizens prefer to express social solidarity with one another. It approaches these questions by drawing on, and developing, T.H. Marshall's (1950 [1992]) conception of citizenship rights, in particular his understanding of citizenship as composed not just of civil and political rights, but also social rights. Marshall has increasingly become conscripted into debates about whether equitable, national social rights of citizenship, as institutionalised in the postwar welfare state, are eroded by the policy diversity implied by decentralised government.

The chapter starts with a reflection on Marshall's conception of how the content of citizenship evolves over time, as different forms of citizenship rights interact and 'spill over' into one another. Marshall's focus was on such interactions at a *national* scale. The discussion here takes forward the logic of Marshall's arguments, but extends them to the *regional* scale. Drawing on recent contributions both to comparative analysis and to discussions about the tensions of welfare equity and political diversity in post-devolution UK, it sets out a number of interpretations of how political and social rights might interact with each other across the UK's national (that is, UK-wide) and regional (that is, devolved) scales.

Those interpretations are then used to frame an analysis, based in public attitudes research, of how citizens perceive and negotiate any tensions between the social rights of the UK-wide welfare state and the new, regionalised political rights of the devolution era. The focus on public attitudes is intended both to introduce a *citizen*-centred perspective on citizen*ship* – which is, perhaps oddly, absent from almost all Marshall-inspired work – and, in that way, to build a sense of how far public views appear either to endorse the current ways in which the devolved UK state expresses equity–diversity tensions, or to signal future alternatives.

Rescaling citizenship

Marshall's conception of citizenship was national. He, along with contemporaries such as Stein Rokkan (Flora et al, 1999), evoked an imagery of how, over centuries, functions of government and rights of citizenship accumulated at the scale and within the institutions of the democratic 'nation-state'. Marshall – working in a narrower, UK-focused frame than the comparativist Rokkan – distinguished three components of the citizenship of this national democracy in the UK: civil rights, political rights and social rights. In their modern form these emerged in sequence, each the precondition of the next. Civil rights, protecting individual freedoms, emerged in something like the modern form in the 18th century, in part as a set of defences of individual liberty versus the state, in part as a set of abolitions of restrictive practices that opened up the space for a market economy. Modern political rights – the right to participate in the exercise of political power through voting or standing as a candidate – emerged during the 19th century as new social interests exploited freedoms of speech and association to

Table 5.1: The evolution of the national rights of citizenship in the UK

UK	18th century	19th century	20th century
Civil rights	Yes	Yes	Yes
Political rights		Yes	Yes
Social rights			Yes

open up a political system dominated up to then by privileged groups of aristocrats, landowners and industrialists.

Social rights followed the final expansions of the franchise in the early 20th century that, by 1945, had enabled a majority Labour government buoyed by working-class votes to come to power. Social rights consisted of minimum standards of welfare, guaranteed by the state, so that the working class in particular was protected from risks of ill health, old age, unemployment and so on. These minimum standards were funded, as an expression of state-wide social solidarity, through general taxation. Social rights, in other words, were guaranteed by the postwar national welfare state.

This is, in many respects a compelling analysis and remains highly influential (cf Flora and Alber, 1981; King, 1987; Pateman, 1988; Rieger, 1992; Lister, 2005; Banting, 2006). But there are important caveats. A first is Marshall's elusiveness on the 'nation'. Marshall claimed that the citizenship whose history he wanted to trace was 'by definition, national' (1950 [1992], p 9). That 'nation' might appear to be the UK as a whole. But as Wincott (2006, p 181) has stressed, Marshall in fact 'equates the nation with England'. Unlike Rokkan, with his enduring focus on the persistence of the 'periphery', Marshall simply ignores Scotland, Wales and Northern Ireland, and in doing so the 'differentiated welfare states' (Wincott, 2006, p 176) that existed even before devolution as a product of the long-standing patterns of asymmetric territorial administration that had always been a feature of government in the UK (Mitchell, 2006). Even in England itself there had never been a simple, uniform, 'national' pattern of policy outputs, as Bulpitt's (1983) innovative work in the 1980s showed.

Marshall, in other words, was presenting less an empirically underpinned account than an idealised vision, even a political project for a state-wide national citizenship. There is a line here between advocacy and social science which was blurred in Marshall's own work, but also a good deal of successor analysis, which appears underpinned by a 'methodological nationalism' (cf Martins, 1974; Beck, 2000): a presumption that the national state is a 'natural' scale for the organisation of political and social life. Such presumptions help to conceal a second caveat about possible interactions between Marshall's different components of citizenship. Marshall viewed citizenship as dynamic, ever changing, as its various components interacted to produce shifting outcomes. But there is a tendency in readings of Marshall to 'freeze-frame' understanding of social rights to support a particular construction of the national welfare state that emerged after the Second World War. It is worth referring back to Marshall (1950 [1992], p 9) on this point, from his celebrated lectures on citizenship delivered in 1949, shortly after the National Health Service (NHS) had been established, when he described his three sets of citizenship rights as a kind of championship steeplechase extending over centuries:

> Before long they were spread far out along the course, and it is only in the present century, in fact I might say only within the last few months, that the three runners have come abreast of one another.

Of course, if the three sets of citizenship rights only came abreast of one another at a national scale in 1949, there is no reason that they should have trotted along in a synchronised canter *at a national scale* ever since. And clearly they have not. For example, important aspects of civil, political and social rights are now realised at a European Union (EU) scale (see Table 5.2). Marshall's civil rights included freedoms to trade without restrictive practices. The main framework for realising such freedoms in the UK and other EU member states has long been a European one, beginning with the first steps in European economic integration in the 1950s, and now significantly more important in regulating economic activity than national law. Should the Lisbon Treaty come into force, European citizens will have a charter of fundamental rights as a guarantee of their civil rights additional to national-level guarantees. While few yet see the EU as the primary arena for exercising their political rights, there is a framework for political participation on an EU scale through the European Parliament and transnational processes of interest intermediation. And there are also examples of social rights beginning to take on a European dimension alongside their national ones, often – as Marshall might have suggested – as a consequence of EU-level civil rights such as freedom of movement, which have begun to make access to social rights portable across national borders within the EU (Greer, 2006b).

This EU-scale example of one set of (civil) rights shaping the availability to citizens of another set of (social) rights has echoes in

Table 5.2: The diffusion of citizenship rights to the EU

21st century	Nation-state	European Union
Civil rights	Yes	Yes
Political rights	Yes	Yes
Social rights	Yes	Yes

Lister's recent attempt to update thinking on Marshall. Lister (2005, p 473) stresses the 'need to consider civil, political and social rights in relation to, not isolation from, one another'. He stresses Marshall's underlying principle of citizenship as one of 'equality of status' and how 'once the principle is grounded in one area, such as the civil sphere, it "spills over" into other spheres'. In that sense:

> Citizenship is not a simple, one-size-fits-all category, but is rather a contingent set of accommodations of the underlying principle of equality of status. This means that citizenship is a contested concept, where different spheres ground the idea of equality of status differently and where different facets of citizenship are prioritized over others. Hence citizenship takes different forms at different places at different times. (Lister, 2005, p 474)

Lister's focus on how citizenship is contested and therefore contingent in Marshall's conception raises the question of who does the contesting. Marshall's (and Lister's) answer has to do with class. UK citizenship evolved as excluded social groups exploited the opportunities of one sphere of citizenship rights to open up a new sphere that then empowered and included them (but also opened up new possibilities for other excluded groups). Marshall's conception is one of non-territorial groups, that is, social classes created by the relationships of the market economy that are present across the whole territory of the national state. Others have focused on other non-territorial and in some way excluded groups in projecting forward Marshall's thinking – including visible minority ethnic groups and women – and how these groups also have the potential to transform the content of national citizenship (Bottomore, 1992).

But what has generally been absent in this conception of contested and evolving citizenship is a sense of what impact *territorially* defined groups located in one part of the national state might have in renewing the content of citizenship and, perhaps, stripping it of some aspects of its state-wide reach; 'equality of status' might, for example, be understood as something achievable at smaller, regional scales. Banting and Simeon (1985, p 11) noted over two decades ago how territorial questions – in particular the demand for self-government – had emerged as the 'major sources of demands for constitutional change', superceding earlier debates driven by class cleavages and relationships. These demands were, in general, for new and additional forms of political rights that could be exercised at regional scales within states (sometimes extending to demands for independence).

Many of those demands have been realised. Marks et al (2008) show in their comprehensive index of regional authorities in 42 established democracies in the period 1950–2006 that 'regional authority' – a combined measure of regional-level democracy, policy competences, tax-raising powers and roles in co-determining central government policy – was broadly stable from 1950–70, but has since grown steadily (especially in terms of the growth of elected regional assemblies and the widening of regional policy competences). Of the 42 states in the index, 20 became more regionalised and only four (marginally) less regionalised. Political rights of citizenship are in many states now exercised also at a regional scale, either in state-wide systems of federal or regional government, or in forms of asymmetrical regional government in which citizens in some regions have different and/or fuller political rights than those in other regions in the same state.

This growth in regional political rights raises, *pace* Marshall, questions about whether the exercise of political rights at that regional scale has 'spilt over' into other spheres of citizenship, and, in particular, has reframed social citizenship – equality of status regarding social rights – as something that should be, or is, also realised at a regional rather than a national scale.

Regionalising social citizenship

This imagery of citizenship 'spillovers' offers a potentially fruitful way of approaching the enduring debate in decentralised states about the tension between equity and diversity, of exploring the extent to which the principles of equity in the postwar welfare state and the political diversity of regional government are or are not compatible. Two notable attempts have been made through comparative analysis to recast this debate in Marshallian terms. In his work on the scope and resilience of state-wide healthcare and income replacement programmes, Banting (2006) argues that equity and diversity are reconcilable. He finds that while regional government may offer opportunities to use regional-scale political rights to express territorial social distinctiveness in areas like education, language policy and the media, it is striking how far a state-wide understanding of equity in health policy and social security persists: 'The norm of the similar treatment of citizens, which lies at the heart of the welfare state, has trumped the full promise of federalism in the largest social programs, income security and health care' (Banting, 2006, p 64). Put more bluntly, the logic of equity inherent in social citizenship is 'winning hands down' (Banting, 2006, p 44) in any tensions with the logic of regional diversity inherent in decentralised government.

Drawing on evidence from public attitudes research Jeffery (2006a, pp 89-91) has put forward a more qualified view which suggests that opportunities for political participation at a regional scale may open up scope for defining social rights as something also to be realised at a regional scale. He argues that this is likely to happen if one or both of two conditions are present which foster a regional frame of reference for social solidarity and may then trump any logic of state-wide equity – where territorial identities underpin a sense of distinctive political community and/or where there are concerns about inter-regional inequities in the distribution of resources.

The surge of scholarly and policy analysis that has accompanied UK devolution has picked up on these themes, although without a consensus view emerging. Rather, three broad interpretations have emerged of how the diffusion of rights of political participation to devolved arenas might impact on the scale at which social rights are realised. The first – consistent with Banting – is that devolved political rights are compatible with state-wide social rights. Some academic commentators – notably Hazell and O'Leary (1999, p 42) – have pointed, for example, to the possibility of identifying and understanding 'what items need to be held in common throughout the kingdom as constants of UK citizenship; and what items can be allowed to vary'. But probably the most consistent advocate of the compatibility of devolution and the British welfare state has been Gordon Brown, one of the leading figures in the Labour governments since 1997, and Prime Minister since 2007. In a series of speeches on 'Britishness' he has emphasised how core components of the welfare state need to retain a state-wide reach even after devolution: an equal right to health treatment 'regardless of wealth, position or race ... in any part of Britain'; 'the ideal that every child in Britain should have an equal opportunity in education'; equal rights of access to the labour market for the 'Scottish, Welsh or English miner, computer technician, nurse or teacher'; and so on (Brown, 1999).

The second interpretation focuses on the renegotiation of the roles and relationships of UK central government and devolved governments in specifying and delivering social rights. Put simply, devolved governments may wish to define social rights in different ways than central government. Mooney et al (2006, p 492) point to the scope devolution has created for the renegotiation of welfare arrangements in Scotland and Wales and the questions this raises about 'the nature of

UK citizenship – and of citizenship in the devolved nations'. Rachel Simeon (2003, p 232) notes the scope for 'conflict over the appropriate boundaries of social citizenship, with the devolved administrations defining it more broadly than London'. In other words, state-wide and regional citizenships may coexist, with devolved governments offering variations from a UK baseline (and so far with a tendency to vary upwards). As Richard Simeon (2006b, p 27) puts it, 'social citizenship may be more fully developed in local than in national communities, especially those engaged in a nation-building project'. To revert to Marshall's terminology, there may be a general, or minimum, equality of status at the state-wide scale alongside coexistent and varying equalities of status at devolved scales. Citizenship may not need to be 'by definition, national'.

This second interpretation chimes with Jeffery's view that in some conditions the devolution of political rights may open up opportunities to pursue the rescaling of social rights to the devolved level. So, in a different way, does the third: that the devolution of political rights, and any consequent territorial differentiation of social rights, may prompt inter-regional tensions which undermine shared commitments to a state-wide social citizenship. Such tensions have emerged, in outline at least, in thinking about the relationship of England to Scotland, especially since 2005 or so, as conservative media and political opinion has articulated a sense of resentment in England about the perceived privileges of Scots after devolution. One outcome has been the evocation of a stronger sense of an English territorial interest defined against a Scottish 'other', especially in relation to the territorial distribution of public spending and the 'West Lothian Question' – the 'double' representation of Scots in the Scottish Parliament and at Westminster. Such resentments point to a potential for devolution to fragment citizenship as something understood within, rather than across, the bounds of the perceived territorial interests of the different nations that make up the UK.

Whether or not the UK's citizens want to see some kind of regionalisation of social citizenship (as implied by the latter two interpretations) or a continued, UK-wide social citizenship (as implied by the first) following devolution is unclear. It may be that citizens are adherents of uniform, state-wide social rights, and that their preferences act as a constraint on the leeway of governments to pursue or allow regional variations in social rights. It may be that citizens are unconcerned about, or even actively favour, greater regional variation in rights packages. In that case citizens' views may facilitate the erosion of uniformity and the emergence of new, regionalised practices of social citizenship. In either respect a better understanding of citizens' views would appear to be important in assessing the possible future trajectories of the post-devolution UK state. The following begins to build such an understanding on the basis of public attitudes data collected in all nations of the UK over the post-1999 devolution era by a number of periodic surveys: the British Social Attitudes Survey, the Scottish Social Attitudes Survey, the Northern Ireland Life and Times Survey and the Wales Life and Times Survey. These data have two main advantages over commercial opinion polls: high and consistent methodological standards and repetition to produce time series data, which opens up the possibility of capturing changes that have emerged since and as a result of devolution.

Devolution and political rights

The UK has only partial devolution. Political citizenship is now exercised in Scotland, Wales and Northern Ireland through rights of participation in devolved electoral processes as well as those at UK level. England has no devolved structures at regional level or at England-wide level equivalent to those outside England and remains governed directly by UK institutions in Westminster. This territorial asymmetry of political rights is by and large endorsed in public opinion across the UK.

Devolution is strongly supported in Scotland and Wales. It is consistently the most popular constitutional preference in Scotland, with some evidence of growing support in the last few years (support has risen from a post-1999 low point of 44% in 2005 to a post-1999 high point of 63% in 2007). At the same time support for the second-most popular option, Scottish independence, has fallen from its post-1999 peak of 35% in 2005 to 23% in 2007 (this despite the election of a pro-independence Scottish National Party [SNP] government in 2007) (Curtice, 2008, p 40). In Wales the devolution variant of 'parliament' (that is, the more powerful model of devolution that exists in Scotland) is more popular than the 'assembly' variant (that is, the less powerful model of devolution that applies currently in Wales). Forty-four per cent supported a Welsh parliament in 2007, and 28% the current assembly, giving a grand total of 72% in favour of devolution of some sort (Wyn Jones and Scully, 2008, p 68). The greater popularity of the 'parliament' model in Wales suggests an appetite for further-reaching devolution. That appetite is even more voracious in Scotland: a majority of at least 54% and at most 68% has agreed in surveys since 1999 that the Scottish Parliament should have 'more powers'. Although there is less data on precisely which additional powers Scots would like to have, since 2001 over 50% of Scots have consistently favoured greater tax-raising powers, and data from the 2007 Scottish Social Attitudes Survey suggests some appetite for additional powers in social security (Curtice, 2008, p 43).

The situation in Northern Ireland is rather more ambiguous. Given a choice in principle, over 80% of Protestants consistently prefer continued membership of the UK, while around half of Catholics consistently prefer reunification with the Republic of Ireland (Mac Ginty, 2006, p 35). But given the current options, *in practice*, of either the Northern Ireland Assembly or Westminster having 'most influence over how Northern Ireland is run', support for the Assembly far outweighs Westminster in *both* communities (see Table 5.3).

In similar vein large majorities of the Scots and (especially) the Welsh feel that devolved government *ought to* have 'most influence' over the way their part of Britain is run. More think Westminster actually does have more influence than the devolved institutions, although with a notable decline in recent years in Scotland, suggesting that the Scottish Parliament at least is coming to be recognised as a key decision-making body (see Table 5.4).

If these data provide a clear endorsement of decisions to locate new political rights of citizenship at the devolved level outside of England, England itself provides a marked contrast. The English are generally, and consistently, happy with centralised government from London, agree that it both does and ought to have most influence on the way England is run, and, as shown in Table 5.5, are not persuaded by the devolution options of an England-wide parliament or elected regional government. The latter view on regional government was given vivid confirmation in the 78:22 rejection of regional devolution in North East England in November 2004.

Table 5.3: Which institution ought to have most influence over the way Northern Ireland is run? (2003) (%)

	All	Catholic	Protestant
Northern Ireland Assembly	50	55	46
UK government	18	8	27
Local government	15	15	16
European Union	4	7	1

Source: Northern Ireland Life and Times Survey

Table 5.4: Which institution does/ought to have 'most influence' over 'the way Scotland/Wales is run'? (%)

	Does have most influence		Ought to have most influence	
	2003	2006	2003	2006
Scotland				
Devolved	17	24	66	64
UK	64	38	20	11
Local	7	18	9	19
EU	5	11	1	1
Wales				
Devolved	22	36	56	74
UK	58	53	29	18
Local	15	5	14	8
EU	5	6	1	0

Sources: Curtice (2008, pp 45-6); Wyn Jones and Scully (2008, p 69)

Table 5.5: Constitutional preferences for England (1999–2007) (%)

With all the changes going on in the way different parts of Great Britain are run, which of the following do you think would be best for England?	1999	2000	2001	2002	2003	2005	2006	2007
England should be governed as it is now, with laws made by the UK Parliament	62	54	59	56	55	54	54	58
Each region of England should have its own assembly that runs services like health	15	18	21	20	24	20	17	14
England as a whole should have its own new parliament with law-making powers	18	19	13	17	16	18	22	17

Source: Curtice (2008)

The current situation of 'asymmetrical' devolution implemented outside of England only is in other words strongly endorsed in public opinion everywhere. The Scots, Welsh and Northern Irish endorse the devolved political rights they have won, and would like more, while the English are content with the status quo position of political rights exercised at the UK-level alone.

Devolved political rights and UK-wide social rights

The potential spillover implications those endorsements have for reframing social rights as devolved, rather than UK, goals depends on the purposes to which citizens outside England wish to deploy their political rights (and on any consequential impacts in England). Do people in Scotland, Wales and Northern Ireland want political rights in order to pursue different policy agendas? Are political rights in that sense a means to the end of a distinctive, devolved social citizenship? The answer is quite clearly no. Survey data show that there are remarkably few territorial differences between the Scots, Welsh and English on questions on basic values about the role of the state or on more specific policy preferences (Jeffery, 2006a, pp 78-80). Table 5.6 gives one example from a question that taps values on social solidarity. A recent, detailed analysis of public views of the NHS in Scotland and England came to a similar conclusion about one of the keystone areas of social citizenship: notwithstanding policy differences on waiting times and healthcare choice that have opened up in the English and Scottish variants of the NHS, 'what matters to the public is much the same in Scotland as it is in England' (Ormston and Curtice, 2007, p 69).

In other words, people in all parts of the UK appear to want the state to do much the same things on their behalf. When asked about their attitude to the possibility of divergences of policy from one part of

Table 5.6: 'Ordinary people do not get their fair share of the nation's wealth' (% agree/agree strongly)

	1999	2000	2001	2002	2003	2005
Scotland	58	71	61	64	54	57
England	60	61	58	61	60	55
Wales	61	–	61	60	59	–
Northern Ireland	62	60	55	62	59	52

Sources: British Social Attitudes, Scottish Social Attitudes, Welsh Life and Times Survey, Northern Ireland Life and Times Survey, Devolved Election Studies

Britain to another, most people in Scotland, Wales and England prefer uniform provision (see Table 5.7). There is little appetite across Britain for territorial policy variation. The public appears to continue to favour a state-wide conception of social citizenship *despite* the creation of an extensive political citizenship at the devolved scale.

These findings are not terribly surprising. Mitchell (2006, pp 165-6) has noted how the devolution reforms in Scotland and Wales had above all to do with reclaiming *ownership* of politics. They were about reconnecting the Scots and Welsh with a political system felt during the years of Conservative UK government from 1979 to 1997 to have become closed, even hostile to Scottish and Welsh concerns. Devolution in that sense was about providing some level of protection against majoritisation by the more numerous English. What it was not about was a distinctive policy agenda. The campaigns for devolution in Scotland and Wales did not mobilise around distinctive policy programmes. The Scottish Constitutional Convention (1995), which

Table 5.7: Attitudes towards territorial policy variation in Britain (2003) (%)

	Should be the same in every part of Britain	Should be allowed to vary
England		
Standards for services such as health, schools, roads and police	66	33
Scotland		
Standards for services such as health, schools, roads and police	59	40
Level of unemployment benefit	56	42
University tuition fees	56	40
Wales		
Standards for services such as health, schools, roads and police	55	44
Level of unemployment benefit	57	41
University tuition fees	58	40
Cost of NHS prescriptions	63	37

Sources: Data collated by John Curtice from British and Scottish Social Attitudes Survey (2003); Wales Life and Times Survey (2003)

animated the devolution debate in Scotland, built a vision of devolution that was much more about symbolic politics, grounded in a claim of popular sovereignty on a Scottish territorial scale (the 'claim of right') and suffused with a rhetoric of civic inclusion, participation and consultation. Wales had a paler version of the same debate, focused on inclusiveness and accountability, the latter focused in particular on making the 'quango state' in Wales accountable to a Welsh political process. In Northern Ireland, for different reasons driven by the peace process, devolution was also about returning decision making to a system of regional accountability.

Table 5.8 gives an example of this rationale for devolution based in proximity and accountability, contrasting levels of trust among Scots in the UK and Scottish governments to 'work in Scotland's interests'. Over three quarters of Scots trust the UK government to act in their interests 'only some of the time' or 'almost never'. By contrast, 55%+ trust devolved government to act in Scotland's interest. In Wales and Northern Ireland there are similar trust gaps. But the English, confirming a pattern of attachment to the status quo, continue to have substantially greater trust in Westminster: 57% 'always' or 'mostly' trusted the UK government to work in England's interest in 2001, 53% in 2003 and 50% in 2007.

These institutional trust differentials do not mean that the Scots, Welsh and Northern Irish are necessarily enthused by what their devolved

Table 5.8: Trust in the UK and Scottish governments to work in Scotland's interests (%)

	2001	2003	2005
UK government			
Just about always	2	2	2
Most of the time	20	19	20
Only some of the time	55	58	52
Almost never	22	20	22
Scottish government			
Just about always	13	10	10
Most of the time	52	52	45
Only some of the time	28	31	34
Almost never	4	4	8

Source: Scottish Social Attitudes Surveys

institutions have achieved; in many respects they feel devolution has not made that much difference in terms of policy outcomes; but 'whatever the controversy or disappointment that may surround decisions made by the [Scottish] parliament, they are thought to have the crucial virtue of being decisions made at home rather than imported from England' (Bromley et al, 2006, p 188).

This understanding of devolution as a means of achieving proximity of decision making rather than difference in policy substance is underpinned by the distinctive senses of political community that exist in Scotland, Wales and Northern Ireland as compared with England. The Scots and Welsh are less likely than the English to identify themselves as British and more likely to claim an exclusively or predominantly Scottish or Welsh identity (see Table 5.9). This different balance of Scottish/Welshness and Britishness is not an effect of devolution, but

Table 5.9: National identities in England, Scotland and Wales (%)

	1997	1999	2001	2003	2007
England					
English not British	7	17	17	17	19
More English than British	17	15	13	19	14
Equally English and British	45	34	42	31	31
More British than English	14	11	9	13	14
British not English	9	14	11	10	12
Scotland					
Scottish not British	23	32	36	31	26
More Scottish than British	38	35	30	34	30
Equally Scottish and British	27	22	24	22	28
More British than Scottish	4	3	3	4	5
British not Scottish	4	4	3	4	6
Wales					
Welsh not British	17	17	24	21	25
More Welsh than British	26	19	23	27	21
Equally Welsh and British	34	37	28	29	34
More British than Welsh	10	8	11	8	10
British not Welsh	12	14	11	9	10

Sources: British Social Attitudes Survey, Scottish Social Attitudes Survey, Wales Life and Times Survey, Devolved Election Studies

rather a long-term trend extending back at least to the 1970s (Heath, 2005). But it has implications for devolution. Devolution squares a problematic circle. It provides an acceptable form of government both for those who claim a distinctive Welshness or Scottishness (by expressing that distinctiveness through institutions of self-government), and for those who feel equally or more British (by containing self-government within the UK).

Table 5.10 illustrates how devolution 'satisfices' in this way, providing an adequate arrangement for a wide range of identity types. Although 'Scottish/Welsh not British' identifiers in Scotland and Wales are more likely to favour independence than other identity types, even among that group opinion on independence is split in Scotland and a minority option in Wales. In all other categories, devolution is the majority option. Devolution is a political framework capable of expressing a sense of political community that bridges different identity groups. Identity structures in Northern Ireland are different, with a stark polarisation between British and Irish identifiers with loyalties to different states. But there is a sense even there that devolution 'satisfices' by bridging

Table 5.10: National identities and constitutional preference in Scotland and Wales (2003) (%)

Constitutional preference	National identity				
Scotland	Scottish not British	More Scottish than British	Equally Scottish and British	More British than Scottish	British not Scottish
Independence	47	22	8	5	10
Devolution	41	63	62	66	68
No devolution	5	10	26	23	21
Wales	Welsh not British	More Welsh than British	Equally Welsh and British	More British than Welsh	British not Welsh
Independence	27	11	11	7	6
Devolution	58	69	59	69	51
No devolution	11	14	28	21	39

Sources: Scottish Social Attitudes Survey, Wales Life and Times Survey

communities which are polarised by identity but share a pragmatic desire for a functioning local politics set aside from the more existential constitutional debates which disabled devolution until its relaunch in 2007 (Jeffery, 2008).

The relative weakness of predominantly English identifiers, the relative strength of British identifiers and their relatively even distribution around an 'equally English and British' middle ground in England (see Table 5.9) suggest that there is no equivalent 'bridging' need in England. This confirms the attachment there to the status quo of direct rule by the UK government.

Challenges to UK-wide social citizenship

The devolution of political rights appears to satisfy, or at least satisfice , demands for expression of distinctive political community in Scotland, Wales and Northern Ireland without undermining what appears to be a continuing preference for UK-wide social rights. In England there is no pressing demand for even the devolution of political rights. Diversity of political rights and equity of social rights appear reconcilable from the perspective of citizens around the UK. That perspective offers some encouragement to Gordon Brown and others who have argued that devolution need not and does not undermine the UK's social citizenship.

There are some signs in public opinion, however, of at least two kinds of challenge to the maintenance of a UK-wide social citizenship. The first is a reflection of the political structure of UK devolution, which tends to segment opinion formation in different parts of the UK and could lead to an erosion of UK-wide social rights more or less by default. The second – in part a consequence of the first – is a potential for the political mobilisation of territorial cleavages, in particular between England and Scotland, to undermine the inter-regional solidarity on which UK-wide conceptions of social rights rest.

Disconnected devolutions

The territorial constitution of the UK is curiously unsystematic. The UK evolved as a union state in a series of accommodations of the non-English component nations, over centuries, with its English core. The series of unions struck and periodically remade between the non-English nations and the core UK state have evolved in distinctive (in current terminology: asymmetric) ways, with relatively little synchronisation between them. Prior to devolution non-English interests were accommodated through territorial departments of UK government, with intra-governmental coordination and collective cabinet responsibility providing at least some sense of, and capacity to pursue, pan-territorial, UK-wide objectives.

Devolution has removed much of that sense and capacity. There is no systematic pan-territorial coordination at the UK centre. There is no forum in which UK and devolved governments convene to identify and commit to pursuing shared UK-wide objectives in fields where responsibilities are now devolved. The devolved governments have little grip at the UK centre, and central government lacks many of the mechanisms that in other decentralised states give the centre leverage over the regions in pursuing state-wide objectives, such as state-wide framework legislation or conditional financial transfers. The political structure of devolution is, in many ways, disconnected and centrifugal.

That centrifugalism is underlined by the dynamics of devolved democratic processes. Scotland and Wales have distinctive party systems in which nationalist parties whose influence is marginal at a UK electoral scale are key players (and, after the 2007 devolved elections, parties of government) at the devolved scale. Electoral systems are different at UK and devolved scales; the semi-proportional systems used in devolved elections in Scotland and Wales bring cross-party cooperation and compromise much more strongly into decision making than majoritarian Westminster. Northern Ireland's party system and electoral system are even more divergent from the UK-level pattern. In addition, patterns of interest intermediation in all the devolved jurisdictions have become more distinctive; public, private and voluntary sector interests have refocused to varying extents on opportunities to influence devolved decision making, fragmenting their capacities to articulate genuinely UK-wide objectives.

One outcome has been growing territorial policy variation, extending some way beyond the differentiations of the territorial policy portfolio that existed before devolution. Some of the headline variations reflect the party system dynamics and cross-party compromises of devolved politics: long-term care for older people, prescription charging, tuition fees, and so on. Others have emerged as the UK government has introduced policies in England – notably on the financing and delivery of public services in health and education – which were rejected as options by devolved governments. In many fields there now exist, as a result, four different policy regimes across the UK. In other words, equality of status regarding some social rights (social security as a

UK-level responsibility is the most comprehensive exception) is now scaled at, and differentiated by, the UK's component nations.

This differentiated practice of social citizenship does not, of course, match with the public preferences for uniformity discussed in the last section. That mismatch is interesting. It might suggest that public opinion is not much of a constraint on the regionalisation of social citizenship. It might alternatively (or also) suggest that a system of disconnected devolutions does not provide much opportunity for the comparison, and therefore problematisation, of cross-jurisdictional policy difference by the UK's publics.

There is some evidence of this kind of territorial compartmentalisation of public debate in research on voting behaviour in devolved elections. The common denominator of most research on devolved elections has been to test the assumption that these would be 'second order' elections, that is reflections of and responses to the issues and personalities that drive voting behaviour in the more important, 'first order' UK elections (Hough and Jeffery, 2006). Although it is clear that 'first order' issues do play a role – for example, controversies over the Iraq War, or Tony Blair's increasing unpopularity in the mid-2000s – UK-level issues certainly have no systematic impact on devolved election processes, and are often marginal to them. In their modelling of voting behaviour in the 2003 Scottish and Welsh devolved elections Wyn Jones and Scully (2006, p 129) found that:

> Voters in Scotland and Wales can, and often do, make different electoral choices for devolved elections from Westminster ones ... they are often guided by factors specific to Scotland and Wales when making such choices.... Significant numbers of voters in Wales and Scotland appear to recognise Westminster and devolved levels as distinct political arenas, to evaluate parties differently for those respective arenas, and to vote accordingly.

Denver et al's (2007) rather different approach to analysing the 2007 devolved election in Scotland confirms broadly the same point. They applied a 'valence' model of voting to that election, using a public attitudes survey to explore how far questions of performance, competence and leadership of the leading parties in dealing with Scottish issues shaped voting behaviour. They found that these valence variables, focused on the Scottish context, were important determinants of how Scots voted, with the SNP holding leads over Labour on issue competence, leadership and campaigning. UK-level factors by contrast were subordinate in explaining the election outcome (or, to put it another way, UK factors were second order; the devolved election was in this instance a first order contest).

These accounts of devolved elections confirm a sense that devolved politics has become increasingly self-contained, focused, as Bromley et al (2003) put it, on 'Scottish answers to Scottish questions'. Despite having similar views to citizens in other jurisdictions on political values and policy preferences, and despite disliking cross-jurisdictional policy variation, there appears to be a tendency to reframe politics, through the lens of the democratic process, at smaller, distinctive devolved scales. The possibility that emerges from this is that the UK's social citizenship may be eroded by default, as policy changes introduced by devolved institutions accumulate, as these are judged in compartmentalised, jurisdiction-specific terms, and in the absence of political structures which facilitate UK-wide thinking and comparison. Greer (2007b, p 159), for example, concludes that devolution, for such reasons, has 'already had an impact on the meaning and rights associated with citizenship in the UK'. Jeffery (2006a, p 90) echoes the point, arguing that social citizenship has become less UK-wide and increasingly 'territorialised'.

Anglo-Scottish contentions

Even though there has been little UK-wide consideration of the implications of post-devolution policy variation, there has emerged one notable example of cross-jurisdictional comparison: that between England and Scotland. The English editions of some of the main conservative newspapers – the *Daily Mail* and the *Daily Telegraph* in particular – have begun to articulate a sense of English territorial interest defined against the 'other' of post-devolution Scotland. The key issues have been threefold:

- The perceived injustice of the 'West Lothian Question' (Scottish MPs continuing to vote on English domestic matters, when English MPs cannot on equivalent Scottish matters now devolved to the Scottish Parliament).
- The pattern of territorial public spending under which Scotland (and Wales and Northern Ireland) receive more spending per head than England.
- The view that higher public spending enables Scotland in particular to fund more generous social policies than those available to the English.

The articulation of this threefold sense that devolution to the Scots is unfair to the English intensified with the prospect (from 2006) and then appointment (in 2007) of the Scottish MP, Gordon Brown, as UK Prime Minister, and the election of the SNP minority government in Scotland in 2007. There have been echoes in Conservative Party opinion, with some English MPs like John Redwood rehearsing some of the cruder themes pursued in the conservative press, and others like Lord (Ken) Baker, Sir Malcolm Rifkind and Ken Clarke rehearsing solutions to the 'English question', in particular various schemes to limit the involvement of Scottish MPs in English business at Westminster.

There is a sense in all this that the Conservative Party is pondering the scope to mobilise support in England by engaging in Scotland-bashing. So far, the Conservative leader, David Cameron, has rejected any official move of the party in this direction. But what is interesting to note is that there appears to be a significant resonance in English public opinion with themes that articulate, and could be used to mobilise, the Anglo-Scottish cleavage. Very clear majorities of the English – consistently around 60% since 2000 – agree that Scottish MPs should not vote on English business at Westminster. There are quite distinct patterns of opinion between England and Scotland about the territorial distribution of public spending (see Table 5.11), with twice as many English as Scots agreeing that the Scots get 'more than their fair share' of public spending, and around five times as many Scots as English thinking the Scots get less then their fair share.

There is a similarly divergent pattern of opinion on the question of whose economy – England's or Scotland's – benefits most from the UK

Table 5.11: The perceived fairness of Scotland's share of government spending (%)

Is Scotland's share ...	2000	2001	2003	2007
England				
More than fair?	20	24	22	32
Pretty much fair?	42	44	45	38
Less than fair?	12	9	9	7
Scotland				
More than fair?	10	10	11	16
Pretty much fair?	27	36	35	37
Less than fair?	58	47	48	37

Sources: British Social Attitudes Survey; Scottish Social Attitudes Survey

union. From 2000 to 2007, 40% or more of the English consistently thought Scotland's economy benefits. In 2000 a similar proportion of Scots felt that England had the most benefit, though that figure has now fallen to under 30%. The English perception that Scots get too much spending and more economic benefit from the union is underlined by the very high levels of agreement with the proposition that 'now Scotland has its own Parliament, it should pay for its services out of taxes collected in Scotland': consistently around three quarters of English respondents agree with that proposition (Curtice, 2008, p 43).

These data suggest that there is, at least in outline, some kind of conception among the English that they have a set of interests which are different from those of the Scots, that they are currently disadvantaged relative to the Scots and that changes in how Westminster is organised and/or how public spending is financed might rebalance territorial interests in England's favour. There appears to be an openness to compartmentalising the government of England and Scotland more fully and disentangling Anglo-Scottish interdependencies as a means of securing English territorial interests better.

There are two caveats to add to this analysis. The first is that it does not appear that these concerns are especially salient; although attitudes appear to be held in some cases by very large majorities, they are not necessarily priority issues. There is, however, a reserve of opinion that resonates with territorial themes in conservative media and political opinion; a potential for territorial mobilisation is there, even if currently it is latent. The second caveat is that on two of the issues discussed above majorities of the Scots agree with majorities of the English, albeit rather smaller ones: 57% of the Scots and 75% of the English agree that the Scottish Parliament should raise its own taxes; and 50% of the Scots and 60% of the English that Scottish MPs should not vote on English business at Westminster (see Table 5.12).

Conclusion

Table 5.12 points to a shared concern among the English and the Scots to disentangle the ways in which they are governed. Public opinion appears to endorse the further compartmentalisation of the different territorial politics of the nations of the UK and, in that way, to increase the scope for framing collective goals − including social rights of citizenship − in territorial settings within the UK state, rather than as state-wide objectives. This may in one sense appear perverse, given the lack of (social) policy content in the political projects of devolution outside of England, the existence of common social values across the

Table 5.12: Shared concerns across the Anglo-Scottish border (%)

2007	England	Scotland
Scottish services to be paid out of Scottish taxes		
Agree strongly	28	8
Agree	47	49
Neither agree nor disagree	14	16
Disagree	5	20
Disagree strongly	1	2
Scottish MPs not to vote on English laws		
Agree strongly	23	14
Agree	37	36
Neither agree nor disagree	16	26
Disagree	10	18
Disagree strongly	1	4

Sources: British Social Attitudes Survey; Scottish Social Attitudes Survey

UK nations and the continued preference of citizens across the UK for uniform policy provision. But it may also be a logical consequence of approaching, and structuring, devolution on a nation-by-nation basis within the UK rather than as a systematic and integrated reform of the UK's territorial constitution.

In the absence of a more systematic reform process, the post-devolution UK lacks the institutional fabric that might continue to frame social rights as most appropriately pursued at a state-wide scale. As the UK operates as a series of disconnected political arenas – with signs also that the English are beginning to frame their collective goals in an English territorial frame – it appears likely that the frame of reference for citizens to articulate collective social goals, and the policy products that emerge, will become increasingly divergent. To cast this in Marshallian terms, the regionalisation of political rights of citizenship appears likely to spill over *by default* into a growing regionalisation of social rights. 'Equality of status' of both political and social rights is set increasingly to be defined within the UK's different territorial jurisdictions rather than state-wide. Citizenship 'spillovers' are not restricted just to interactions between different types of citizenship rights, but also the different scales at which they might be realised. The UK seems set, in consequence, to have not a single social citizenship, but a series of regional social citizenships.

SIX

Social citizenship, devolution and policy divergence

Michael Keating

Civil, political and social rights in the British state

Marshall's essay on civil, political and social rights is framed by the nation-state. While many readers will find his reference to this state as England irritating, he does at least implicitly make a correct point, that by his time these rights were largely equalised over Great Britain (although not the United Kingdom). Civil rights were achieved during the 18th and 19th century. Political rights were equalised among the constituent nations with the uniform franchise provisions of 1884. The foundations of the welfare state under the Liberal government after 1906 and its development by the Labour government after 1945 were British in scope, and even the devolved government of Northern Ireland chose to shadow them. Yet we now know that this did not reflect a deep national integration as imagined by certain observers in the 1960s and early 1970s (Blondel, 1974; Finer, 1974), but rather a historical contingency, an alignment of social forces and demands that would not necessarily persist. Even as Marshall wrote, there was a revived Scottish home rule movement, arguing that political rights for Scotland must include a parliament of its own, against the main political parties who continued to insist that they could be realised by Scots as British citizens within a unitary polity. Marshall does draw attention to a tension between social rights and the market economy, a tension that has since increased and taken on a territorial dimension. He does not, on the other hand, mention a classic tension (identified in de Tocqueville, 1981) between political and civil rights, as democracy threatens to turn into the dictatorship of the majority or encourage populist policies aimed at whoever might be identified as deviant. Nor does he explore the relationship between social and civil rights as exemplified in the debate over whether to deal with various forms of misbehaviour as social or criminal issues. Devolution since 1999 has brought all these issues to the fore.

It is commonplace nowadays to note that devolution in the UK did not start from a clean slate. There was administrative devolution to all three peripheral territories and Northern Ireland had had home rule between 1922 and 1971. Institutions had survived the various unions and there were distinct interest groups and networks. Scotland and Northern Ireland had their own statute book. Administrative devolution was not merely a survival of the past but developed steadily over a hundred years and, indeed, gained a new lease of life during the 1990s under the late period of a Conservative government passionately opposed to political devolution (except for Northern Ireland and this not for reasons to do with policy divergence). In this chapter I will argue, however, that this did not add up to a differential welfare state or distinct forms of social citizenship in the component parts of the Union. Devolution does offer for the first time the opportunity for such differentiated citizenship; but a review of policy development shows that constitutional change has produced divergence in some policy fields, but convergence in others. New conceptions of social citizenship are emerging but they are poorly articulated and often confused. To understand this, we need to consider carefully the situation before devolution and that post-devolution, getting away from over-simplified categories and recognising the complexities of policy making in modern government. Since the scope for policy divergence in Scotland is greater than in Wales, the analysis inevitably has more Scottish material. Northern Ireland is absent from the practical examples, given the repeated failures to put devolution into operation.

While Scotland since 1885 and Wales since 1965 had their own departments and Secretaries of State, these were not, in general, policy makers. The Secretaries of State were members of the UK Cabinet, appointed and removed by the Prime Minister and chosen among the Scottish and (where possible) the Welsh MPs of the governing parties. The policy-making capacity of the Offices was limited, as experience since devolution has shown, and their main task was to put a Scottish or Welsh face on Whitehall policy, adapting it to the local institutional forms and delivering it with the right accent. Social entitlements in cash were not even administratively devolved, the Scottish Office having lost this battle to Whitehall in the 1940s. The basic principle of services funded by general taxation and free at the point of use, with charging at the margins, was applied to the National Health Service (NHS) across the UK. Labour market regulation was centralised and uniform. Education was universal and free. Remaining peculiarities like the Scottish fee-paying state schools and the system for subsidising council housing were removed during the 1970s. The welfare state was, indeed, a British institution.

There were, of course, disparities in the distribution of resources. This will happen in any welfare state, especially perhaps in centralised ones where the disparities can more easily be concealed. Overall spending in Scotland and Wales was higher than in England, not as part of the welfare state design to give the Scots and Welsh more, but for institutional and political reasons. Scottish spending was slow to respond to falls in relative population and one skill that Secretaries of State did develop was that of protecting their own budget totals – indeed this was arguably their main task. Other spatial disparities were more random. Patterns of demand vary, driving up provision of demand-led services. Policy implementation is subject to the activities of multiple levels of administration and the activities of 'street-level bureaucrats'. Professionals often had a lot of discretion over the details of provision. The location of major installations like teaching hospitals and universities affected both provision and demand. Municipal governments traditionally had a large role in deciding priorities and patterns of provision. None of this, however, added up to a systematic differentiation of the welfare state on territorial grounds. Disparities were found as much within as between the nations of the UK and most disparities were not spatial at all.

There were two key exceptions to this picture of overall uniformity and random disparity. One is the Scottish education system, which has a long tradition of distinctiveness and survived incorporation efforts in the 19th and 20th centuries. It did represent a distinct Scottish ethos and assumptions and was a badge of national identity. Even here, it should be noted, there were assimilationist trends, especially in the universities. The second field is Scots law that, exceptionally for unifying European states, retained almost all its own institutions, with the key exception of a legislature. Scots law has developed in its own way, with important repercussions in the field of social intervention, notably the pioneering Social Work (Scotland) Act of 1968. These two fields did not, however, represent Scottish self-government in the home rule meaning. Rather they were professional enclaves within the Scottish/British system of government, enjoying a degree of autonomy from politics as a whole, even from the politicians in the Scottish Office. Within these two fields there developed what the policy specialists call policy communities and epistemic communities, united by shared perceptions of problems and solutions and with dense networks of communication. I would argue that one condition for this was precisely their insulation from political life and public and party opinion, whether Scottish or British.

This created a double democratic deficit in Scotland. Politicians were insulated from control and accountability since they answered only to Westminster, and these self-regulating elites were insulated from political control, as long as they stayed within the broad parameters of government policy. The results could in turn be backward and conservative, as in the delay in modernising the law on divorce or homosexual relations, or progressive and enlightened as in the Social Work Act (Keating, 1975).

Another myth recurrently told (most recently by Gamble, 2006) is that Scottish and Welsh ministers protected their territories from the ravages of Thatcherism. The myth seems to have its origins in the self-justifying accounts that the ministers had to spread about in order to boost their slender standing in Scotland and Wales. Detailed policy studies, however, show a rather uniform application of the main Conservative measures (Midwinter et al, 1991; Griffiths, 1995). Internal markets were introduced to the NHS, schools were allowed to opt out of local authority control, transport was deregulated, compulsory competitive tendering was applied to local authorities and labour market policy developed on the same lines. The Poll Tax, in spite of claims that it was invented in Scotland (at the University of St Andrews), was always intended to apply across the whole state in the same way. It is true that the feared 'Barnett squeeze' did not materialise as the Secretaries of State were able to find ways to by-pass it and the formula was not adjusted fully to population changes. Scotland, Wales and Northern Ireland did not therefore suffer disproportionately, merely to the same degree. This defence of spending levels is, however, part of the old politics of territorial defence and lobbying and does not represent a distinct model of welfare state.

It is also true that take-up of the various measures was often less in Scotland and Wales. For example, GP fundholding was poorly developed and only two Scottish schools opted out of local authority control. Attempts to collect the Poll Tax in the cities were an abysmal failure. What this shows is that government policy was the same across the UK but that it was seriously out of line with public demand and the preferences and structures of the professional communities. This, of course, is exactly what fuelled the demand for devolution, which reached a peak in the mid-1990s.

We would therefore expect devolution to lead to policy changes. It is not, however, obvious what these will be and whether they will amount to divergence or convergence among the constituent nations of the UK. Devolution represents a twofold shift in power: from Westminster to Scotland and Wales; and within Scotland and Wales from existing policy networks into new ones and into the Parliament and Assembly. It also introduces an electoral dimension to policy choice, which had almost disappeared during the 1980s when the way Scotland and Wales voted was largely irrelevant to the policies they got. The outcome has been complex. In some fields there has been divergence, reflecting opinion, policy communities and structural factors. There are some signs of a distinct Scottish and Welsh welfare model, with its own assumptions and ways of working, to be measured not just against England but in a comparative European context. In other areas there is convergence, as old self-governing Scottish enclaves are subject to populist political pressures.

The devolution settlement

The allocation of powers in the three devolution settlements generally followed the existing responsibilities of the territorial departments, but there is an underlying logic to them, shared by other European devolutionary schemes. The main redistributive services are reserved for the centre, along with market regulation and nearly all taxes. Cash transfers are reserved, while service provision is widely devolved. In this way, a single British social citizenship could be maintained. There was little debate about this at the time, since all the British parties favour keeping a centralised social security system both to cushion asymmetrical shocks and as an expression of social solidarity. Yet, while this follows general practice, there are three striking differences from other European schemes. First, there are no state-wide framework laws covering matters devolved to Scotland and Northern Ireland, setting limits to divergence. Second, there are no UK-wide ministers in devolved matters and so no 'centre'; indeed Whitehall ministers are not allowed to intervene or spend money in the devolved territories unless there is an express reservation of the competence to them. Third is the financing of the devolved institutions almost completely from central transfers, together with no provision for the centre to influence the allocation of the transferred money; in fact it is now technically almost impossible to compare the functional allocations and priorities across the four parts of the UK. Some people regard this absent centre as a deficiency in the settlement. For my part, I do not. The settlement gives a high degree of self-government to Scotland without the disruption and strife of separation and, potentially at least, allows it to develop its own policy mix.

The devolution settlement also has consequences for civil rights. Scotland and Northern Ireland, although not Wales, gained control of most of the criminal law. On the other hand, all three devolution Acts incorporated the European Convention for the Protection of Human Rights and Fundamental Freedoms, allowing the courts to strike down legislative and executive acts. While Westminster can opt out of large parts of the Charter and court rulings on its legislation can be reversed, this is not the case for the devolved territories. This potentially detaches considerable areas of civil rights from British citizenship and makes possible the development of distinct forms of Scottish and Northern Irish civil rights, within a European framework. The reservation of anti-terrorism law to Westminster may limit this in practice, although this too will be applied by the Scottish and Northern Ireland courts.

The potential for divergence is, of course, limited in practice. In an earlier contribution to the debate, I cited the common UK market, common security area and welfare state as constraining factors (Keating, 2002). This remains largely true but, against most expectations, some of the critical issues in devolution have arisen precisely around the welfare state, its design and underlying assumptions. While conflicts have occurred only around marginal issues, they have taken on a large symbolic and political significance. The scope for welfare differentiation is potentially quite large. Taxation remained, for the first two terms of devolution, off bounds. The Labour Party in power at both levels between 1999 and 2007 shares the same broad vision of the welfare state. Yet the effort to keep redistributive services at the central level has not quite worked, since almost any public service can have redistributive effects. More broadly, questions have been posed not just about redistribution but about universalism versus selectivism and their relationship to community. These have produced some odd alliances across the political spectrum, often very opportunistic but sometimes posing interesting questions about understandings of community, solidarity and social citizenship.

Devolution is about shifting the territorial boundaries for communities and services, part of a general process of unbundling of territory across European states. This followed a period, since the 19th century, of boundary building, in which state institutions, systems of economic regulation, social welfare and culture, representation and social mobilisation, were enclosed within the same boundaries. The result was the Keynesian welfare state, in which social compromises were reached between capital and labour, and the dis-equalising effects of the market mitigated by the welfare state albeit, as Marshall noted, not without tensions. The modern transformation of the state has allowed different functions to take different boundaries, so that social interests and groups can engage in partial exit (Bartolini, 2005). Policy communities have been rebuilt at different territorial levels (Keating, 2005a; Keating et al, forthcoming) and new social compromises are being sought. It is not therefore obvious in advance just how patterns of citizenship will change under devolution. There next sections give two contrasting examples, of divergence and of convergence.

Public services

Some of the most important instances of divergence since devolution have come in the field of public services, although mostly this has involved Scotland and Wales opting not to follow innovations pioneered in England, rather than preferring to strike out on their own.

New Labour governments at the UK level and in England have been strongly committed to public service reform following the broad lines of the new public management (NPM). This emphasises differentiation in provision, privatisation and contracting-out of services, competition among service providers and choice for service users. There is a distrust of public service professionals and trade unions and an instinctive preference for market-type solutions. Semantic changes are important here, as the language of social citizenship is replaced by that of consumerism. In a further semantic shift, public servants become 'producer interests' and 'modernisation' is redefined to mean marketisation and competition. A favourite metaphor has it that governments should confine themselves to 'steering' while other service providers do the 'rowing' (Osborne and Gaebler, 1992).[1] Prominent examples of the application of NPM are the re-introduction of the internal market in the NHS, including foundation hospitals; and competition among schools including quasi-privatisation and (city) academies. Unable to manage public services in a place the size of England from one place and unwilling to allow local autonomy, the government has generated a proliferation of service delivery targets which local governments, the NHS and other agencies must compete to reach. Even local governments are given summary star ratings, with the best ones allowed to have a limited 'earned autonomy'. Welfare services, including pension enhancements and personal care for older people, are allocated on a selective basis to those in most need, rather than according to the universalist principles of the earlier welfare state.[2]

Scotland and Wales between 1999 and 2007 went in a somewhat different direction. They too embarked on public service reform, often informed by the same New Labour ideas. Performance targets proliferated, with the same perverse results. Yet there were significant differences in policy style and in substance (Keating, 2007). There is much less demonisation of public sector workers and professionals and a more collaborative style of working with them. Delivery targets tend to be worked out with the deliverers and assessed collaboratively. There are few summary measures of performance or 'star' systems and more use of narrative accounts of complex problems. There is a stronger emphasis on collaboration and partnership and less competition among service providers. So there is no internal market in the NHS and no foundation hospitals (Greer, 2004, 2006a). Comprehensive education has been firmly retained (Raffe, 2005), and, while there is some private money in schools, private donors are not allowed to take over schools entirely as with the English academies. University policy has been more collaborative and also placed less emphasis on 'naming and shaming' alleged under-performers than in England (Keating, 2005b).

There is also a tendency to universal rather than selective provision. The opportunities to demonstrate this are few but two have been symbolically important. Scotland decided to implement the recommendations of the Sutherland Royal Commission to provide free personal care for older people, while the UK government declined to do so for England. Scotland also abolished up-front tuition fees for universities and did not follow England in introducing the £3,000 top-up fee. Wales, within the limits of its powers, has gone down the same route, and has abolished prescription charges.

The NPM model of service delivery and the general approach started by the Conservatives and continued under New Labour has been criticised for undermining the public domain and devaluing the concept of citizenship, which traditionally has been associated with participation and public engagement (Crouch, 2003; Marquand, 2004). NPM replaces 'voice' as the way of improving public services with 'exit', the opportunity to find another provider. So hospitals and schools are supposedly improved by the threat of their customers leaving them. Service providers and professionals are assumed to be motivated by their own self-interest rather than any concern for their clients or the public as a whole. Professional ethics and motivations are devalued in favour of material incentives. Now there is no doubt that much of this is true and that base motives do underpin performance in many cases. In the past, however, this has been seen as a problem rather than the basis for policy design; and the more it becomes the basis for policy, the more professionals will shed any vestige of ethical motive and seek to do as little work as possible for as much reward as is available. Scotland's distinct trajectory is evident not only in the policy choices and instruments but also at the discursive level, since there has not been the semantic shift away from citizenship to consumerism, and professionals are still accorded a degree of respect. There is also some scattered, but consistent evidence of a greater public service ethos there than in England as a whole (Keating, 2005a).

These policy patterns in Scotland and Wales reflect a realignment of public demand, parliamentary majorities and professional opinion around a distinct (if inchoate) vision of public services. The emphasis is on the public sector and universal provision, rather than privatisation and selectivity. Free personal care has provoked furious attacks from New Labour ideologues, far out of proportion indeed to the extent of actual policy divergence,[3] suggesting that this is a raw nerve in the repositioning of social democracy. Supporters of the Scottish line on this (and tuition fees) will claim that it is more progressive, in line with traditional understandings of social democracy and inclusion; they are supported by the Scottish Socialists, the Labour Left and the Nationalists. New Labour acolytes attack the model precisely on these grounds, claiming that it is regressive since both policies benefit the wealthy more than the poor; indeed they are supported by the Scottish Conservatives. If this criticism is a pragmatic one, about the best use of resources, then it should give rise to a calm debate, and careful study of how the rival systems work in practice. If it is a criticism of principle (as the strident tone of the debate suggests), then it is bogus and hypocritical, since the principle would require charging for secondary schools as well as universities, and for hospital treatment as well as personal care. In fact the argument is not so much about distribution (or Left and Right in the traditional sense) as about underlying attitudes to the state, shared welfare values and citizenship.

Marshall is on stronger ground here, in pointing out that universal services may indeed benefit the middle classes economically, by relieving them of the need to pay for services that they previously bought for themselves; but that socially and politically they represent a powerful equalising force. After 1945 for the first time, all classes used the same health service. This was less true in education, given the existence of a private sector (albeit smaller than in most European countries) and an effective social segregation in the state sector (especially in England). Yet most pupils were enrolled within the state sector, and comprehensive education from the 1960s was aimed at achieving equality of status. Much of the New Labour agenda in England seems to be dedicated to keeping the middle classes within the welfare state, since their defection could undermine public provision in general. Marshall also recognised that getting the middle classes into common institutions might require a special status for them, his aim not being assimilation but integration of the classes. Council housing, in Marshall's day, was also seen as an option for all classes, not to abolish class differences but to break down class segregation. Only later did it become a residual service for the poor and a strong indicator of class status.

Nowadays the cost of keeping the middle classes in may be to provide them with their own niche in the form of foundation hospitals and elite schools, leaving the second-rate services to the masses. Of course, ministers do not put it quite this way and talk of driving up standards across the board, but inherent in the whole idea of competition is that some will come out ahead of others – the idea that everyone can win and get a prize is confined to the Red Queen and certain management gurus. In Scotland, conditions are different. For example, only one in ten Scots have private medical insurance, compared with around a quarter in the south east of England. Private schools enrol 3.9% of Scottish pupils, against 11% in the South East. This does not mean that educational opportunities are equal for all in Scotland, nor that there are no status differences, but they are worked out largely in a unified system.

A more subtle process of divergence is visible in the area of anti-poverty policies. In the early days of the Labour government, a strong emphasis was placed on reducing social exclusion. This concept was originally devised in France to replace what we used to call 'multiple deprivation'. 'Social exclusion' was preferred because it helped redefine the problem for an age in which class and other distinctions no longer worked and in which the poor were a relatively small minority unable to rely on wider conceptions of solidarity. Social exclusion also linked directly to citizenship, since the exclusion referred to was precisely the range of social, economic and political rights provided by the modern state and economy. A socially excluded person was not an active citizen and thus an affront to the idea of national society. When the idea was imported into Scotland a subtle relabelling took place to put the emphasis on social *in*clusion, and this was pronounced to be the underlying theme of the whole of the Scottish Executive's policies. Some of the work has been rather traditional, taking the form of area initiatives (social inclusion partnerships). Other initiatives involve working closely with UK departments and welfare agencies. Social inclusion seems to be more mainstreamed within other policies in Scotland (Keating et al, 2003b) and there is an emphasis on social justice rather than just tacking identified concentrations of poverty (Lohde, 2005). The UK government's insistence on detaching the issue of poverty from that of social equality, on the other hand, is visible in its refusal to increase the highest marginal rate of taxation even to the levels it was during most of the Thatcher years, and in repeated statements by ministers that their aims are limited to those at the bottom and that they have no problems at all with very high incomes. Of course this matter might be largely a matter of rhetoric but it does at least represent an appeal to a distinct set of community values.

Many of the decisions made in Scotland have been the result of political opportunism and unlikely alliances including the Conservatives and the Scottish Socialist Party. There is also an element of pork-barrel politics, especially under coalition government. In Wales they owe more to the persistence of traditional Labour traditions and the desire of Rhodri Morgan to put 'clear red water' between Cardiff and London. Yet there are some consistencies, rooted in ideas of community and service or older notions of 'moral economy' (Hearn, 2000) and summed up in conceptions of fairness. The basis does exist then for a Scottish and Welsh conception of social citizenship, which can draw in its own traditions and institutions as well as contemporary demands. There is an alignment here between political support and the policy communities and a potentially strong commitment on the part of public service professionals. Some may interpret this in a social democratic mode, emphasising equality of outcome, while others may link it to traditional conservative ideas of organic society – that is a matter for political debate within the common culture. Yet this conception of citizenship has not been articulated by any of the political parties, analysed systematically by intellectuals, or extended consistently across policy domains. Instead, Scottish and Welsh particularism is a series of deviations from English innovations, advanced defensively and under constant attack from defenders of the new orthodoxy, as the extraordinarily resilient campaign against free personal care illustrates.

The populist turn

The second example of change concerns the balance between democratic and populist pressures and liberal conceptions of penal policy. Law and order policy in Scotland shows a convergence after devolution as old policy communities come under attack from populist ideas brought in by the process of democratisation and sweeping the UK (and indeed the western world) as a whole. Wales does not feature here, since criminal law is not devolved there. Scotland before devolution had developed a rather progressive set of policies in regard to criminal justice and especially youth offenders. The Children's Panel system sought to integrate social work with youth justice in order to reduce the incidence of crime and catch problems at an early stage. This 'penal-welfarism' (McAra, 2007) had attracted international attention and admiration in England and elsewhere. It was developed within a distinct policy community, bounded by the system of Scots law from external interference and supported in the 1960s by progressive officials and ministers in the Scottish Office. Key elements of this tradition survived the Conservative years, although the prison population did rocket at the same rate as in England and Wales and innovations like the Special Unit at Barlinnie were forced to close.

In the first session of the Scottish Parliament, the Justice Portfolio was held by the Liberal Democrats, who were able to a degree to resist the massive spawning of criminal justice bills seen at Westminster under David Blunkett. The populist rhetoric and anti-civil liberties provocations of Blunkett also found little echo in Scotland. Labour politicians in Scotland were not all happy with this and Henry McLeish (2004) in his memoirs complains about the Liberal Democrats being soft on law and order. With the arrival of Jack McConnell as First Minister, the decision was taken to go down the populist road and to build a political support base on a law-and-order platform, with a particular emphasis on visible and often petty crime.[4]

Following the 2003 Scottish elections, during which McConnell and Liberal Democrat leader and Justice Minister Jim Wallace had clashed on punishing the parents of delinquent children, the Justice portfolio was taken by Labour in the person of Cathy Jamieson. A tough campaign against anti-social behaviour (the 'war on needs') was launched, and policy came into line with that of England (for a list of measures, see McAra, 2007). Powers to disperse groups of young people, that even the police said that they did not need, were taken and the use of Anti-social Behaviour Orders (ASBOs) extended. Indeed First Minister Jack McConnell constantly complained about the failure of local authorities to issue enough ASBOs and Dispersal Orders. The Children's Hearing System, a centrepiece of the Social Work (Scotland) Act of 1968, survived, but was gradually eroded at the edges down as a more punitive approach was adopted.

There is no doubt that these measures proved massively popular, as they did in England, although many elements have been opposed by the old policy community of penal reformers, civil libertarians, the legal profession and even the police. A previously cohesive policy community insulated from populist politics gave way to a politically driven strategy using the new institutions of devolved government. In the pursuit of political support in a much more competitive electoral climate, ministers played up the problem of crime and helped stoke popular fears. The essentially political nature of the game was revealed at one point when ministers, faced with evidence that crime was actually declining, stated their goal as that of reducing perceptions of crime – this, it has to be said, was laughed out of court.

These new policies also change the relationship between the citizen and state in Scotland in a more authoritarian direction with overspills into other fields. As mentioned above, social inclusion was taken as a thread to run through the policies of the Scottish Executive. In practice, it is a whole range of specific policies, of varying degrees of effectiveness, but as a theme it gave a distinct narrative to these policies. The new emphasis on law and order runs in the contrary direction, with the labelling of deviants, the punitive elements and exclusions. It conjures up a different conception of citizenship that might not be in concord with those we identified above.

Is divergence a problem?

Until the 1990s, a standard criticism of devolution was that it would exacerbate spatial inequalities and fragment social citizenship. Leftist critics talked of dividing the working class, the fundamental basis for solidarity. Perhaps more important, however, was the fear of undermining Britishness as the basis for solidarity – this could perhaps explain why leftist anti-devolutionism so easily combined with anti-Europeanism in those days. In some cases, class and Britishness were vaguely fused as the enemies of 'divisive' nationalism. This opposition has greatly dissipated. Class rhetoric has largely gone from the social democratic lexicon and if it is still confounded with a national identity it is the Scottish or Welsh one (McCrone and Keating, 2007). State restructuring and the rediscovery of the decentralised strand in social democracy have vanquished the idea that social solidarity requires a centralised and uniform system of government. Yet many of the underlying concerns remain. New Labour, like the Conservatives before it, has engaged in frantic and sometimes ludicrous efforts to rebuild Britishness around its own values. In a more restrained tone, commentators on the devolution settlement have pointed to three ways in which the weakness of the centre and increased divergence may be a problem. The first is the evidence that citizens of the nations and regions have the same aspirations and that specifically they do not want differences in service provision (Jeffery, 2006a, 2006b). The second is a more general concern about the lack of an overall vision and conceptualisation of British social citizenship, an increase in spatial inequalities and the lack of a central policy frame within which divergence could be situated (Adams and Schmuecker, 2005; Jeffery, 2006a, 2006b). The third is the existence of spillovers, which mean that decisions taken in one jurisdiction will affect the others (Ashcroft et al, 2005).

The first point is mainly empirical but also conceptual. It is true that citizens of the UK have similar aspirations, but so do those of other European societies; this is the basis of the 'European social model', identifiable beneath the detailed institutional and policy differences of welfare states. Beyond this, however, it is difficult to read directly from public opinion onto public policy, since the latter involves trade-offs and policy emerges in specific contexts and circumstances. The question as to whether people favour uniformity or variation is a particularly abstract one once we get beyond the most basic entitlements, and it is likely to be tapping a general sense of territorial equity or a desire not to be worse off in any particular.[5] The trade-offs are worked out in the policy communities. Putting it more (perhaps excessively) idealistically, citizenship is about working out rights and obligations and sustaining debate about the conditions and content of policy. Citizenship is more than public opinion and is always mediated by institutions and social practices. Political rights are transformed into social rights through working on specific problems with particular instruments and in determined contexts. Devolution has created a new set of institutions and practices, which need to be evaluated as a whole. In the example of public services, it was the coincidence of public opinion, policy communities and political leadership that produced the effects. The alternative might be the sort of populist politics noted above in relation to law and order.

The second criticism raises the question of what is the relevant unit of social solidarity. To stipulate that it should be Great Britain or the UK is a legitimate value judgement, but a Scottish or Welsh nationalist could as plausibly answer that it is Scotland, without excluding a European, global, or even a British dimension.[6] Developments in international and European political economy mean that the 'region' (admittedly variously defined) has become a key level for the understanding of and in the management of economic change. Regions are portrayed (with a strong element of truth) as being in competition. As welfare states are still largely based on the central state, this has produced a disjuncture between market-making powers (regional and European) and market-correcting welfare systems designed to counteract the inequalities and social disequilibria provoked by markets, where Marshall assumed that these would coincide. The smaller European states, themselves of regional scale and with highly networked policy-making systems, seem better able to face these global challenges than the larger ones. It is not surprising that there should be systematic pressures to design 'regional' welfare states to capture some of these benefits for devolved and federated units.

A standard criticism of devolution in welfare states, certainly, is that devolved units, in their eagerness to attract investment and remain competitive, will cut social spending and, where permitted, taxation, and seek instead to subsidise capital. The evidence for this is inconsistent (Banting, 2006; Simeon, Richard, 2006b), and where it is most convincing, involves local governments in close spatial proximity, such as municipalities in fragmented US metropolitan areas. Against this, however, it is noted that some devolved areas may themselves be more solidaristic than larger states, or at least able to frame their own social compromises (Noël, 1999). Scotland and Wales may, potentially, be such places. This is not an inherent quality of the Scots or Welsh and not revealed in individual-level opinion data, but stems from the structures and nature of articulated demands and institutions.

So I see nothing inherently wrong in the weakening of social solidarity and citizenship at the UK level, if it is being reconstructed elsewhere. There remains the matter of spillovers and externalities when the policies of one jurisdiction impinge on those of another. This problem is less than it might have been in the past, and this is one explanation of the more permissive nature of the 1998 devolution settlement compared with the proposals of 1978. Europe, through the single market, EU competition policy and the European Convention for the Protection of Human Rights (from the Council of Europe but embedded in the devolution settlements) deals with some of the externalities. The decentralist turn in regional policy has removed other obstacles, while the international transfer of policy ideas often means that divergence leads to convergence in a continual circle. There remain problems, as in any territorial division of competences.

It is difficult, however, to see how any system at the UK level for managing these could have other than re-centralising effects given the dominance of England within the system. Scottish and Welsh devolved institutions are still fledgling and the practice of policy making for Scotland and Wales in its infancy. It needs to grow and mature and work out its own welfare model and governing assumptions first, then perhaps enter into intergovernmental discussions with other parts of the UK about common interests. This itself should be balanced with an insertion into European and international policy networks both to learn and to export Scottish and Welsh policy innovations. Otherwise the Scottish and Welsh policy models risk strangulation at birth.

Towards a new social citizenship

Scotland and Wales have new forms of political citizenship in the form of devolved bodies representing a territorial electorate and filling what was perceived before 1999 as a political deficit. While these bodies are functionally restricted, the implications of the new politics are wider, creating new expectations across the spectrum. The devolved territories have the basis for their own conception of social citizenship within a broader UK and European framework. This emerges partly from the pattern of public opinion, which may on individual issues be close to England, but is desirous of settling the main questions on a Scottish and Welsh basis to judge from the majorities in favour of giving more powers to the devolved institutions. It emerges from policy communities, stronger in Scotland than in Wales, and some of which pre-date devolution and which have been reshaped in various ways since; and from the way that institutions frame choices and sustain norms. It also stems from shared national identity (although see below). Individually the differences on public service provision are often small but they point in a consistent direction, towards more universalism, less privatisation, less competition and more collaboration among government, professions and citizens. Yet this social citizenship is poorly articulated and the devolution settlement itself does not always facilitate its expression in coherent policies.

On the devolution settlement, let us consider two examples. The first is the financial settlement, which provides nearly all Scottish and Welsh funding as a block grant from Westminster. The lack of earmarking, almost unique in intergovernmental transfers in the world, has allowed Scotland and Wales to go a different way in organising their public services. Yet only at the margin does it allow Scotland to make the crucial decision on whether to finance public services by taxes or by fees or leave them to the market. The benign state of public finances in the first few years of devolution and the recent conversion of all the UK parties to the model of taxpayer-funded social services has postponed the impact of this question, but it will re-emerge at some point. As noted above, neither the Scottish and Welsh nor the Westminster side has a coherent or consistent argument on free personal care, prescription charges or university fees but the funding for the welfare state is an issue that can only become more acute with time.

The second issue concerns the link between Income Support policies, social inclusion and economic development. Marshall noted that social citizenship could destroy the incentives on which the market economy depends, although arguing that in practice this was the sort of issue on which politics could arrive at compromises. The Keynesian welfare state, with the problem of unemployment apparently solved, provided one model for reconciling economic competition with social solidarity. We now know that this depended on rather benign external conditions and since the 1970s states have been searching for a new formula. Small European states have not been able to afford sustained periods of high unemployment and have needed to respond rapidly to asymmetrical shocks. The answer is either emigration (Ireland until the 1980s) or active labour market policy linked to the welfare state (the Nordic countries). Scotland and Wales, however, share the cost of their unemployment, disability and old age policies with the rest of the UK, insulating them from shocks. On the other side of the equation, the devolved institutions do not gain revenues from increases in economic activity even when this is the result of their own expenditures on supply-side measures and active labour market policies. There may be good reasons for spreading social insurance across wider areas and a complete devolution of social security would appear a poisoned chalice to the Scottish and Welsh political class, but the present system does seem to create a strange system of incentives. For example, the current effort to move people off disability benefit (an important form of disguised unemployment in Glasgow and the Welsh Valleys) will result in a loss of spending flows into Scotland and Wales. One answer to this may be institutional, a new division of competences and financial responsibilities to bring social inclusion and economic development more closely together.

The failure to articulate a coherent Scottish or Welsh conception of social citizenship, or indeed a narrative around economic development, is in striking contrast to other stateless nations and historic reasons. Nationality here is an advantage, since it is clear that shared national identity provided a focus for defence of the welfare state under Thatcherism. It can also provide a basis for collective action around economic development in the 'new regionalist' mode, which stresses networks, shared aims and a balance of competition and cooperation (Keating et al, 2003a). Yet national*ism* is a political cleavage within Scotland. Labour is afraid to stress the Scottish dimension for fear of stoking nationalism to the benefit of the Scottish National Party. The latter has failed for its part to develop a concept of social citizenship to broaden and deepen its appeal. Indeed, unlike its counterparts elsewhere it seems to see the nation as complete rather than a work in progress. Its policy prospectus evades the question of a Scottish social model by promising Scandinavian-level welfare services with Irish-like taxation levels. In office since May 2007, it has continued to extend universalism without seriously considering its relationship to a new social citizenship, for example in the abolition of the graduate endowment (the postponed university tuition fee) and of bridge tolls. Labour, for its part, seems dedicated to reconstructing Britishness. Scotland lacks a concept equivalent to *catalanismo*, in which all the parties in Catalonia with the exception of the conservative Partido Popular (PP) (and even some of them) share a commitment to the nation and its promotion, while remaining divided on the constitutional question and the matter of nationalism. Wales is less sharply divided on the national question, but it too has failed to use Welshness as a mobilising theme. Such a concept would certainly be viable, to judge both by public opinion and the structure of civil society. It is inhibited by a structure of party politics designed for another age and other issues, but which itself may be dying as a result of the new politics of devolution.

We are seeing a gradual reconstruction of politics in Scotland and Wales in response to devolution. Changes in the political superstructure are followed by slower changes in the infrastructure of policy communities and processes. As elsewhere in Europe, civil, political and social rights are being reconfigured at different levels. It is too soon to say that there are distinct Scottish and Welsh models, but the old British model, captured by Marshall at the moment of its completion, is becoming a thing of the past.

Notes

[1] This aphorism, that has become a favoured NPM cliché, is one of the most misleading analogies in management theory, a field notorious for misleading comparisons. Anyone familiar with boats knows that most of the steering is done by the oarsmen.

[2] This is not entirely true. The otherwise austere Chancellor of the Exchequer has given winter fuel payments and help with Council Tax payments to all pensioners in the UK, irrespective of means or condition.

[3] It is not actually free anywhere. Rather there is a complex matter of deciding who pays for what in what circumstances, which differs somewhat between England and Scotland.

[4] The formula has been tried in many jurisdictions, most famously in New York under Rudolph Giuliani, who was able to take credit for a declining crime rate (itself due to demographic change and reduced unemployment) by targeting visible things like graffiti and youths jumping subway barriers, and claiming that this was somehow affecting

big crime as well. Indeed law and order is one of those issues on which populist politicians can hardly lose. If crime is falling, then whatever policy they have in place can be credited with the success. If crime is rising, then they can claim that their policies are needed all the more. Whether the policies actually work is, politically, almost irrelevant.

[5] The test would be to ask a question like: 'Do you think that Scotland should be able to decide to spend less on, say, roads and put the money into health instead?'.

[6] Segall (2007) misses this point in a criticism of an earlier contribution of mine (Keating, 2003). He insists that solidarity should be at the level of the political community. My point is that Scotland is such a political community and not the sort of ethnic segment at which his criticisms are addressed.

SEVEN

Un-joined-up government: intergovernmental relations and citizenship rights[1]

Alan Trench

While there are obvious connections between devolution in general and citizenship rights, the relationship between intergovernmental relations and citizenship rights is not immediately evident. At least between 1999 and 2007, intergovernmental relations were a relatively obscure and technical aspect of the working of devolution in the United Kingdom (as it is in many federal systems), more suited to discussions of the practicalities of public administration than to issues of principle like citizenship rights, or the macro-level discussions of the working of welfare states that often accompany them. However, this chapter will argue that the two are connected; that the UK's approach to intergovernmental relations helps to explain the disjointed approach to citizenship rights that has manifested itself since devolution and reinforces such a trend.

This chapter will look at two aspects of intergovernmental relations. First, there is the division of powers between the UK parliament and government and the devolved institutions of Scotland, Wales and (intermittently) Northern Ireland. Second, there is the nature of those relations – the substance of negotiations and agreements reached between governments, how the substantive relationship changes over time, and the processes by which those governments involved deal with each other. This approach has a long pedigree in understanding the working of federal systems (see, for example, Watts, 1989, for comparative discussion; Simeon, Richard, 2006b, or Stevenson, 2005, for Canada; Galligan et al, 1991, for Australia; or Jeffery, 1999, for Germany), which can also be applied to the very different conditions of the UK (as in Trench, 2007). (It has been used, although with less success, in understanding relations between central and local government in the UK; see Rhodes, 1988, for a discussion.) Such relations are particularly important for states undergoing a process of decentralisation or devolution, because of the often-limited powers available to constituent unit governments in such systems and the dynamic nature of the process of constitutional change (Agranoff, 2004). In this context, the UK is rather unusual, as unlike most welfare states in federal or decentralised systems (such as those discussed in Obinger et al, 2005), it is decentralising a welfare state that has already been built around the institutional framework of a unitary or union state, rather than building its welfare state to take account of a division of powers between federal and state governments. Comparatively speaking, the only other state to attempt such a process is Belgium, itself a distinctive case for numerous reasons. Moreover, as McEwan (2002) points out, the creation of the UK's welfare state has itself played an important role in reinforcing citizenship and loyalty to that broader union state in the period since the Second World War.

Devolution, however, has been carried out with little regard to issues of citizenship generally, and particularly social citizenship in Marshall's (1950 [1992]) conception of it. Devolution is concerned principally with political rights rather than civil or social ones, although the relation between civil and political rights is itself a potentially difficult one, eased by the fact that legal primacy was given to the European Convention on Human Rights (which addresses individual rather than group rights, and is principally concerned with civil rights) by the 1998 Scotland Act, 1998 Government of Wales Act and 1998 Northern Ireland Act.[2] (For further discussion, see Himsworth, 2001.) Indeed, there has long been a problem in the UK, and particularly for academic lawyers, in construing social rights as a form of constitutional rights (rare contrary examples are Ewing, 1999, 2000). As a result, it is little surprise that not much attention was given to the impact of devolution on social citizenship before now.

This chapter will begin by surveying the division of powers between the UK government and parliament, on the one hand, and the devolved legislatures and administrations on the other. It will discuss how the UK's system of intergovernmental relations has functioned between 1999 and 2007, the problems that this presents for citizenship rights within the UK and the nature of the constraints on both the UK government and devolved administrations regarding social policy, and concludes with a discussion of the implications of different ways of managing such relations for citizenship rights.

How devolution works: the devolved division of powers and what it means

The fundamental principle of devolution is the conferring of certain governmental powers to elected legislatures (and governments accountable to those legislatures) in three parts of the UK. This is accompanied by the assumption that devolved matters will be the responsibility of the devolved institutions, but that is not explicitly laid down anywhere, and indeed Westminster retains legal sovereignty across the UK. Devolution is profoundly asymmetric, with the powers devolved varying from territory to territory, as does the structure of the devolved institutions.[3] The different political backgrounds in Scotland and Wales (political nationalism and the need to respond to distinctive senses of national identity) help explain the differences between the scope of devolution in each country. In Northern Ireland, devolution was only one of three 'strands' in the 1998 Belfast Agreement, and derived not from distinctive national politics but from attempts to find common ground between two different, and conflicting, national traditions. England has remained outside this picture, at least for the time being; there were hopes if not expectations that increased functions would be devolved to elected regional governments, but progress in this direction was slow and came to a halt after the defeat of such proposals at a referendum in the North East in October 2004. However, this has not slowed the progress of administrative regionalisation (Sandford and Hetherington, 2005).

Although the functions devolved vary a good deal from territory to territory, several key areas of social policy are devolved. Education, health, personal social services and housing are all the responsibilities of the Scottish Parliament and Executive, National Assembly for Wales and Welsh Assembly Government, and Northern Ireland Assembly and Executive, in Scotland, Wales or Northern Ireland respectively. Education includes primary, secondary and tertiary (higher) education; health includes all aspects of primary and secondary health services, and most (although not quite all) aspects of health promotion and disease control. In health, this creates a degree of divergence that amounts to the existence of four different national health services, sharing little in common beyond the name (Greer, 2004). However, although the division of powers creates an impression of very extensive devolved autonomy, it is easy to misread the formal division of powers to assume that devolved autonomy is greater than it actually is. The apparent neatness and breadth of the powers devolved in Scotland, Wales and Northern Ireland should not mask the complexities and restrictions that exist in practice, which are discussed further below. Speaking generally, the pattern can be understood as the range of 'social, health, education and welfare', or SHEW, services commonly given to meso-level governments (Sharpe, 1993). On the constitutional level, the extent of devolution is considerable, arguably more so than in many regionalised systems.

In two major areas, however, the devolved administrations have no autonomy. One relates to the social security system, which remains a reserved (UK) matter. Thus the nature of welfare benefits, the conditions or events that trigger them, and the levels of payments made are all determined by the UK government on a UK-wide basis.[4] Given the interactions between the social security system and other aspects of the welfare state, this is a major potential source of problems, with incompatible policies either removing eligibility for social security benefits for those intended to receive them or conferring benefits on those also receiving assistance in some other form. The former has already arisen, in the loss of entitlement to Attendance Allowance of claimants in Scotland who can take advantage of the Scottish policy of 'free' long-term care for the older people (Simeon, Rachel, 2003). (That care provided under this policy can be patchy in its application, and sometimes fails to deliver the level of care that the cash benefit was expected to provide, makes the double whammy of loss of eligibility the worse.) A similar row, but with much more money at stake, has arisen in 2007-08 regarding Council Tax benefit if the Scottish government proceeds with the Scottish National Party's (SNP) manifesto commitment to replace the Council Tax as a source of revenue for local government with a uniform local income tax. If governments take different approaches to the exercise of their powers, informed by different ideological approaches, this sort of problem is likely to continue to arise.

The second major limitation on devolved powers is finance. The devolved administrations have minimal financial autonomy: the Scottish Parliament can vary the standard rate of income tax by 3%, and through their control of local government grant and spending they have scope to increase overall revenues by allowing local authorities to increase the money they raise.[5] Otherwise the funding of the devolved administrations is controlled by the UK government, determined through the Barnett formula as a consequence of spending decisions made by the UK government for 'comparable functions' in England. (For general discussions, see Heald and McLeod, 2002b, or McLean and McMillan, 2003.) Elsewhere in this book Iain McLean, Guy Lodge and Katie Schmuecker (Chapter Eight) argue that the UK's financial system fails to deliver territorial equity, by failing to allocate public spending to the parts of the UK that appear to have greatest need of it and (in particular) giving Scotland a generous share when its level of needs is relatively low. This is far from the only ground on which to criticise the UK's present arrangements. The economics literature suggests ways in which fiscal decentralisation can promote economic efficiency while not undermining (and perhaps enhancing) equity, primarily by governments having greater responsibility for raising revenue to pay for the services they provide. The UK's system does not deliver this; it pays unconditional grants, calculated on criteria that are hard to justify objectively or rationally (because the baseline is a historic one) to devolved administrations that, as a result, are effectively just spending agencies. There are strong arguments, rooted in both politics and economics, that this inherently undermines devolved financial and policy-making autonomy.

However, the implications of the UK's financing system are not entirely straightforward. Funding provided by the Treasury is unconditional; it takes the form of a block grant that can be allocated as the devolved institutions see fit, according to their priorities, not anyone else's. The financial arrangements for devolution therefore facilitate devolved autonomy and allow the devolved administrations extensive freedom in policy making, with the scope for different approaches to social welfare that this implies. Moreover, the funding that Barnett provides is remarkably stable – while in theory it could go down, that has not yet happened, and the amount of increases is generally predictable (although problems can arise when the Treasury announces in-year changes in English spending). This is a significant advantage, and one that systems more closely tied to need cannot deliver (contrast it with the various needs-based formulae used to calculate local government spending in England, Scotland and Wales). Yet the formal foundation of that grant – a Treasury 'statement of policy' (now HM Treasury, 2007b) – is weak. It has no statutory (let alone constitutional) basis, but is a policy that takes effect through annual Appropriation Acts, and so affords little guarantee to the devolved administrations despite its importance to them.

A further consequence is that the devolved administrations have a continuing, close, if somewhat ambivalent, relationship with the Treasury. The Treasury accepts its relationship with the devolved administrations is necessarily a more distant one than with Whitehall spending departments, but nonetheless it keeps a close interest in and eye on their spending policies, if only to compare them with those adopted for England. It cannot impose public spending agreements on the devolved administrations (although when those were still in fashion in the early 2000s it appears to have wanted to, and had reluctantly to accept the political impossibility of that). (See generally Trench, 2007, pp 86-112) Over the last few years the Treasury has sought to control devolved activities over such matters as the use of end-year flexibility to carry unspent money from one year to the next, the introduction of resource accounting and budgeting with its implications for the use of capital assets (in each successfully), and the split between capital and current spending within the devolved block (unsuccessfully in 2004, but not because of the way the devolved institutions used their powers, but successfully in the 2007 Comprehensive Spending Review). On the technical level, too, the devolved administrations remain deeply integrated into the UK system of public finances (Heald and Macleod, 2005).

In the real world of policy making, devolved powers regularly interact with non-devolved or reserved ones. This creates a pattern of considerable complexity, often not appreciated by the general public (and sometimes not by officials either, particularly London-based ones). So far, such overlaps have been resolved between governments (usually informally, between officials), in order for the devolved administrations to be able to develop their own approaches to policy making (Trench, 2007). The upshot is a system in which the practical exercise of devolved autonomy depends on the ability to reach an accommodation with the UK government – which, given the inequality of bargaining power of each level, means at least ensuring that the UK government does not obstruct devolved proposals (and ensuring it takes devolved policies into account in its own policies). Devolved autonomy cannot simply be asserted on the basis of constitutional powers, nor judged to exist from the ability of the devolved administrations to depart from 'norms' of the UK government, whether applied for England or in relation to reserved/non-devolved matters. That goodwill in turn depended heavily on the political goodwill that Labour dominance of all three British governments between 1999 and 2007 generated, but which has been much weaker (if it exists at all) with the entry of nationalist parties into office after the 2007 elections.

This sort of complex interaction arises in many areas. A good example is higher education. Policy in Scotland and Wales has already diverged a significant way from that for England, with both countries adopting more generous policies for supporting students and less onerous ones for fees, in order to increase participation particularly from poorer families (Keating, 2005b; Trench, 2008b). These are at odds with the UK government's policy of expanding resources for higher education by charging graduates a 'deferred flexible fee' after graduation (so-called 'top-up fees'), a policy that meshes poorly with devolved powers and policies (see McLean, 2005, for a discussion). There have been extensive changes in administrative arrangements (for example, establishing a single funding council for both further and higher education in Scotland), fees (the adoption of deferred variable fees in England, the establishment of the graduate endowment in Scotland in 2001 as an alternative to upfront fees and its subsequent abolition by the incoming SNP government in 2008, or Assembly fees grants for Welsh-domiciled students attending Welsh universities), and student support (for example, Assembly Learning Grants in Wales). These mean that the costs to students and their families of attending university vary a good deal across the UK.

However, while these aspects of higher education are devolved, research – or at least the research councils – is not. This money is allocated on a UK-wide basis, by UK-wide criteria, depending in part on the outcome of the UK-wide Research Assessment Exercise (RAE) (which is run by the Higher Education Funding Council for England and remains UK-wide only because the devolved administrations have chosen to remain part of it). The importance of research council funding varies from institution to institution, and Scotland appears to receive somewhat more than its pro-rata share on a population basis might indicate: 11% of the UK's research council funding for 9% of the population. (Wales receives less than its population share.) However, research council spending accounts for nearly two thirds of total public sector funding of research in the UK, and for research-oriented universities (meaning, outside England, principally Edinburgh, Glasgow, Cardiff and Queen's University Belfast) it accounts for 25%-30% of total income. As the amounts involved are substantial, and have significant impacts on what are key institutions (for teaching as well as research) in each country, those concerned with higher education as a whole have to be concerned about how research spending is allocated. Yet this is in the hands of arm's-length research councils, which (with one exception, the Economic and Social Research Council [ESRC], which is also one of the smallest of the research councils) do not even publish figures on the allocation of their funding in territorial terms. The research councils were formerly under the aegis of the Department for Trade and Industry (DTI), and when problems in policy for England (in particular, the costs of Rover Group's insolvency) led in 2007 to cuts in DTI spending generally, these fell on the research councils as well as other parts of that department – and so Scotland and Wales paid a price for problems that related only to England. Moreover, UK government policy for research is territory-blind, allocated according to perceptions of merit, and the officials involved in it are conspicuously proud of doing so. The result is a policy that gives increasing rewards to the already successful, and locks out the less successful – which includes many institutions in Scotland and Wales (and indeed England outside the South East).

Attempts to mitigate this within Scotland or Wales are necessarily modest. The higher education funding councils provide funds for 'quality research' as part of their grants to universities, and have sought to encourage some research activities such as collaboration within disciplines across institutions, and to allocate funds more generously to departments that have performed less well in the RAE (departments rated 4 and 4A in the 2001 RAE still get meaningful research allocations in Scotland and Wales, but not England), but the amounts involved cannot compensate for research council funding.

The result is that neither UK nor devolved levels of government 'owns' the policy domain of higher education – each has control of part of it, can try to use that control for different (and possibly conflicting) ends, and can interfere with the others' policy in doing so. When it comes to individual citizens, the sort of access to education one has, and what one's experience of university study is, will vary according to where one lives and where one studies. Moreover, it will vary in ways that are haphazard and hard to understand or rationalise. That has implications for the governments involved, but also for the rights of those wanting higher education (and indeed for society at large). Whatever outcome one wishes to see – whether it be a common policy across the UK that delivers a single package of citizenship rights across the whole country, or to maximise devolved autonomy to enable distinct forms of Scottish, Welsh, Northern Irish or English social citizenship to emerge – this is no way to achieve it.

Higher education is not unique in this. A similar pattern develops, for example, in relation to controlling contagious diseases – a convoluted administrative arrangement, understood only by insiders if by anyone, which relies on practical cooperation and goodwill to work effectively. This arises from two sources: the interaction between devolved and non-devolved policies in the same field, and between financial matters that are reserved to the UK level (including social security) and devolved policy functions.

Nor are policy interactions the only way in which the UK government can affect the devolved administrations, or vice versa. The sheer size of England (with 85% of the whole of the UK's population, and somewhat more of its GDP) means that decisions taken for England have a major impact on Scotland, Wales and Northern Ireland. Particularly in border areas, policies of one government can affect the others. Decisions about National Health Service (NHS) pay in England will affect staffing and recruitment in border areas, for example; in many ways, the Avon area and South East Wales as far as Cardiff form a common labour market. NHS patients similarly move across borders.[6] The influence can also go the other way, although more as an example of different approaches to policy that can be taken.

Making sense of the pattern of devolved and non-devolved powers is not, then, straightforward. Perhaps more useful than considering these simply as 'SHEW' functions in Sharpe's (1993) terms is to draw on Lowi's (1972) distinction between distributive, redistributive and regulatory functions, as James Mitchell (2004) has done. The devolved administrations are largely confined to 'SHEW' functions of distributive or regulatory character, and not granted redistributive ones such as social security (Mitchell, 2004; Trench, 2007). In this context, the extent devolved administrations can create a distinctive form of social citizenship is a limited one, but one which has curious spillovers between levels of government. The intention lying behind devolution appears to have been to maintain a single welfare state, while allowing relatively minor variations in policy making and implementation by the devolved administrations. However, this is not what was in fact created. While the devolved administrations may be limited to being spending agencies rather than fully fledged governments with fiscal and financial responsibility to match their legal powers, those powers are sufficiently extensive that they can use them to create different sets of benefits from the welfare state. To the extent that there remains a common UK social citizenship, it is institutionally fragmented, and so incomplete and haphazard.

Formal intergovernmental relations and social policy

The practice of intergovernmental relations since devolution in the UK has been characterised by informality, limited use of formal mechanisms and frameworks and a heavy reliance on 'goodwill' (House of Lords, 2003). As Parry (2004) notes, these relations are 'interdepartmental' rather than 'quasi-diplomatic' in character.

The arrangements made in 1998–99 for intergovernmental relations were modest in their scope. They included an agreement between governments – the *Memorandum of understanding* (now DCA, 2001) – setting out the basic principles for conducting relations.[7] Key to this was an understanding that relations would be governed by the maxim 'no surprises', and by articulating as key principles those of consultation, communication, cooperation (especially in sharing information) and confidentiality. This was to be supplemented by specific bilateral 'concordats' between particular UK government departments and devolved administrations, and dealing with particular issues in the context of that area of government. The *Memorandum of understanding* created a framework for intergovernmental ministerial meetings by establishing the Joint Ministerial Committee (JMC), comprising an unspecified number of functional formats and a plenary JMC to meet at least annually consisting of heads of government from the four governments, along with the Secretaries of State for Scotland, Wales and Northern Ireland in the UK government. The posts of those Secretaries of State, and their Offices, were retained as key liaison figures to manage relations, under overarching guidance from a central section originally in the Cabinet Office. The role of that section (since 2007 part of the Ministry of Justice) has been limited to coordination, however.

In practice, relations have not worked quite as anticipated. Ministerial meetings have largely ground to a halt, and often take place outside the JMC framework. The plenary JMC has not met since October 2002 despite the requirement for an annual meeting (also demonstrating that breach of the *Memorandum of understanding* is acceptable). Few bilateral meetings between subject ministers take place either, and these meetings are ad hoc ones rather than being arranged as part of the normal routine of doing business. Territorial Secretaries of State and First Ministers have kept in contact (closer for Wales than Scotland), but hitherto, when both have been Labour, this has been driven as much by party concerns as policy matters.

The most effective meetings that do take place regularly relate to European Union (EU) matters: EU policy itself, meaning particularly the Constitutional Treaty (and more recently the Reform Treaty) and agriculture. Clearly the existence of external constraints, and the need to coordinate UK policy to respond to those constraints, is a significant factor. Even here, however, there are reasons to believe that the system does not work perfectly.[8] There are also six-monthly meetings of finance ministers, convened by the Chief Secretary to the Treasury, which appear to be concerned with the practicalities of financial management.

What is notable is that hardly any of these areas relate to issues of welfare and social citizenship. These fall outside the framework of formal coordination. 'Functional' formats of the JMC for areas such as health, the knowledge economy or poverty were created in 1999, but ceased relatively quickly. There has been no meaningful discussion of education (although the 'knowledge economy' format did touch on this), or any of housing matters. A functional JMC for health was established in 2000 but has not met since 2001 (and there have been no ministerial meetings outside the JMC framework). It was clear from the communiqués that the last meetings were devoted to 'sharing experiences' rather than substantive discussion – not the sort of activity that a minister with much to do is likely to find rewarding or useful.

The most direct attempt to use formal intergovernmental mechanisms for social policy matters was the JMC's functional format for poverty. Like several 'functional' formats of the JMC, this was established in 1999, chaired by Gordon Brown, Chancellor of the Exchequer, with a remit 'to consider joint or coordinated action by the UK government and the Devolved Administrations to tackle poverty and social exclusion; and to facilitate exchanging information and best practice' (Trench, 2007, ch 8). After a flurry of initial activity when experiences were exchanged but otherwise little accomplished, it ceased meeting in 2001. What was most interesting about its work was the further meeting that took place in September 2002, and its aftermath. The 2002 meeting had a wide-ranging agenda concentrating chiefly on social exclusion, child poverty and data collection, and resulted in a communiqué that set out an ambitious work programme and announced two further planned meetings for the first half of 2003 (HM Treasury, 2002). There was little further work on that agenda; the planned subsequent meetings never happened and UK officials interviewed were unable to explain why.

While civil servants may be unable to say so, it is not hard to see reasons for the reluctance of the devolved administrations to embrace this UK initiative. According to the Treasury press notice of the meeting, Brown said:

> The government has set the framework for tackling poverty and improving childcare through, for example, reforms to the tax and benefit system, especially the introduction of the Child and Working Tax Credits from April 2003. All four administrations across the UK are committed to tackling poverty and social exclusion. Yet all too often we measure our progress to those goals in different ways. Establishing a key set of indicators and, where relevant, a common approach is not an academic issue; it is the bedrock upon which different policy approaches can be tried and tested.
>
> Devolution brings new opportunities for the development of policies better suited to local needs across the UK. We need to learn what policies work best in tackling poverty

and social exclusion. The Joint Ministerial Committee on Poverty is an ideal forum for sharing best practice and policy innovation among the UK government and the devolved administrations in Scotland, Wales and Northern Ireland. (HM Treasury, 2002)

The remit and agenda of this form of the JMC were strongly influenced by Brownite ideas of what needed to be done to tackle poverty (ideas not always shared by the devolved governments, even under Labour). The devolved administrations were being asked to commit themselves to Brownite policies and approach, and to common data collection and benchmarks for success, with the implication that any failures would be highlighted – exposing them to potential political embarrassment, especially if they had in fact pursued distinctive policies rather than followed London's lead. Worse, this was proposed without any extra funding being made available, or any other sort of benefit or reward for devolved compliance. It is not surprising that the devolved administrations simply sought to avoid engagement in this policy initiative, which subtracted from devolved autonomy without offering anything in return.

Managing intergovernmental relations informally

As a result of the disuse of formal mechanisms, routine coordination of intergovernmental relations has fallen to officials. They have been expected to keep in regular touch with each other and by and large have done so, but there have been cases where this arrangement has failed to work effectively, and one government has been caught on the hop by an initiative of the other. This has generally arisen much more often with UK government initiatives than devolved ones, as the UK government looms much larger in the devolved view than the devolved administrations do in London's eyes (Trench, 2005).

The result is that on the process level intergovernmental relations have been overwhelmingly bilateral, and had only limited involvement from ministers. They have been largely unstructured, and dominated by the 'issues of the day' rather than anything more strategic or long term. Such relations have largely taken place in private and far away from the public gaze, with only very limited information made public about what has been happening or the nature of any bargains or agreements struck between governments. When such relations have become matters of public interest this has usually been because rumours of a 'row' or 'split' have reached the press. This public perception is far from the reality of a process of routine disagreements and differences between governments, which have been resolved thanks to the mediation and brokerage of the offices of the territorial Secretaries of State (and sometimes the Secretaries of State themselves) (Trench, 2007, ch 3).

The backdrop to this – and a large part of the reason why so few formal meetings have taken place and relations have generally been so harmonious – was the dominance of Labour across the three governments in Britain. Even when government has been devolved to Northern Ireland, the parties elected have not competed with Labour, which does not campaign there. The UK government also has the means to inconvenience and perhaps to obstruct the devolved administrations if it wishes to do so – whether through finance, through taking a narrow and obstructive view of their legal powers, or through failing to create space in UK legislation or programmes for devolved policies. In this context, it is easiest to understand the outcome as a form of 'permissive' or 'contingent' autonomy (Trench, 2007, especially chs 1 and 12). This has been underpinned by Labour's dominance. The effect of this was not simply to create a climate of political accord between governments (although it did do that to an extent). It was also to create conditions where politicians had sufficient common interest that when they had dealings with each other they knew that they were 'among friends' (as the Rt Hon Helen Liddell once put it). Furthermore, it created a desire to make devolution (like other Labour policies) appear to be a success, and the absence of disagreement, or at least public disagreement, was seen as the measure of that. Consequently, there was a shared desire to reach agreement, quietly and away from the public gaze, when there were differences between governments. This has started to decline with the arrival of nationalist parties in government, particularly in Scotland. Despite protestations of overall good relations (for example, Cairns, 2008), it has been clear that difficulties are emerging in many policy areas. However, the framework for managing relations has not changed, although the UK government conceded in the spring of 2008 that a revival of the JMC was needed and set about that in a rather slow and cautious way.[9]

Such arrangements have placed a heavy burden on what the UK government seeks to do and how it seeks to do it. That the UK government has dominated intergovernmental relations is not in itself a surprise, given the various powers it has retained under each devolution settlement. Its lack of a reconstructed internal structure means that there are no systematic arrangements, on the administrative or political levels, for dealing with devolution questions as part of its own processes. While various forms of procedural guidance about how to deal with devolution matters have been issued (such as the 'Devolution Guidance Notes' for which the Ministry of Justice is now responsible), compliance with these has been variable and sometimes they are not even referred to. Consequently its record for 'devolution awareness' has been patchy and inconsistent at best, with variations from department to department, between different parts of departments and between individual officials (Trench, 2005).

The result is a system of intergovernmental relations that does not seek to establish common standards or policies across the UK. It does not coordinate policy, or manage differences between governments or policies. Neither does it attempt to apply general principles of the devolution settlement in the various cases that arise (because there are no such principles). The result is that the devolved administrations have largely been left free to develop their approaches to policy in devolved areas, the UK government has developed its own approaches and any connection between the two has either arisen because of shared Labour priorities and outlook on the world or been coincidental. Differences between governments have been dealt with in private, and resolved with little publicity and (so far as one can tell) little attention to broader implications. The consequences can be unintended or even perverse. As discussed above, the Scottish introduction of free personal care for older people meant that claimants in Scotland lost their entitlement to Attendance Allowance, a social security benefit and so a reserved matter. When the Scots sought to recoup this money from the Department for Work and Pensions and the Treasury, they were rebuffed. For political reasons, the Scottish Executive decided not to press the point and did not use the appeal arrangements that exist for finance matters (to the UK Cabinet), nor did they ask that the matter be considered by the (plenary) JMC. Frail older people in Scotland therefore receive a different package of rights from their English or Welsh peers, but to provide this the Scottish Executive has to shoulder a financial burden. While one can argue that Scotland is generously funded and can afford to do so, none of those involved appear to have tried to take an overall view of what this meant; they merely dealt with particular issues as they arose.

In general terms the devolved administrations have done reasonably well out of this arrangement, certainly up to 2007. That has been the consequence of favourable circumstances, however. Nowhere in this pattern of relations is there any entity or institution concerned with articulating what devolution means in social terms for citizens individually or collectively, whether in the constituent parts of the UK or for the UK as a whole.

The non-use of the JMC both for summit meetings of the UK's various governments, and as a framework for interministerial meetings at working level, worsens this. It means intergovernmental relations consist of nothing other than ad hoc interactions triggered by the issues of the day (which usually arise in London rather than in the devolved capitals). It means that there is no setting to deal with one of the key functions of the JMC – to consider how non-devolved functions affect devolved matters and vice versa. Given the structure of the devolution settlement (as discussed above) this is a serious absence; not only is it harmful in itself, but it sends a signal to Whitehall officials that such issues are unimportant. The informality of intergovernmental relations makes it all the harder for the devolved administrations to make their voices heard on matters which affect them but which are retained at UK level – an issue of greater concern given the expectations of the public (discussed by Charlie Jeffery, Chapter Five, this volume) about the greater 'voice' that devolution was expected to give their parts of the UK, within the UK's institutions.

Social citizenship and intergovernmental relations

What the UK has ended up with is a situation in which social rights are starting to vary significantly across the UK's territory, and have probably already reached the point at which variations in specific entitlements are turning into variations in the overall nature of social citizenship. That trend is likely to continue, and means one has to consider whether social citizenship is now a UK-wide matter (with certain acceptable but limited departures from a UK-wide norm), or an English/UK, Scottish, Welsh or Northern Irish matter, connected on certain institutional levels. At present it has elements of both, but verges more towards the latter. As political differences become increasingly marked between the various governments, that trend is likely to increase over time. The means available to the UK government to restrain divergence may be powerful ones, but they are also rather hard to use. They are essentially political in nature, at least to the extent that they require political will to be used – and use of them for such reasons risks being regarded by electors in the devolved territories as an act of political vindictiveness on London's part which will strengthen the popular appeal of nationalist parties as the ones best able to 'stand up' for Scotland or Wales. (The dynamics in Northern Ireland are somewhat different, and both Sinn Féin and the Democratic Unionist Party [DUP] would be able to make similar claims there.)

Underlying this is a further problem. The UK's system has so far rested on a set of tacit understandings about the nature of social citizenship and its territorial extent. This is manifest in Marshall (1950 [1992]) himself; he takes for granted 'the state' in which his package of rights will apply, and his historical discussions of the development of various sorts of rights relate to England rather than the UK as a whole. The welfare state he discusses was, however, essentially a *British* affair, and those understandings are unarticulated and implicit. What welfare means in a post-devolution UK has been similarly left to a series of such understandings, which there are neither the administrative nor intergovernmental mechanisms to address, nor any other document (whether constitutional or something else) to explain. That may be convenient for governments, but it is not good for citizens. The original Labour expectation may have been that devolution would simply result in different administration of common, UK-wide, services without changing the nature of those services or the conception of citizenship underlying them. However, Labour created a system that created no guarantees of this other than political ones – and also created political conditions that, in the medium term (if not immediately), would undermine the effectiveness of that political guarantee.

The entry of nationalist parties into government has other political implications. Neither the SNP nor Plaid Cymru shares the view that the UK rather than Scotland or Wales is the appropriate locus for expressing social solidarity, and each takes a more generous view of what welfare should involve than the UK Labour government does. Quite apart from views within Labour in Scotland or Wales (whether they are to the left of the UK leadership or not), this compels a political response from the other parties there. In Wales, the attempt to put 'clear red water' between it and London appeared in late 2002, and the Conservatives there have also responded by becoming a pro-welfare party of the centre-right, which would sit comfortably with or perhaps to the left of many continental European Christian democratic parties. Labour's response has been more tentative and uncertain, although clearly it is underpinned by traditional Labour views of cross-UK redistribution and common citizenship that is better protected and more responsively implemented in Scotland or Wales. That is more expressly articulated in Wales than Scotland. In Wales, Labour politicians have been keen to point out the virtues of the Barnett formula in the way funds are allocated, and to stress that they might do no better under alternative arrangements.[10] In Scotland, the issue tends to be handled with more care and in a more coded way, to avoid sending messages to voters in England (especially southern England) that their taxes are, in effect, subsidising a higher level of social welfare in Scotland and a more universalist approach to welfare than those taxpayers can expect to receive themselves. Yet this is a point loudly made by the right-wing press in London, with some political resonance. Whether the implicit redistribution achieved by the Barnett formula can last is therefore in doubt, and any successor will need to be more explicit about its purposes, and the rationale for those purposes.

Conclusion

A different approach to the practice of intergovernmental relations in the UK could help resolve some of these problems. It could do so in four ways. First, the greater use of formal mechanisms of intergovernmental relations would create a forum to air and resolve some of the thorny issues of divergent citizenship rights that are starting to emerge. In this context, it is worth looking at comparative experience. In most federal systems, the practice of intergovernmental relations (sometimes called executive or cooperative federalism) enables governments to manage the interface between their various powers and functions, and the policies they have adopted in these areas (see generally Watts, 1989). Such a process obstructs the taking of rapid decisions by one government alone, but can result in overall better policies being adopted, and this happening in a form that all governments can accept. A notable example is the adoption of the pensions plans in Canada, an initiative of both the federal government and the Québec government during the early 1960s, during which the federal government completely revised and made more extensive its scheme, and developed an innovative constitutional framework to enable the federal government to create a scheme for the English-speaking provinces while Québec established its own system (Simeon, Richard, 2006b, especially ch 3; and more generally, Banting, 2005). All this is a far cry from the disjointed approach that generally prevails in the UK at present, or the sort of attempt to co-opt the devolved governments to a UK policy agenda that the 2002 revival of the JMC (poverty) signified. It is understandable that few governments wish to embark on such a way of governing if they have a choice. It involves the commitment of significant administrative and political resources, slows down decision making and builds compromise into the fabric of that decision making. A combination of inertia and a belief in government (particularly in London) that this is a matter of choice has created considerable resistance to such a change.

Second, such an approach would alter the way the UK government considers such issues. It would have to address the implications of divisions of power for social rights, and might become more effective in addressing these in its internal arrangements. Given the weight attached to those internal arrangements in the management of devolution, that would be a significant potential advantage. Whether the UK or the constituent units are considered to be the appropriate locus, that would result in more coherent and consistent policy making.

Third, it would create a framework for governments and legislators (whether in UK or devolved institutions) and society more generally to reflect on what, in social terms, the UK is now *for*, and which level of government should do what. This would imply a broader deliberative approach to what sorts of policy differentiation there ought to be, and what sorts of financial redistribution across the various parts of the UK. In other words, it would involve openly thinking about the nature of social and economic equity in the UK, and seeking to reach agreement based on some broader principles about what the various governments in the UK should and should not do, and how they should (or should not) do it. This need not necessarily have a centralising effect. A systematic approach to the practice of intergovernmental relations in Canada has not centralised government there, nor do unsystematic intergovernmental relations contribute to decentralisation in the US – both have different causes (Trench, 2006a). What it would do is to structure existing relations between UK and devolved administrations, enable policies to be coordinated better where that is possible and appropriate, and enable differences to be managed when it is not. That in turn would improve public transparency and public understanding of decisions presently being reached in private, in an opaque and uncoordinated way. Such a change would improve the rights of citizens, and possibly of governments too.

Fourth, it would both create an appropriate forum to resolve the financial issues that underpin questions of social citizenship, and help ensure that the financial arrangements commanded broader legitimacy and better fitted the institutional and political conditions in which they now have to function.

To put matters slightly differently: it is impossible to reach a conclusion now about the nature of social and economic equity in the UK and its constituent parts, if such a conclusion is to command broad support and be reasonably durable, without using intergovernmental processes. Like it or not, territorial interests are now central to determining citizenship rights in the UK. That needs to be dealt with openly, explicitly and on a UK-wide basis if the UK is to remain the locus of social citizenship. And if a shift in the locus is to happen, there still needs to be better ways of managing the differences in policy that arise as a result.

Notes

[1] This chapter draws on interviews that were carried out as part of a project on 'Intergovernmental relations in the United Kingdom', funded by the Leverhulme Trust through the research programme 'Nations and Regions: The Dynamics of Devolution', based at the Constitution Unit at University College London (UCL). It also draws on work on higher education and devolution, funded by Universities UK, and on finance and welfare arrangements in federal and decentralised systems, funded by the Swiss Confederation. I am grateful to all these organisations for their support. I remain solely responsible for the arguments presented here, however. This chapter was finalised in June 2008 and does not cover developments after then.

[2] The legislation governing devolution to Wales is now the 2006 Government of Wales Act.

[3] A further variation was that Wales had only executive, not legislative, devolution, until May 2007. The 2006 Government of Wales Act separated the executive functions of the National Assembly from its legislative ones, and legally conferred the former on the Welsh Assembly Government. It also provided for the National Assembly to acquire legislative powers on specific matters in 20 'fields' with Westminster's approval, either through 'legislative competence orders' sought by the Assembly itself, or by Acts of Parliament. The Assembly could also acquire legislative power over 20 fields set out in the Act if popular support for that is given in a referendum. (See generally Trench, 2006b.)

[4] Technically, social security is devolved in Northern Ireland. However, this is a case of formal not real devolution, as the 1998 Northern Ireland Act provides that parity is to be maintained between benefits paid there and those paid in Great Britain.

[5] In 2007, use of the three percentage points to increase taxes would produce about £1.1 billion in extra revenue, according to UK budget documents (HM Treasury, 2007a, para A.8), compared with a total budget for the Scottish Executive/Government of about £21 billion.

[6] The long border between England and Wales, and the fact that much of it is densely populated, make this more of an issue there than between England and Scotland or Northern Ireland.

[7] The first version of the *Memorandum of understanding* was published in 1999 as Cm 4444. The present version is the third, although in substance it does not differ from that issued in 1999 (DCA, 2001).

[8] In January 2007 a draft report being prepared by Michael Aron, head of the Scottish Executive's office in Brussels, was leaked to *The Herald* newspaper. The report suggested that problems in getting the UK government to take seriously Scottish concerns and to incorporate these into its negotiating positions were much more widespread than had hitherto been indicated, and that Scottish interests were coming off badly as a result.

[9] This involved announcements that the JMC would be revived, followed by visits by Paul Murphy, the new Secretary of State for Wales, to discuss with the devolved governments how this would work.

[10] As part of the process of forming a coalition with Plaid Cymru, Labour in Wales agreed to establish a commission to look at the Barnett formula and the spending needs of the National Assembly. In announcing this, however, Jane Hutt (the then Minister for Assembly Business and Budget) was keen to point out the benefits of the Barnett formula. See *Assembly Record*, 20 June 2007, pp 106-9. The Commission had still not been established by June 2008, however.

EIGHT

Social citizenship and intergovernmental finance

Iain McLean, Guy Lodge and Katie Schmuecker

Social citizenship rights only become meaningful when there is money to make them a reality. In federal or devolved political systems intergovernmental finances can determine who sets social citizenship rights. For instance, a system that provides devolved administrations with an unconditional block grant, when combined with substantial devolution of political powers, enables the administration to alter the citizenship rights available to its citizens. On the other hand, in a system where devolved administrations' grants are conditional and key legislative powers remain with the federal or central government, it is central government that will dominate the country's social citizenship agenda. But shared standards, declarations of intent, public expectations and administrative efforts to create equal outcomes will all fail if the money is missing.

To understand intergovernmental finance and its consequences for social citizenship in the UK, we need to understand the extent of the powers and functions available to the devolved administrations in Scotland, Wales and Northern Ireland, and the way in which the UK intergovernmental finance system works – basically how the UK government taxes and spends. This is important for social citizenship for two reasons. First, where the power lies determines which administration has policy-making competence in the key areas for social citizenship, which will give an indication of whether it is the UK as a whole or the devolved administrations that are setting the social citizenship agenda. Second, how public spending is distributed has implications for social citizenship, as an equitable distribution of public spending can enable shared social citizenship.

This chapter explores the impact of the UK's devolution and intergovernmental finance arrangements on shared social citizenship in the UK. First, we give an overview of the degree of devolution, using public spending as a proxy for the degree of devolved powers, to explore whether it is the UK or the devolved territories that constitute a 'sharing community' (Banting, 2005a). Second, we outline how public spending is distributed in the UK, explaining the much misunderstood 'Barnett formula', how it works and why it is a source of political tension. Then we analyse where the spending actually goes, before considering whether the current distribution of public spending is equitable and promotes shared UK citizenship. The conclusion returns to the question of whether it is the UK or the devolved territories that constitute sharing communities, and we offer some thoughts on future developments.

Is the UK a sharing community?

Most theorists would say that social citizenship is supposed to be insensitive to territory, as much as class (see Chapters Two to Four in Part I of this volume). Within a given 'sharing community' (Banting, 2005a), residential location should not affect that 'common minimum' that Marshall defined as the basis of citizenship. The consequence for the UK is simple: *if* the UK is the sharing community, *then* its internal fiscal arrangements should enable equal access to a certain set of services. This section looks at the UK devolution settlement through the lens of finance, by analysing how spending power is devolved. The picture that emerges is a mixed one.

Table 8.1 sets out the extent of financial devolution within the UK. It is taken from HM Treasury's *A statement of funding policy*, published with each spending review (HM Treasury, 2007a). This document sets out some of the arrangements that apply in deciding the budgets of the devolved institutions, and details the extent to which the services delivered by UK government departments correspond to services for which the devolved administrations are responsible. The Treasury uses the term 'comparability' to describe this. In practice it means if a programme is devolved, the devolved administration will be provided with monies (through the Barnett formula, which we discuss further below) to fund a comparable programme (although in reality whether the devolved administration actually uses the monies to fund a comparable programme or something different is by and large up to them). If a programme is devolved the 'comparability percentage' is 100; if it is not devolved, the 'comparability percentage' is zero.

What this table shows is that in the core social citizenship area of welfare and benefits – the main redistribution mechanisms controlled by the Department for Work and Pensions – the UK government reserves power, in this area the UK is the sharing community. However, there is substantial devolution in the delivery of public services, most notably health, education and the functions of local authorities, and frequently

Table 8.1: The extent of financial devolution: comparability percentages[a] from the 2007 Spending Review

	Scotland	Wales	Northern Ireland
Children, Schools and Families	100	100	100
Innovation, Universities and Skills	79.3	79.3	79.3
Health	99.3	99.3	99.3
Transport	91.5	68.3	94.0
Communities (not including Local Government)	99.6	99.6	99.6
Local Government[b]	19.4	100	17.3
Home Office	99.8	0	0.4
Legal departments	99.7	0	0.6
Business Enterprise and Regulatory Reform	31.9	28.8	32.6
Environment and Rural Affairs	95.2	93.6	95.2
Culture, Media and Sport	95.8	90.6	98.5
Work and Pensions	0.8	0.8	100
Chancellor's departments	0.8	0.8	4.5
Cabinet Office	7.2	7.2	18.3

Notes: [a] At the programme level there either is or is not devolution, so the comparability percentage is either 0 or 100. These figures are an aggregation of programmes to the UK government department level.
[b] Non-domestic rates are accounted for differently in Wales compared with Scotland and Northern Ireland, and actually the figure of 100 should be taken as applying to all three nations.

it is these services that make social citizenship tangible. Through these public services the devolved territories can arguably create a distinctive social citizenship agenda.

This is further complicated as the devolved administrations are mainly funded through a block grant determined by the Barnett formula. There are no conditions attached to the grant, enabling the devolved administrations to switch money between different policy objectives within their competence depending on their priorities (although in practice this is tempered by the UK's incremental finance system). On the one hand, this is right, as devolution is fundamentally a recognition of diversity, and territories should be able to vary their spending and tailor their policy programmes to ensure they are able to address local problems. On the other hand, the devolved territories remain part of a single state, and citizens should expect certain state-wide guarantees. While the UK as a Union state maintains popular support, which it currently does (Curtice, 2007), it is right that risk is shared across the state.

This is the tension between the logic of citizenship and the logic of devolution. Keith Banting makes the point powerfully with a question about a sick baby. If the logic of devolution prevails, its treatment and chances of survival should vary with its parents' residence. If the logic of social citizenship prevails, then its treatment and survival should not depend on location (Banting, 2005b). Managing this tension is a major challenge to the progressive state (Morgan, 2001; Schmuecker and Adams, 2005).

Intergovernmental finance in the UK

UK taxation is *formally* insensitive to territory and remains centralised despite a high degree of devolution in spending, as outlined above. Major tax bases such as corporation tax, income tax and National Insurance are reserved to the UK government, with the exception that the Scottish Parliament can vary income tax rates by up to 3%, a power that is yet to be used. Council Tax is the main exception; while local governments levy it, they are creatures of the devolved governments (and the UK Parliament in England). This means that the UK (for England) and the devolved administrations are free to change the basis and use of Council Tax in their territories. Currently a debate is under way in Scotland about abolishing the (property-based) Council Tax in favour of a local income tax.

In this chapter we focus on spending rather than revenue for two reasons. First, the centralised nature of the tax system means that the devolved administrations do not currently have the powers to vary their revenue, beyond what is outlined above. Second, revenue data are far more contested and less reliable than data on spending. These data problems put consideration of revenue beyond the scope of this chapter. However, it is important to note that this chapter therefore only gives a partial picture of finance in the UK. It is also important to note that there is currently a lively political debate taking place in the UK about greater fiscal decentralisation, with the UK government-backed Calman Commission looking into the issues in Scotland. The Scottish Government's 'National Conversation' is also considering issues of finance (Scottish Government, 2007).

The remainder of this chapter focuses on spending, looking first at how public spending is distributed among the nations of the UK, focusing particularly on the Barnett formula and how it works. We then analyse where the money actually goes, before finally considering whether the distribution promotes a shared social citizenship. But before doing this we consider the political tension that intergovernmental finance is creating within the UK.

The distribution of public spending among the nations of the UK: a source of political tension

The Barnett formula governs the distribution of spending to Scotland, Wales and Northern Ireland, based on spending in England. It has been a source of political tension for years, and is regularly vilified as a device that over-rewards Scotland, Wales and Northern Ireland at the expense of England. Indeed the issue of territorial finance seems to be one of the key issues driving English dissatisfaction with the devolution settlement and the Union itself. Recent data from the British Social Attitudes Survey suggest that the proportion of people in England who think Scotland receives 'more than its fair share' of public spending has risen sharply from one in five in 2000 to one in three in 2007 (Curtice, 2008). This sense of injustice is compounded by a perception that additional funding translates into policy divergence and enables the Scots to enjoy popular policies like free personal care for older people, and the abolition of prescription charges and university tuition fees.

Within England, the poorer regions of the North complain that objectively their needs are greater than those of Scotland, yet they receive less spending per head, while the Greater South East complains that it subsidises everyone else. But to blame the Barnett formula for spending disparities within England is to blame the wrong device: Barnett only covers the distribution of public spending between Scotland, Wales and Northern Ireland based on spending in England – where the latter is treated as a single block. Nonetheless, this has not prevented the idea that the Barnett formula punishes the English regions from entering the public imagination.

But it is not just the English who have a problem with Barnett. In Wales a commission is being established to review whether the funding formula is denying the nation its fair share of the public spending cake and whether it should be replaced. In Northern Ireland too there are concerns about whether the level of spending is keeping pace with need, and the Finance Committee of the Northern Ireland Assembly is currently urging the Executive to examine the implications of the

Barnett formula and scenarios for reform (Committee for Finance and Personnel, Northern Ireland Assembly, 2007).

In Scotland a different but related debate is emerging over fiscal decentralisation, with growing calls for Scotland to have more power to raise revenue, with both the Scottish Government's National Conversation and the Unionist parties' Calman Commission considering greater fiscal decentralisation and greater fiscal responsibility for the Scottish Parliament (Scottish Government, 2007). However, it is likely that any such change would have to be accompanied by a change in the way spending is distributed in the UK in order to accommodate Scotland's greater autonomy. Wendy Alexander, then Leader of the Labour Party in the Scottish Parliament, has also argued that not only would greater fiscal responsibility be good for Scotland, but it may help defuse English dissatisfaction with the distribution of spending too (Alexander, 2008). This sentiment is supported by the British Social Attitudes Survey of English opinion, which found three quarters of those surveyed agreed with the statement that 'now Scotland has its own parliament, it should pay for its services out of taxes collected in Scotland' (Curtice, 2008).

There are clearly political pressures to reform the distribution of spending in the UK. But before looking at these issues in more detail it is helpful first to understand a bit more about the much misunderstood Barnett formula and how it works.

The Barnett formula: what it is and what it is not

The Barnett formula governs the allocation of spending blocks from HM Treasury to the devolved administrations in Scotland, Wales and Northern Ireland. The spending block it distributes constitutes the majority of the unconditional block grant available to the devolved administrations. It also constitutes the majority of the public money spent in each devolved territory, although the UK government also spends public money on reserved functions in or for each territory. The Barnett formula does not govern the allocation of spending within England, either to regional bodies or local authorities. Nor is it based on any assessment of either relative needs or of costs of services: instead it is based on relative populations. In this respect it is unlikely to be a suitable basis for social citizenship in a devolved UK.

The Barnett formula succeeded another allocation formula, known as the Goschen proportion, which goes all the way back to 1888. To understand the current distribution of spending and the Barnett formula, a bit of history is required. Scotland has enjoyed higher public spending per head than England since about 1900. There has been one big reason for this: Scotland poses a credible threat to the UK. When the Goschen proportion was established the big problem facing the Union was Ireland, not Scotland. To try (vainly in the end) to keep Ireland in the Union, the Unionists threw money at it. This was called killing home rule by kindness. Not many people in Scotland wanted to secede, and almost none of them were violent. But governments decided to placate them too just in case.

The Goschen proportion assigned £11 to Scotland for every £80 assigned to England and Wales on particular programmes, to be spent by the already-devolved Scottish administration under the Secretary (of State) for Scotland. The proportion was based on share of the population, but by 1901 Scotland had dropped to below 11/80 of the population of England and Wales, and has continued to drop further below. By the time the ghost of Goschen finally vanished in the 1970s, public spending per head in Scotland was about 20% above that in England (and substantially higher than in Wales, which was as poor and almost as sparsely populated as Scotland, although it has fewer midges). But the Secretary of State could protect the Goschen proportion because he had a credible threat at his back. He could tell the Cabinet that unless they protected Scotland's spending share the Nationalists would start winning elections, and where would the UK be then?[1]

The prospect of a Scottish National Party (SNP) triumph began to look more plausible in the 1970s, leading Prime Minister Harold Wilson to announce plans for devolution in summer 1974.[2] As it was, the 1979 referendum in Wales led to a crashing No vote. In Scotland there was a faint Yes, but far below the 40% threshold that had been set following a backlash by English MPs.[3]

During this period, as part of its plans for life after devolution, the Treasury conducted (some would say bullied the Scottish and Welsh Offices into) a Needs Assessment, to inform the design of a needs-based funding formula for devolution. This assessment, not published until 1979, gave the following numbers for the relative needs and the actual spending in the four countries of the UK, for the services that the Scotland and Wales Acts would have devolved (see Table 8.2). This suggests that Scotland and Northern Ireland were receiving more than their need would suggest, while Wales was receiving less.

Treasury papers released to us under a Freedom of Information (FoI) request in March 2005 include the service-by-service assessments that led to these summary numbers. Hints in the published document already suggested that there was a fight between the Treasury and the territorial departments. The FoI release confirms this. The Scots fought

Table 8.2: Relative needs: HM Treasury data for 1976/77

	England	Scotland	Wales	Northern Ireland
Relative Needs Assessment	100	116	109	131
Actual spending levels 1976/77	100	122	106	135

Source: HM Treasury (1979, especially para 6.5)

for a health formula that would record Scotland's 'needs' as being higher than the Treasury was prepared to concede. They were still stalemated when Margaret Thatcher won the 1979 General Election, and so a needs-based system has never been implemented.

However, the Treasury's other preparative step has lasted. This was the Barnett formula. Treasury officials had designed the formula as a temporary expedient to reduce Scotland's relative spending advantage until a needs-based formula could be introduced. Lord Barnett, as he now is, told a Commons Select Committee in 1997 that he expected 'his' formula would not last more than 'a year or even twenty minutes' (House of Commons Treasury Committee, 1998). It has not only lasted, but it is still used today, although the formula is not statutory, and a future UK government could revoke it unilaterally. Lord Barnett used to be proud of the fame his formula had brought him, but he now dislikes its unfairness so much that he would like to remove his name from it.

The Barnett formula is not about needs. It is based solely on relative population. It leaves unchanged the baseline block grant from year to year. It merely stipulates that for every £1 of extra spending in England each year on a service that is devolved in the rest of the UK, Scotland (and Wales and Northern Ireland) will get an increase in their block grant proportionate to their relative populations. Originally the proportions were set arbitrarily at 85:10:5 for England, Scotland and Wales. So, for every 85p of extra spending in England, Scotland would get 10p added to its block grant and Wales 5p. These population proportions were too generous to Scotland (and too mean to Wales) until altered by Michael Portillo, Chief Secretary to the Treasury in 1992, to the correct population proportions. Now they are rebased after every spending review for the next two or three years.

But while the Barnett formula was not about needs it was, importantly, designed to reduce the spending disparities across the nations of the

UK over time. The formula was supposed to ensure that in the long run spending per head would converge until it was the same in all four countries of the UK. In the long run, the original 1979 baseline, under which each country got more per head than England, becomes swamped by the successive increments added every year, until spending per head is imperceptibly different from identical in all four countries. This is known as the 'Barnett squeeze', a process that should occur when public spending increases.

The long run, however, has been longer than anyone anticipated in 1978. Up to 1999 there was no perceptible convergence, even though the Barnett formula supposedly operated throughout. For all but the last two years of that period, the Conservatives were in office. As the pre-eminently unionist party, they so feared a nationalist threat to the continuation of the UK that whenever Barnett threatened to produce embarrassing results they bypassed it and found a way to supply off-Barnett goodies to Scotland. The change of government in 1997 caused no immediate change due to the decision not to increase the Conservatives' planned spending totals for two years – and if public spending does not increase in England there is nothing for Barnett to bite on. In the next section we analyse the distribution of spending for the last five financial years, from 2002/03 to 2007/08.

Where public spending goes

In this section we show where public money is actually being distributed across the nations and regions of the UK. To do so we use HM Treasury's *Public Expenditure: Statistical Analyses* (PESA). PESA does not give exact figures for how much spending flows to the devolved territories via the Barnett formula; instead it gives figures for *identifiable* public spending per head across the nations and regions of the UK.[4]

Identifiable public spending is that which can be identified as benefiting the population of a particular region. For Scotland, Wales and Northern Ireland identifiable public spending figures include all spending through the Barnett formula *plus* other central government spending in those territories (but minus unidentifiable expenditure, which refers to items like defence and international development, deemed to benefit all equally). To get closer to the amount distributed through the Barnett formula, we remove expenditure under the headings 'social protection' (benefits and pensions) and 'agriculture' (farm payments). We do this because these categories of expenditure are entitlements – meaning anyone who is entitled to claim can do so. Social protection is by far the largest category of UK government expenditure in the devolved territories (over 80%). In the absence of figures for spending through the Barnett formula, this manipulation of the data gives us the most accurate picture that is possible and in a way that is directly comparable. The data are also available to make these same calculations for the English regions, so we also include these in our analysis below. While the Barnett formula does not allocate spending to England or the English regions, including the regions in the analysis paints a richer picture of how public spending is distributed around the UK.

Figure 8.1 gives data for 'identifiable' public expenditure in England, Scotland, Wales and Northern Ireland, minus entitlements, for the last five years. The data are presented as an index, where the UK average is 100. Over this period the level of public spending in Northern Ireland and Wales has declined, which may be evidence of the Barnett squeeze. But in Scotland, while spending per head declined between 2002/03 and 2004/05, it increased again sharply from 2004/05 onwards. Why the Barnett squeeze is not evident in Scotland is not clear. Overall, the long-term goal of bringing each of the three devolved administrations

Figure 8.1: Index of identifiable public expenditure per head in the UK nations, not including social protection and agriculture

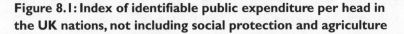

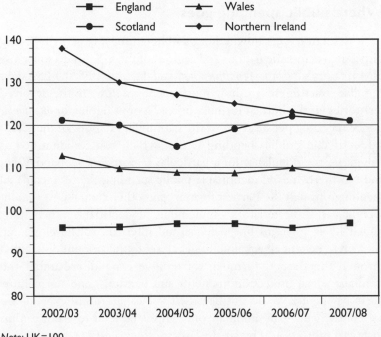

Note: UK=100.

to a position of equal per capita spending with England still seems far away, and the disparities in spending per head, particularly between England and Scotland, speak to why the distribution of public spending is becoming an increasingly live political issue. In 2007/08 spending per head in Northern Ireland and Scotland was 21% above the UK average, and Wales 8% above, while England is 3% below the UK average. This works out as £1,161 per head more spend in Northern Ireland compared with England, £1,153 more per head in Scotland than England, and £527 per head more in Wales than England.

Figure 8.2 shows the identifiable public spending per head across the nations and regions of the UK for the last five financial years. Again, expenditure per head for each region is expressed in relation

Figure 8.2: Identifiable public expenditure per head across the nations and regions, minus social protection and agriculture

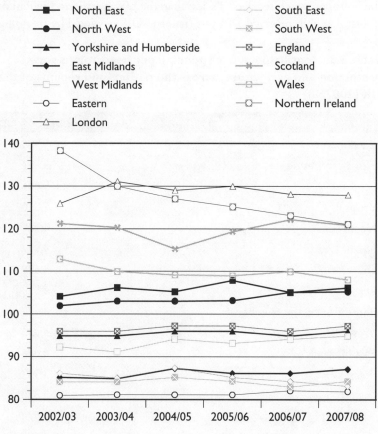

Note: UK=100.

to the UK average, which is set to 100. Therefore a region with above average expenditure per head is above the 100 line, and the others are below it.

The results are fairly stable. From 2003-04 onwards London received the highest public expenditure per head, a mantle held by Northern Ireland for many years. In 2007-08 spending per head in London was 28% above the UK average. In Northern Ireland and Scotland it was 21% above. Wales, the North East and North West of England were the only other regions in receipt of spending above the UK average, but received considerably less than that received by Scotland, Northern Ireland and London – as Table 8.3 suggests. To take the North East for example, in 2007/08 London received £1,025 per head more than the North East, Northern Ireland £724 per head more and Scotland £716 per head more. England as a whole and all the English regions other than the North East, North West and London received public spending per head below the UK average, ranging from Yorkshire and the Humber which received 4% less than the UK average, to the East of England, which received 18% less than the UK average. The spending

Table 8.3: Identifiable public spending per head, minus social protection and agriculture, across the nations and regions of the UK (2007/08)

	£
London	5,985
Northern Ireland	5,684
Scotland	5,676
Wales	5,050
North East	4,960
North West	4,927
UK	4,679
England	4,523
Yorkshire and the Humber	4,477
West Midlands	4,430
East Midlands	4,086
South West	3,947
Eastern	3,820
South East	3,874

Source: HM Treasury (2007a)

gap between the top (London) and the bottom (East of England) is £2,165 per head.

Does UK spending promote shared social citizenship?

Having established how and where public money is distributed in the UK, this section seeks to assess whether the distribution of public spending in the UK is equitable. This is important as an equitable distribution of public spending can enable shared social citizenship. We have argued elsewhere that equity is a core principle for the progressive distribution of public spending. By equity we mean sharing risk across a state, so that each area can provide quality public services regardless of the wealth of the area or if delivery costs more in some areas (for example, due to higher wages or sparsity) (for more on this see McLean et al, 2008). The most basic – although admittedly crude – way to assess whether spending promotes shared social citizenship is to see if, in general, poor people (and therefore poor places) receive more money than rich people (and places). Such a redistribution ensures all areas can enjoy a common minimum of service provision and social citizenship no matter where they live. A more sophisticated way to assess equity would be to ask whether public expenditures secure an equivalent level of public services to citizens all over the UK, irrespective of the region they inhabit and their wealth.

There are of course other principles that should underpin a progressive system of intergovernmental finance. For example, it should be efficient, so public money is well spent, and it should be transparent and accountable to the public (for more on this see McLean et al, 2008). However, with regard to social citizenship it is equity that is of primary interest.

In this section we therefore seek to test the correlation between public spending and need, using wealth and poverty as two measures of need. The often heard argument from those who object to the UK's distribution of public spending is that greater spending should go to economically poorer regions. As an indicator of wealth we use gross value added (GVA) per head as it is a measure of economic output and a good general measure of economic well-being. However, its use is somewhat limited as it does not give an indication of how wealth is distributed within a region. This is a particular problem for a region like London where there is a wide disparity in prosperity.

We also, therefore, provide an analysis of spending compared with poverty, as a more widely accepted indicator of need, and one which is concerned with the relative distribution of income. While both these indicators are important, and ones that a progressive distribution of public spending should be concerned with, they still only give a partial picture. A full needs assessment would have to include a range of other measures, such as demographics, mortality rates and sparsity, weighted by their importance. Such a complex calculation is beyond the scope of this chapter, but the following analysis will give an indication of how spending and need correlate.

For each measure, we first present the rank order of how the nations and regions perform on that indicator. We then provide a more sophisticated picture of how spending and need correspond by combining the datasets and conducting a mental experiment: we ask what the distribution of spending would look like if all identifiable expenditure was designed to assuage need. In that case, it would be perfectly inverse to GVA or the prevalence of poverty. The richer a region, or the less impoverished a region, the less public expenditure per head it would receive. The poorer or more impoverished a region, the more public expenditure per head it would receive. The formula we use to calculate the correlation can be found in the Appendix to this chapter.

Comparing the distribution of public spending with wealth

To assess the correlation between the distribution of public spending and wealth we have used the Office for National Statistics (ONS) income statistics for the UK's 12 standard regions, under the heading of GVA per head. GVA is a standard output measure used by the government to analyse economic performance over time and across regions and industries. The reliability and comparability at the regional level are of particular importance for this analysis. But as a measure it does have its limitations in that it includes only goods and services sold in the market sector of the economy, or those not sold on the market but whose value is imputed by ONS (for example, public services like health and state education). It therefore misses out household production, and includes no measure for many things that people value in life, like the environment and relationships with friends and family.

As with PESA, we need to know something about how the figures are compiled before we can safely use them. Whereas the PESA figures relate to expenditure over a financial year, the GVA per head figures are collected annually to relate to a single point in the year (December). Because of the interdependent nature of the nations and regions there has to be some uncertainty about the figures. As far as possible, the value added by people (labour income) has been assigned to the place they live rather than the place they work. Getting this right is most important for the three south-eastern regions, since millions of people commute from the South East and the eastern region to London (and a non-trivial number commute the other way). The value added by capital is more difficult to calculate, as one needs to know not only where firms' headquarters are located, but where their plants are located, and which plants are adding value within the firm. Therefore, through no fault of the ONS, it is necessary to treat the GVA per head figures with more caution than the public expenditure figures.

One more qualification is important especially for Scotland. The ONS classifies some GVA as 'extra regio'.[5] This refers to value added outside the territory of the UK. The main category is the processing of oil in the North Sea. The Scottish Nationalists would, of course, prefer it to be assigned to Scotland, and the tax proceeds from it retained in Scotland. If it is, it makes Scotland appear a relatively wealthier part of the UK than in Figure 8.3. However, this cuts both ways. If Scotland is (even) wealthier than shown in Figure 8.3, then its high public spending per head (Figure 8.2) is (even) more anomalous.[6]

Figure 8.3 provides an index of GVA per head for the nations and regions of the UK, where 100 is the average GVA per head for the UK. Therefore regions that lie above the 100 line are those adding more value per head than average for the UK, and the remaining regions add less. The richest region (alternatively, the region adding the most value) by far is London (41% above the UK average in 2006), and its relative advantage is increasing. The two other southern regions, the South East and East, come second and third, respectively 15% and 5% above the UK average. Scotland comes next, just 5% below the UK average, and is followed by the South West and the two Midlands regions. The trailing regions are those that have trailed for decades: the North West (13% below the UK average in 2006), Yorkshire and the Humber (14% below), Northern Ireland and the North East (both at 19% below) and Wales (23% below the UK average).

Figure 8.4 goes on to compare this ranking of GVA per head with the distribution of public spending for the year 2006/07 (the most recent year GVA per head figures are available for), to see whether spending and need correlate. Here, the 100 line represents where spending and need correspond, those above the 100 line are receiving more than their 'need' would suggest and those below the line, less. To do this we first slot the wealth figures into the financial year in which they belong. Thus GVA for December 2006 is assigned to financial year 2006/07,

Figure 8.3: Index of GVA per head across the nations and regions of the UK (2001–06)

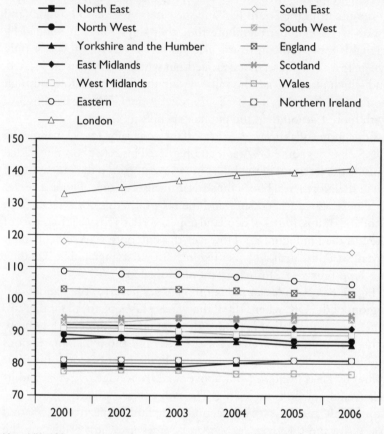

Note: UK=100.

the December 2005 figure to financial year 2005/06, and so on. Then we apply our formula.

The two regions above the line in Figure 8.4 (London and Scotland) are therefore those that are receiving more than they would get if all public spending were designed on the basis of GVA per head. On this basis, in 2006/07 London received 65% more, and Scotland 11% more than they would do if all public spending was based on GVA per head. Wales, Northern Ireland, England as a whole, and all the English regions other than London received less than they would do if spending was based on GVA per head. The region that did 'least well' on this measure was the East Midlands, which received 19% less than it would if all spending was based on GVA per head. It was closely followed by

Figure 8.4: Identifiable public spending per head compared with GVA per head (2006/07)

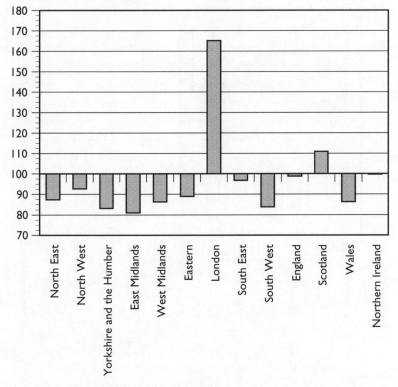

Note: 100 = public spending in line with 'need'.

Yorkshire and the Humber (17% less), the South West (16% less) and the West Midlands (14% less).

Next, we refine the figures somewhat. As discussed above we remove social protection and agriculture from the spending figures, in order to get an idea of the correlation without entitlements in case this is skewing our findings. The result is Figure 8.5.

The effect of this change is to sharpen the distinction between London and all other regions. On this basis, in 2006/07 London received 80% more spending per head than would be predicted if all controllable public expenditure were assigned on the basis of GVA per head. Scotland is also still ahead (by 16%). As with Figure 8.4, all other regions are below the index level where public spending and 'need' are in line. The regions that do the 'worst' are the East Midlands and the South West, which both received 22% less spending per head that would be predicted if expenditure were assigned on the basis of GVA

Figure 8.5: Public expenditure compared with GVA, excluding social protection and agriculture (2006/07)

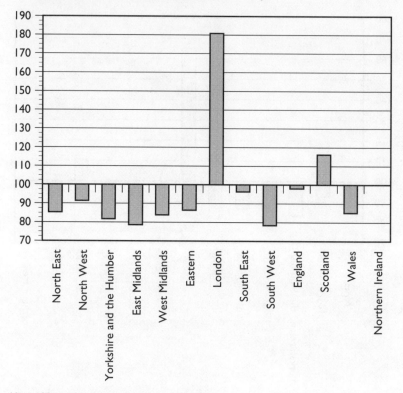

Note: 100 = public spending in line with need.

per head. They were closely followed by Yorkshire and the Humber (18% less) and the West Midlands (16% less).

It would be premature to jump to the conclusion from this that London receives far too much public spending, and the East Midlands far too little, as this is based on only one imperfect measure of need. This is particularly the case for London, where there are wide wealth disparities, particularly with the City of London cheek by jowl with some of the country's poorest communities. These disparities will be masked by using GVA per head as an indicator. In the next section we therefore repeat the analysis using poverty as an indicator of need.

Comparing the distribution of public spending with poverty

In order to compare the distribution of public spending with poverty we use the Department for Work and Pensions' annual Households

Below Average Income (HBAI) series. This dataset provides income data at a household level based on the Family Resources Survey (FRS). HBAI data, despite its name, cover all income at a household level, not just households with low income. However, the key figures that are of interest for our purposes are those on poverty, understood as households with an income below 60% of median income, either before or after housing costs (BHC or AHC).

The large sample size of the FRS (over 28,000 households were interviewed across the UK in 2005/06) provides a robust dataset that can be analysed at the national and regional level. However, the regional averages are presented as three-year averages to smooth out year-on-year variation as the single-year regional estimates are considered too volatile. The UK data are presented as a single-year average. HBAI provides data on poverty among the general population and among children at the national and regional level. As a general measure of need we use the data for poverty among the general population for our calculations below.

Figure 8.6 provides an index for those not at risk of poverty across the nations and regions in 2005/06 both BHC and AHC. The inclusion of both BHC and AHC is important, as while the former gives an overall picture of income levels, the latter allows some indication of the cost of living as housing is generally the most sizeable item of expenditure (and there are not currently robust data on the overall cost of living). As above, the UK average risk of poverty is set at 100. Regions that lie above the 100 line are those where there is *less* risk of poverty, those below the line have a *higher than average* risk of poverty.

This provides a different picture from that in Figure 8.3. On this measure the regions least in need are the South East (7% less likely to be at risk of poverty than the UK average BHC and 6% less likely AHC in 2005-06), the East of England (5% both BHC and AHC) and the South West (4% both BHC and AHC). In Scotland the risk of poverty is 3% less than the UK average AHC, but is the same as the national average BHC. There are also interesting variations in Northern Ireland, the West Midlands and the East Midlands, where the risk of poverty is greater than the national average BHC, but lower than the national average after housing costs are included. The regions where the risk of poverty is the greatest are the North East (4% greater than the UK average BHC and 1% AHC), Wales (4% BHC, and at the UK average AHC) and Northern Ireland (but only BHC when the risk is 4% greater than the UK average). Housing costs are a significant factor in London, where the risk of being in poverty is the same as the UK

Figure 8.6: Index of those not at risk of poverty (2005/06)

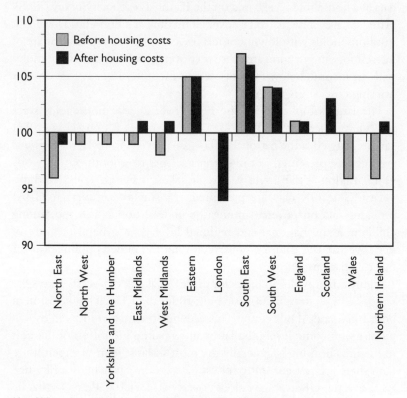

Note: Where bars cannot be seen they equal 100; 100 = UK average.

average BHC, but is 6% greater than the national average AHC, greater than anywhere else in the UK.

The next step is again to compare spending with our measure of need, in this case the risk of poverty in the general population. And again, if all spending were designed to assuage poverty then we would expect spending to be higher where the risk of poverty is higher. To test whether this is the case we use the same formula as before, comparing HBAI data for 2005/06 with spending data for the same year. For the purposes of this calculation we leave entitlements in with the spending figures as social protection payments are fundamentally important to tackling poverty. If public spending was correlated to poverty rates, we would expect all the nations and regions to converge on the 100 line in Figure 8.7.

On this measure, the nations and regions receiving 'more' than their need would suggest if spending was based on poverty are Northern Ireland (10% more BHC, 25% more AHC), Scotland (15% more

Figure 8.7: Public spending compared to poverty before and after housing costs (2005/06)

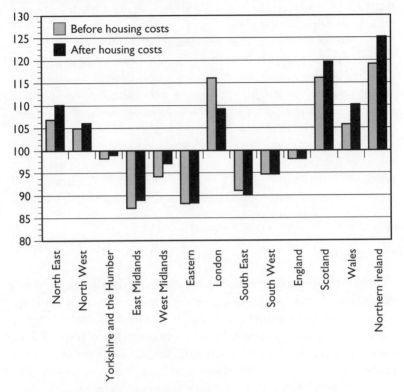

Note: 100 = public spending in line with need.

BHC and 19% more AHC) and London (18% more BHC and 11% more AHC). It is notable that London emerges from our analysis as still receiving more than its poverty need would suggest AHC, as it has the highest level of poverty AHC in the UK by quite a margin. This serves to underline the very high level of public spending in the capital. Wales, the North East and the North West are all also receiving more than their need would suggest. The regions furthest below the line, and receiving less public spending than their 'need' would suggest, are the East Midlands (12% less BHC and 10% less AHC), the East of England (12% less both BHC and AHC) and the South East (10% less BHC and 11% less AHC).

While the analysis of GVA per head and poverty reach different conclusions about how spending and need correspond, there is nonetheless some common ground between them. First, Scotland, Northern Ireland and London receive high levels of public spending even once our chosen measures of relative need are taken into account. Second, it is the East Midlands region, rather than the northern regions, that fares least well on both of our measures of need when compared with levels of public spending.

The preceding analysis does not constitute a full needs analysis, as such an exercise would have to incorporate a wider range of measures, weighted by their importance. An important consideration in this would almost certainly be the higher costs of delivering services in places like London, where for example the costs of agency staff are higher. Similarly this may explain some of the higher spending in Scotland, where sparsity increases the costs of delivering services outside of the urban areas. However, this analysis demonstrates that there is not a clear relationship between levels of public spending across the nations and regions of the UK and levels of need, suggesting the current distribution of public money is not equitable.

Conclusion

Getting the balance right between social citizenship on the one hand, and the diversity that devolution brings on the other, remains a key challenge for the UK post-devolution, a challenge that has implications for whether it is the UK or the devolved territories that are regarded as the 'sharing community'. In one important sense the UK level remains the sharing community because it is at this level that benefits and pensions policy – the core of the UK social citizenship offer – are decided.

However, it remains the case that in key public services there is a great deal of scope for variation. The permissive nature of the UK's devolution settlement, when combined with the unconditional nature of the block grant delivered to the devolved administrations via the Barnett formula, gives the devolved administrations considerable scope to vary social citizenship on a territorial basis. This could serve to undermine UK social citizenship and the sense of the UK as a sharing community. Already these tensions are beginning to show, embodied in debates about policy divergence and public spending disparities. Increasingly there is media coverage of different policies in Scotland and Wales, from free prescriptions in Wales, to free personal care for older people in Scotland. This becomes entwined with a debate about funding devolution, as the perception is that popular policies not available to citizens in England are the result of higher spending per head in the devolved territories.

Furthermore, as our analysis here shows, the distribution of public spending in the UK is not equitable. Spending per head in Scotland

and Northern Ireland (and in London) is substantially higher than the UK average, and it is not in line with their levels of need when assessed against either GVA per head or levels of poverty. For equity and for shared social citizenship, funding should be based on need, so different areas can experience the same standard of services regardless of geography or wealth. It is in this way that intergovernmental funding provides an important underpinning to social citizenship. The inequitable distribution of public spending in the UK, if not addressed, may serve to further undermine UK social citizenship.

And the time to address the distribution of public spending may be drawing nearer. The Barnett formula is certainly the subject of much heated debate, and pressure for reform is growing on all sides. Barnett is increasingly looking unsustainable and should be replaced with a spending formula based on need.

But even with a more equitable distribution of spending, in a devolved system – especially one as permissive as the UK's – there will always be variations in policy, as enabling a territory to respond to local needs and demands is part of the point of devolution. Devolution is a good thing precisely because it creates space for territories to innovate and find new solutions to old problems. But if the UK is to continue as a Union state, the challenge is to ensure that there are some common minimums in the areas that really matter to people in terms of their social citizenship, while still respecting diversity.

Appendix: Formula for the calculation of Figure 8.3

We apply the following formula to each of the 12 regions in each of the five years for which we have data:

$$R_{ij} = \frac{P_{ij}G_{ij}}{100}$$

where:

R_{ij} = Public expenditure relative to need of territory i in year j
P_{ij} = Identifiable public expenditure per head in territory i in year j (UK=100) (from Figure 8.1)
G_{ij} = GVA per head or risk of poverty in territory i in year j (UK less extra regio=100) (from Figure 8.2)

Because the product $P_{ij}G_{ij}$ is divided by 100, Figure 8.3 is again in index units where the average for the UK is 100.

Data sources

Department for Work and Pensions HBAI 2005/06, available at www.dwp.gov.uk/asd/hbai.asp

HM Treasury PESA 2001/02–2005/06, available at: www.hm-treasury.gov.uk/economic_data_and_tools/finance_spending_statistics/pes_publications/pespub_index.cfm

ONS headline GVA at current basic prices by region 1989–2005, available at www.statistics.gov.uk/statbase/Product.asp?vlnk=14650

Notes

[1] All Secretaries of State have done this, but the supreme practitioners have been Tom Johnston (Labour, in the Churchill wartime coalition 1941–45), Willie Ross (Labour, 1964–70 and 1974–76), Ian Lang (Conservative, 1990-95) and Michael Forsyth (Conservative, 1995–97).

[2] In fact, the electoral system did for them more effectively than Wilson. In October 1974, the SNP got 30% of the vote in Scotland to the Conservatives' 24%, but only 11 seats to the Conservatives' 16. Labour retained the majority of Scottish seats on a minority vote. With 35% of the vote, the SNP would have swept the board, won more than half the seats in Scotland, and started to negotiate independence.

[3] An English backlash caused a government defeat that killed the original flagship bill in 1977. Separate bills for Scotland and Wales were then enacted, but the rebels added sections requiring a referendum on the plans, with a 'Yes' vote not to be confirmed unless at least 40% of the electorate voted Yes.

[4] The nations and regions are: the three devolved administrations in Scotland, Wales and Northern Ireland; and the nine standard regions of England (North East, North West, Yorkshire and Humberside, East Midlands, West Midlands, East of England, London, South East and South West).

[5] If the ONS's Latin were better, it would be 'extra regione'.

[6] The issue is discussed further in the annual *Government Expenditure and Revenue Scotland* (GERS), which enables the analyst to calculate the balance of revenue and spending in Scotland in the event that various proportions (up to 100%) of oil tax revenue were to be assigned to Scotland.

NINE

How uniform are uniform services? Towards a geography of citizenship

Martin Powell

This chapter further explores the thesis in Chapter Two of this volume that Marshallian citizenship cannot be linked with simple notions of equality: that E does not MC (see also Daniel Wincott, Chapter Three, this volume; Christie et al, 2007). It focuses on the geography of citizenship, and examines the question: how uniform are 'uniform' services? Bogdanor (2003, in Wincott, 2006, p 170) asserts that New Labour displays a preference for diversity over uniformity, making it harder for a government of the left to secure equality of conditions in different parts of the UK. The welfare state was based on the principle that benefits and burdens would depend on need, not geography. This principle dates from the time of the Attlee government, if not from the time of Lloyd George (Bogdanor, 2002, para 24). He claims that devolution negates this need not geography principle, and so marks the end of the welfare state and a key strand of social democracy (see Wincott, Chapter Three, this volume, and 2006; Mitchell, 2006). However, this claim is too simplistic. First, it is very difficult to detect 'fundamental' principles in the welfare state as they are complex and varying (see Powell, 1995a). There has certainly been a long-standing objective of reducing geographical inequalities. However, dating this to Lloyd George (due to his national health insurance?) is problematic. Moreover, mention of 'equality of conditions', 'uniform national standards', 'the benefits you get and the service you get should be exactly the same' and securing 'equal social and economic rights' for all citizens (Bogdanor, 2002, 2006) are too vague and too strong claims. Second, the links between principles and service objectives are not obvious: the 'spatial strategy of equality' is far from clear (Powell and Boyne, 2001). Third, even *if* services were meant to depend on need rather than geography, major territorial variations existed throughout the 'golden age' of the British welfare state (see Wincott, Chapter Three, this volume). Finally, this principle may be important for a particular strand of social democracy or democratic socialism (for example, Bevan's National Health Service), but is less relevant to other conceptions such as federalism (see Obinger et al, 2005), Swedish decentralised services or Morrisonian or Robsonian versions of local democracy (see Powell, 1998; Powell and Boyne, 2001). Indeed, localists such as Robson present the reverse argument, that the nationalisation of the 1940s onwards marks the end of the welfare state and social democracy.

This chapter examines these debates using the lens of healthcare. It first explores the spatial development of citizenship, before turning to discuss the geography of national and local services. It then briefly examines some empirical material on how uniform 'uniform' services are before concluding that uniform services were not – and never can be – uniform.

Spatial development of citizenship

Marshall's famous definition is that 'Citizenship is a status bestowed on those who are full members of a community' (1963, p 87). Most accounts of citizenship implicitly or explicitly define the 'community' as national (Crowley, 1998). While some recent accounts go beyond the state (for example, Hoffman, 2004) and focus on 'global' or 'cosmopolitan' citizenship (Isin and Turner, 2002), there is little material on local or municipal citizenship below the national level. However, most citizenship theorists begin their story in the Athenian city state or the European city states. In the early and neglected part of his essay, Marshall (1963) traced the development of citizenship from a local to a national setting. He states that in early times the three strands of citizenship were wound into a single thread. He notes that in feudal society there was no uniform collection of rights and duties, but in the medieval towns, examples of genuine and equal citizenship can be found. 'But its specific rights and duties were strictly local, whereas the citizenship whose history I wish to trace is, *by definition*, national' (Marshall, 1963, p 75; emphasis added). Marshall continues that its evolution involved a double process, of fusion and of separation. The fusion was geographical, the separation functional. He claims that the institutions on which the three elements of citizenship depended – the courts, parliament and the Poor Law – parted company, and each travelled at its own speed under the direction of its peculiar principles. This divorce was followed by the (national) formative period of civil rights in the 18th, political rights in the 19th and social rights in the 20th centuries.

Turning to social rights, Marshall (1963, p 75) argues that they 'had been rooted in membership of the village community, the town and the gild were gradually dissolved by economic change until nothing remained but the Poor Law, again a specialized institution which acquired a national foundation, although it continued to be locally administered'. He regards the 1834 New Poor Law and the Factory Acts as the 'divorce of social rights from the status of citizenship' (1963, p 84). The Poor Law treated the claims of the poor not as an integral part of the rights of the citizen, but as an alternative to them, as claims which could be met only if the claimants ceased to be citizens in the true sense of the word, by forfeiting personal liberty in the workhouse, being politically disenfranchised and being stigmatised. Marshall then moves on to discuss the welfare state introduced by the 1945 Labour government in the period he was writing.

There are three major problems in Marshall's discussion of the movement from local to national citizenship. The first (conceptual) problem is that it is never fully clear what Marshall means by a nationally conceived and locally administered service. This has two elements. The first concerns the definition of the 'nation'. Many commentators point out that Marshall's 'nation' was clearly England (see, for example, Mitchell, 2006; Wincott, 2006). At one point he is explicit on this point: 'So far my aim has been to trace in outline the development of citizenship in England to the end of the nineteenth century' (Marshall, 1963, p 86). However, this leaves unanswered (and unasked) questions about citizenship in the rest of Britain, and the welfare histories of the nations, their 'poor laws' and 'welfare states' varied (for example, Young, 1994; Crossman, 2006). A number of writers point to the nationalisation of social policy in the 20th century, but their 'nation' is usually implicitly England, or the Britain masquerading as England (see Mitchell, 2006; Wincott, 2006; and other chapters in this volume). While much attention has been given to 'political' devolution after 1998, there is much less known about 'administrative devolution' and the diversity in the 'health and welfare states of Britain' (Williamson and Room, 1983), 'variations on a theme' and 'centre–centre relationships' (Hunter and Wistow, 1987) or the 'territorial dimension' (Rose, 1982) in earlier periods. The subtitle of Stewart's book (2004) is *Scottish social welfare after devolution*, but we know much less about Scottish social welfare before devolution.

Relatively little is known about many aspects of administrative devolution before political devolution. Hunter and Wistow (1987, p 3) state that the literature charting intra-UK differences was both sparse and widely scattered. Williamson and Room (1983, p 9) point to a dearth of intra-UK comparative studies. Moreover, these variations between the nations are likely to increase under the 'divergence machine' of political devolution (for example, Greer, 2004; cf Stewart, 2004; Adams and Schmuecker, 2005).

The second concerns the national and local welfare state. While most writers focus on the national welfare state of Titmuss, Marshall and Beveridge, the local 'Robson welfare state' is rarely considered (Powell and Boyne, 2001). W.A. Robson was a powerful advocate of localism and local government, and deplored the loss of powers and functions from the localities to the centre. Robson (1953, p 52) stated that:

> ... just how or why the Labour Party ceased to believe in local government as one of the instruments for realizing the socialist commonwealth is hard to say. One reason is probably an extreme emphasis on equality: if socialists regard the provision of more or better services in one area than another as indefensible anomalies, if, for example, they become indignant if more grammar school places are provided in Surrey than in Cornwall, or if Labour MPs feel they have a genuine grievance if housing is provided on a more lavish scale in Luton than in Glasgow, they have ceased to believe in local government as regards these services. For nothing is plainer than the fact that local self-government is incompatible with uniformity. It is consistent with the imposition by the central government of a national minimum standard below which no local authority may fall. It is not consistent with the imposition of a maximum standard above which no local authority may rise.

He continued that 'The full realization of democratic socialism or even the development of the welfare state, demands a reversal of recent trends, a revitalization of local government, an expansion of its functions and responsibilities' (p 54). In short, *contra* Bogdanor, Robson regards the nationalisation of social policy as the negation of the welfare state and of social democracy.

The third (empirical) problem is that Marshall's brief and sweeping thesis vastly oversimplifies a more complex evolution. As in Athens, 'genuine and equal citizenship' may have existed for some in the medieval towns, but alongside a large 'socially excluded' population who did not enjoy such citizenship. Modern scholarship on the Poor Law suggests a far more complex situation than was accepted at the time that Marshall wrote. In spite of administrative centralism being a major principle of the New Poor Law, there remained significant geographical differences between Poor Law Unions (Lees, 1998; King, 2000; Brundage, 2002). In particular, Marshall appears to leave the history of municipal welfare almost entirely out of his account. The 'national' welfare state appears out of thin air in 1945, with no acknowledgement of significant amounts of geographical variation of municipal and voluntary provision of services such as healthcare, education and housing. As early as 1890 Sidney Webb indicated the importance of municipalism in everyday urban life (quoted in Davis, 2000, p 261). Using a phrase generally linked with the post-1945 welfare state, Mr Marshall, Labour MP and a former Lord Mayor of Sheffield, stated that 'In one way or another, local government touches our lives at all stages from the cradle to the grave' (quoted in Powell, 1995b, p 361).

Geography of citizenship

Powell (1998) and Powell and Boyne (2001) suggest three possible criteria that differentiate national from local services: autonomy, funding and provision. First, a national service is part of a chain of command from national to local levels, a transmission belt for implementing central policy, rather than local government that is able to respond to local wishes. Second, a national service has central as opposed to local funding. Third, a national service has a uniform, as opposed to varying local levels of, provision. Adding the elements together, in a national service geographical location should make no difference to contribution or benefit: two individuals of identical income should pay the same amount towards the service and two individuals in identical need should receive the same amount of benefit regardless of location. The aim of a truly national service would be to make geography irrelevant.

In the UK benefits are 'national' as they tend to be determined by the centre at nationally uniform levels. Local offices have limited discretion over payment levels. However, it is clear that as there are price variations around the country, it could be argued that the same benefit level is worth more in low-cost areas, and there have been some recent calls to localise benefits (coming into line with countries where social assistance is a local system) and to regionalise the national minimum wage. In principle, services such as education and social housing are local services as they are run by local authorities. 'Robsonian' local democracy decides whether areas set high local taxes in order to finance high levels of services. In practice, many critics argue that the nationalisation of local government has taken place. The vast amount of money spent locally comes from centrally allocated grants rather than local taxes, and the centre has attempted to increase the degree of 'territorial justice' by a number of fiscal and regulatory measures such as capping local taxes (Boyne and Powell, 1991, 1993). Control over local services has slipped away from local authorities, with some 'hollowing out' to central quangos (quasi-autonomous non-governmental organisations) and to local boards (such as school governing bodies). Sometimes, powers over institutions such as polytechnics and grant-maintained schools have been taken from local authorities.

We now turn to focus on the quintessential 'national' service of the NHS. However, as we shall see, its degree of 'national-ness' can be disputed. This choice of national versus local can be seen in the debates over the formation of the NHS. Aneurin Bevan nationalised the hospitals, while his Labour Cabinet colleague and Deputy Prime Minister Herbert Morrison, along with powerful voices in the Socialist Medical Association, wished to retain a local service (Stewart, 1999). For many years, Bevan's nationalisation trumped Morrison's localism by default, but some writers have suggested that the Morrison versus Bevan debate should be reassessed. Foster et al (1980, p 58) wrote that Bevan's arguments of variations in size and wealth are not too persuasive at this distance, and also should apply to education (and housing). The most important reason for nationalisation – the medical profession's dislike of local authorities – was not explicitly stated. Campbell (1987, p 177) writes that:

> ... all the fundamental criticisms of the NHS can be traced back to the decision not to base services on local authorities. The various medical services were fragmented instead of unified; the gulf between the GPs and the hospitals widened instead of closed; there was no provision for preventive medicine; there was inadequate financial discipline and no democratic control at local level. In retrospect the case for the local authorities can be made to look formidable, the decision to dispossess them a fateful mistake by a Minister ideologically disposed to centralisation and seduced by the claims of professional expertise.

According to Fraser (2003, p 256), there was a good case to be made for local authorities to run the new health service just as they ran the education service. Although there were problems of finance, the overwhelming argument against the primacy of the local authorities was simply that the medical profession would not wear it. White (2004) argues that the NHS objectives of universal or uniform provision and command and control have proved elusive. Universal or uniform provision has never been achieved in the NHS. Of course to a service predicated as 'national', local differences will usually look like failure, but one wonders whether local government would have evolved a less national service than the one we have now. Centralising power – command and control – has failed, with a democratic deficit and sham local accountability. Again, one wonders whether a service devolved to local government could have brought about less effective control than this? Blunkett and Jackson (1987, p 64) see nationalisation of health as 'Labour's great mistake'. White (2004) argues that the NHS marked the greatest creation of quangos in British administrative history, marking the true beginning of that withering away of local democracy, recognised belatedly by the Royal Commission on Local Government in England in 1969. It called the loss of the hospitals a 'great misfortune' that ought to be reversed, but five years later, the remaining local authority health services were also nationalised. It is no exaggeration to talk of the immersion of local government in its present state, with powers largely abdicated to Whitehall at the centre (the Attlee model) and to school governors, urban regeneration companies, housing associations and so on at the periphery (the Thatcher model, still actively pursued). Blunkett and Jackson (1987, p 55) wrote that the NHS, for all its sophistication and success, has never achieved the same combination of local accountability, sensitivity and innovation as local government services.

In terms of our three criteria of autonomy, funding and provision, the NHS has clearly remained a national service on the second, with the vast majority of money being allocated by formula funding from the centre. However, its 'national-ness' as suggested by the other two criteria is more problematic. While some writers point to a 'command-and-control' system, others argue that it was de facto a series of local services. As one NHS manager put it, it appeared 'that 191 different National Health Services existed in the country, rather than one single NHS operating in 191 districts' (quoted in Jenkins, 1996, p 69). Commentators such as Jenkins (1996), Timmins (2001) and Klein (2006) claim that it was only under the post-1979 Conservative government that the NHS was essentially nationalised. Klein (2006, p 215) notes that a process of centralisation has been gradually creeping up, but 'Almost 50 years after the NHS was first created, in the second half of the 1990s it became a *national* service' (emphasis added). This was due to a unified management structure, where the lines of accountability ran firmly and unambiguously to the centre, that resembled a line management that Stalin might have envied (Timmins, 2001, p 511). This represents the ultimate logic of Bevan's principle that health authority members were the agents or (in Herbert Morrison's words) the creatures of the minister (Klein, 2006, pp 197-8). Jenkins claims that Prime Minister Margaret Thatcher completed what Bevan began: the nationalisation of the NHS. 'His bedpans were not just heard in the Palace of Westminster. They were picked up, emptied, cleaned, counted and given a numbered place on the Whitehall shelf' (Jenkins, 1996, p 88). New Labour continued, and probably strengthened, the performance assessment framework of a tight system of top-down central targets. It also created the Commission for Health Improvement, an inspectorate in all but name (Klein, 2006). However, at the same time it claimed that it was localising the NHS, with the creation of primary care groups and trusts (PCGs and PCTs) and later foundation trusts. Moreover, health policy was a major part of devolved government to the nations, resulting in major variations in terms of prescription charges and long-term care (Greer, 2004).

Turning to uniformity of provision, the NHS inherited a very unequal geographical pattern of facilities (Powell, 1997). Despite claims that equality was a major aim of the welfare state (Le Grand, 1982), quantitative equality played a minor role in the so-called 'strategy of equality' (Powell, 1995a; see also Chapter Two, this volume). Like the other principles of the NHS, the equality principle is problematic (Powell, 1997). As Seedhouse (1994, pp 61-2) puts it, 'contrary to the fashionable belief that equality at least is an unequivocal NHS principle ... the NHS does not have a coherent egalitarian philosophy, and so possesses no practical egalitarian impulse to guide planning. In fact the aspiration to "equality in the health service" could hardly be more vague'. There is no universally agreed interpretation of equity for the allocation of NHS resources, and government policy statements are notoriously ambiguous and inconsistent. It follows that it is necessary to examine the NHS's commitment to equality on the basis of specific policy instruments and mechanisms to achieve objectives as well as on post hoc interpretations of vague statements from official documents. In other words, the NHS should be judged more by its actions than by its words (Powell, 1997, pp 58-60). Certainly, concerns about geographical inequality did not lead to rapid, clear and unambiguous policy responses. Powell and Boyne (2001) and Powell and Exworthy (2003) argue that the spatial strategy of equality is unclear. The geographical aims of the NHS are unclear due to confused policy pronouncements: we do not know what type of geographical equity the NHS is attempting to achieve – equality of provision, access or outcome? The first decade of the NHS was characterised by incremental resource allocation to the hospital sector, which tended to perpetuate existing inequalities. However, the designated area policy aimed to (mildly) redistribute general practitioners (GPs) from 'overdoctored' to 'designated' (that is, underprovided) areas through a system of carrots (financial incentives) and sticks (regulations not allowing new practices in overdoctored areas). The 1962 Hospital Plan aimed to equalise the provision of hospital beds through a series of planning norms. However, the Resource Allocation Working Party of the 1970s aimed to secure 'equal access for equal need', but produced a distribution that aimed for 'equal input for equal need'. In other words, there has not been a clear and consistent territorial dimension of citizenship associated with the NHS, with the aims of geographical equality varying between sectors and over time. Klein (2006, pp 225-6) concluded that 'more than 40 years after its birth, the NHS had yet to offer everyone the same level of service'. New Labour introduced *national* service frameworks (NSFs) and the *National* Institute for Clinical Excellence (NICE) in order to increase the 'national-ness' of the service and reduce the 'postcode lottery'. It was clear that provision in terms of procedures (such as IVF) and prescribed drugs varied from place to place. NSFs set up ('cookbook') guidelines, while NICE was a *de facto* rationing body that determined whether treatments should be funded by the NHS. In principle, if NICE decided that a treatment was not effective, nobody in the NHS would get it, but if it decided a treatment was cost-effective, everybody would get it. In practice, the postcode lottery remains a feature of NHS life. New Labour set out targets to reduce health inequalities between social groups and between areas, although some critics doubt if these long-term targets will be met.

In some ways the NHS has never been clearly a national or a local service, and existing trends seem to lead to the worst of all worlds: the disadvantages of central control and local differentiation without any genuine local autonomy (Powell, 1998). New Labour has displayed a Janus-face over national and local services. While it argues for devolution, decentralisation and the 'new localism' on the one hand, it has increased the 'national-ness' of the NHS on the other, with initiatives such as NICE and NSFs. In other words, Bogdanor's (2003) claim that New Labour displays a preference for diversity over uniformity is only half correct. As White (2004) points out, it is easy for myths to be created: in November 2003 the Blair government was accused in the main local government journal of following through Thatcher's anti-local agenda in contrast to Attlee's and Bevan's protection of local democracy in the

1940s! With such dangers, it is vital that contributions to debate are conceptually and historically informed.

How uniform are uniform services?

While there is a great deal of empirical evidence on geographical inequality, it is difficult to say whether services are becoming more uniform. First, the evidence covers widely different criteria (for example, inputs and outcomes) and different services. Second, there is little longitudinal evidence. Third, the fragments of evidence may point in different directions (Powell and Boyne, 2001). NHS resource allocation policies and NICE have reduced inequalities in England. Moreover, one unexpected side effect of the Conservative desire to control the expenditure of local authorities was to increase territorial justice, as most areas were forced to spend near to their centrally decided level of standard spending assessment (SSA) (Boyne and Powell, 1993). On the other hand, most writers argue that political devolution has resulted in greater differentiation between the nations (Greer, 2004; Schmuecker and Adams, 2005; Wincott, 2006).

However, it can be shown fairly simply that even in a national service such as the NHS, 'uniform' services are not uniform. A great deal of material 'maps inequality' at different spatial scales (Powell and Boyne, 2001). First, as we saw above, there have always been differences between the nations within the NHS, and these differences have increased since political devolution in 1998, with commentators stressing major differences in prescriptions, long-term care and the 'postcode lottery' of eligibility to drugs (for example, Greer, 2004; Stewart, 2004; Schmuecker and Adams, 2005).

Second, there is inter-area variation between different administrative units such as PCTs. These include waiting times for treatment, the availability of treatments such as IVF and the availability of drugs for conditions such as multiple sclerosis. This is often termed the 'postcode lottery' where the place that you live in affects your healthcare. There is anecdotal evidence of people moving house to areas where they can get drugs denied them where they used to live. In other words, there is a lack of national standards (DH, 2000). The creation of NICE was meant to end the postcode lottery, but variations still exist (for example, Bungay, 2005). There is also a 'lottery' in continuing care. A report by Age Concern shows that people in some areas in England are 160 times more likely to get continuing care than others. In March 2007 Derby City PCT had a rate of 0.26 people per 10,000, while Harrow PCT had a rate of 41.75 per 10,000 (www.bbc.co.uk).

A few recent examples should suffice to illustrate the geographical variations in NHS services by area in England. Data on choice for March 2007 (DH, 2007a) show that 38% of patients in England were aware of the government's choice agenda. This varied from 25% (Heart of Birmingham PCT) to 55% (Kensington and Chelsea PCT). Similarly, 48% of patients were offered choice, ranging from 24% (Brighton and Hove City Teaching PCT; South East Essex PCT) to 77% (Blackburn with Darwen Teaching PCT). The regional variation was 58% (East Midlands) to 39% (East of England and South East Coast). In 19% of PCTs, 60% or more of patients were offered choice compared with below 30% in 5% of PCTs. The Health Secretary Alan Johnson announced an initial package of measures to tackle inequalities in GP services in England (DH, 2007b). He was 'particularly concerned about areas of deprivation where there is a greater need for GP services, but fewer available compared to more prosperous parts of the country' (DH, 2007b). For example, in 2006 Barking and Dagenham had 43 GPs per 100,000 of the population while Northumberland PCT had 88, with the England average being 61. Hospital Episode Statistics (HES) data for 2005-06 show that the mean hospital waiting time was 78 days for England, but 55 for Northumberland, Tyne and Wear Strategic Health Authority (SHA) and 103 for Kent and Medway SHA. The mean length of hospital stay was 6.6 days for South East London SHA and 8.3 days for Northumberland, Tyne and Wear SHA. The percentage of day cases was 29%, varying from 26% in Kent and Medway SHA to 38% in Shropshire and Staffordshire SHA (HES, 2007). Finally, the Healthcare Commission (2006) showed a 'mixed picture of quality of services'. Four per cent of the 570 NHS trusts got the highest rating of 'excellent', 36% were 'good', over half (51%) were 'fair' while 9% were 'weak'. The central region had the highest percentage of trusts rated 'excellent' or 'good', while the South West had the highest number rated 'weak'. On a more local scale, within 20 miles of my home, of 33 trusts rated, one was excellent, eight were good, 20 were fair and four were weak.

Third, there is intra-area variation. Because of the 'friction of distance' and 'distance decay' some people will have better access to local services than others (Powell, 1995c). Ceteris paribus, people living closer to facilities will tend to have higher consultation levels. For example, Christie et al (2005) report that access as given by Renal Replacement Therapy point prevalence varied within the 16 unitary authorities of Mid and South Wales from 780 per million population in the major city of Swansea to 256 in rural and remote Powys. Moreover, the rate for those within 30 minutes' travel time of a main unit was 669 compared with 458 for those over 60 minutes.

Provision within the 'National' Health Service, then, varies between the nations, and between and within areas. It is difficult to determine exactly what all these fragments of evidence add up to, but it is clear that the NHS – perhaps the most 'national' of all services in the UK – fails to deliver services on the basis of 'need not geography'. This might be due to the failure of the 'need not geography' policy. However, in my view, it shows that there has never been a clear and consistent 'need not geography' policy in the British welfare state: there is a spatial division of welfare largely because there has been no clear spatial strategy of equality (Powell and Boyne, 2001). 'Territorial justice' (Davies, 1968; Powell and Boyne, 1991, 1993) has never been a major element of the British spatial strategy of equality. First, there have always been differences between the nations, which have been amplified by political devolution. Second, there are differences between national (for example, NHS) and local (for example, local government) services. Third, even within services, there have been different bases of distribution such as equality for GP services and equity for hospital services (since 1976). Fourth, objectives change over time, such as the move to proclaimed 'equal access for equal need' since 1976 in hospital allocations. Finally, there has been confusion about different types of equality objectives (Le Grand, 1982; Powell, 1995a; Powell and Boyne, 2001; Powell and Exworthy, 2003).

Conclusion

Uniform services were not – and never can be – uniform (Powell, 1997). It is difficult to make much headway beyond this fairly obvious point for conceptual and empirical reasons. It has been claimed here that many writers have over-stated the egalitarian nature of both citizenship and welfare state theory, as neither gives us a clear and consistent spatial strategy of equality. The unitary, uniform state is a myth (Mitchell, 2006). Moreover, the claim that 'the welfare state was based on the principle that benefits and burdens would depend on need, not geography' (Bogdanor, 2003) is at best only partially correct, not least because there is no clear 'welfare state principle' (cf Wincott, 2006). Similarly, Bulpitt (1983, p 141) is correct that 'territorial governments did not produce uniform policies or policy standards anywhere in the UK', but for the wrong reasons: he conflates the (local) services of elected local authorities and the (national) nominated ad hoc agencies with some form of territorial organisation.

As Daniel Wincott (Chapter Three, this volume) argues, it is a myth that citizenship and the welfare state involved a strong commitment to territorial egalitarianism, and he shows that major territorial variations continued to exist both within British society and in public policy throughout the purported 'golden age' of its welfare state. It is clear that geography still matters: welfare state provision varies from place to place whether this is in terms of the nations of the UK or local authorities. This picture is blurred as different criteria (such as equality of inputs or outcomes) give somewhat different views. However, it is far from clear to what extent this undermines Marshall's thesis, as we are not sure precisely what criteria matter, which units of analysis are important and how large inequalities between citizens can be before it may be concluded that we have unequal citizenship. New Labour's aim is to reduce 'unacceptable variations' (DH, 1997). However, ministers point to a range of variations, with little indication of prioritisation, and little explanation of why some appear to be more acceptable than others. The NHS has never been, and could never be, a *perfectly* equitable service (Klein, 1988; Powell, 1997). More thought is needed on which variations are unacceptable, and how much variation should be tolerated (Klein, 1988). Given that perfectly uniform services are not possible, how much uniformity can exist before citizenship is undermined?

TEN

Ever closer union: devolution, the European Union and social citizenship rights[1]

Scott L. Greer

Quite often the point of decentralisation is to defend or extend social citizenship. As chapters in this book, and other works, have argued, that is to a large extent the case in the UK. And quite often the point of Europeanisation is said to be the same: to defend or extend social citizenship. The call of a European social model is a powerful one, and so is the call of a Europe of the regions. Put them together and the future for distinctive and extensive social citizenship rights looks bright.

But is it? This chapter asks what effects Europeanisation has on the citizenship rights of the people of the UK's different jurisdictions, focusing not on the thin thing that is European Union (EU) citizenship, but rather on the effects that the EU has on devolved and UK social citizenship. First, it makes the connection between devolution and Europeanisation, which are, between them, the two major developments in the territorial politics of the UK. What does their interaction suggest for the freedom of the UK's polities to develop their own social citizenship regimes, to maintain what they have, or to enhance it? The EU constrains more than it enables regions such as Northern Ireland, Scotland and Wales. The ability of regions in Europe to be independent actors, developing distinctive new social policy arrangements, is limited. So it pays to study the EU's consequences on social citizenship in general.

What are those consequences? For all the important effects the EU has had on various rights (particularly for women), it has overwhelmingly focused on one right – the freedom of movement, whether for goods, services, capital or people. The effects are to regulate the conditions under which states make social rights real by regulating the bureaucracies and rules that provide the benefits.

This chapter concludes with a discussion of the scope that the development of the EU leaves for the development of distinctive social citizenship rights within parts of the UK, or for the UK as a whole.

Overall, there is an upward shift of powers to the EU – directly, insofar as the EU regulates policy decisions, and indirectly, insofar as regional governments in the UK and most of the EU are weaker than the states that now once again vote on their policies.

The rise and fall of the Europe of the regions

> We underestimated the importance of juridical statehood.
> (Nationalist [Convergencia Democratica de Catalunya] Deputy in Catalan Parliament, 2001)

The year 1992 is not a bad date to look at the genuine excitement about a 'Europe of the regions' and the many promising developments that gave rise to it. Start with the constitutional politics of the EU and the Maastricht Treaty of that year, the document that set forth to set Europe's direction in the aftermath of the end of the Cold War and the completion of the Single Market. Its provisions – most notably monetary union but also cooperation in foreign policy and home affairs – presaged a much more tightly integrated continent in which state borders and therefore presumably states mattered less. The symbolism of the organisation's naming says it well enough: what had been a trio of organisations led by the 'European Economic Community' now became the 'European Union'. Equally symbolically, it added a thin 'European citizenship' to that of member state citizenship, with rights such as access to other EU states' consular services.

In all these developments regional politics played a role – institutionally and in policy (this literature is vast – edited collections that were particularly influential include Jones and Keating, 1995; Hooghe, 1996; Jeffery, 1997; the best current summaries of the situation are in Weatherill and Bernitz, 2005). On the level of the EU institutions, regions gained representation with the creation in the Maastricht Treaty of a Committee of the Regions (CoR) to represent them. On an equal status with the moribund corporatist Economic and Social Committee, it brought together regional and local politicians from Greek mayors to the presidents of major stateless nations in one body with a remit to comment on certain proposed EU legislation and a right to discuss any policy that interested it. In countries with very substantial powers on the regional level and regional governments with clout to match – Belgium and Germany – regions also won the right to send their representatives, rather than representatives of the federal state, to relevant meetings of the Council (the EU's final decision-making body).

This increased attention to regional government in the EU's institutions came alongside policies that more closely integrated regional government. One component of Maastricht-era politics was a substantial degree of EU 'structural funds', funding for development of poorer areas. These were organised on the level of standard regions (such as German Länder) and required region-wide development plans. Even in the most centralised countries, such as France, regional governments would have some kind of role. The thought of regions and the European institutions (well, the Commission) establishing a direct connection led to all sorts of interesting possibilities.

In different states, meanwhile, regionalist and nationalist politics were hitting crescendos for different reasons. In Spain, the Barcelona Olympics, object of much public relations by the governing Catalan nationalists, was a fitting match for an important nationalist role in Madrid parliamentary politics and the completion of pacts granting new powers to other regions (Greer, 2007a). In France, the regions were becoming more important after slow starts. And while the 1992 UK elections, won by unionist Conservatives, were hardly a boon for Scottish or Welsh nationalism, at least the national questions in those countries were firmly in the centre of politics. In the background, the collapse of the former Communist bloc was creating a 'springtime of the nations' that inspired nationalists around the world with the potential for liberated civic nationalism. It is hardly surprising that in this environment the result was that the regional leaders of the continent embarked on the endless networking, agreement signing and discussions that still engage them while academics set about writing hundreds of works referring to the 'Europe of the regions' (Kohler-Koch, 2000, p 50).

It is almost something of an anticlimax that, after all this excitement, what we turned out to have was not a Europe of the regions but instead 'multilevel governance', known to aficionados as MLG. MLG was influentially defined by Gary Marks and collaborators in that year, 1992, as a system of governance involving local, regional, state and supranational actors in networks. It was governance by collectivity of governments rather than governance by a single responsible government (Marks et al, 1996; Hooghe and Marks, 2001; Bache and Flinders, 2004). MLG is a phenomenon that is often mistaken for a theory, usually with disastrous consequences. Instead of a zero-sum transfer of powers between different territorial orders of government, the changes in competencies that accompanied Europeanisation and regionalisation merely integrated new actors (such as regional governments and the

EU) with new resources that would give them a voice and that were required to achieve any of the ends of governance.

But 'governance' trumps 'multilevel'. European governance has become more complex, but that does not necessarily mean good things for regional governments. Part of the problem was that many of these changes, such as the deployment of structural funds or direct participation in Council decisions, merely changed the functioning of EU policy to more closely match the existing balances of power within countries. Federal Germany did a great deal to federate its EU representation and Länder took a major role in allocating structural funds. The powerful central French state remained clearly dominant in structural funds, and regions got nothing more than consultation (if they were lucky) in its EU policy making (Smith, 1995).[2] Just as the best explanation of a regional government's outcomes in contests with the central state is its pre-existing political strength, the best predictor of regional governments' successes in fashioning a Europe more to their liking might well have been their pre-existing political strength (Goldsmith, 2003).

The more basic problem, however, lies in the constitution of the EU itself. The EU has four important institutions. One is the European Commission, the executive branch and the only institution with the right to initiate legislation. One is the European Council, the body of member state representatives that decides on whether legislation is passed. One is the European Court of Justice (ECJ), which has been a case study in the expansion of judicial power: from inauspicious beginnings (it was intended as a referee in disputes between different EU institutions) it first arrogated to itself the power to enforce EU law over member states and subsequently built an enormous and important jurisprudence. Finally, there is the European Parliament, a directly elected body that from an exceedingly low base has slowly gained powers (as measured by its blocking role in several different, extremely complex, processes of inter-institutional negotiation and its ability to fire the commissioners). These are all the institutions needed to pass, police and expand the scope of EU law. The Economic and Social Council (ECOSOC) and CoR must be consulted on specified issues but the influence of their opinions is down to their persuasiveness or to some other kind of political power they might muster; nobody else is obliged to listen to them. The history of ECOSOC, powerless even if unions and employers both wield influence in Brussels, and the slow desertion of CoR by major regional politicians, both suggest this is an inefficient way for the strong to argue or project power (Jeffery and Palmer, 2007).

In this system, it is clear that the Commission, the Council and the Court dispose of enormous power, and the Parliament of an ambiguous but steadily increasing amending and veto power. Looking at this structure should give rise to a suspicion: the absence of formal regional representation with amending, proposing or veto powers suggests that the power of a regional government in the EU will be felt through some indirect mechanism if it is to be felt at all.

Given the eternally increasing importance of the EU in policy areas, this has meant a transfer of power from regional governments and intra-state intergovernmental relations to a set of institutions in which states and supranational bureaucrats or jurists dominate. All it requires to come to this conclusion is attention to the point that EU law supersedes regional law and policy and to the fact that the EU is a terrain on which regional governments are institutionally disadvantaged by their lack of significant representation. The best example is fisheries: constitutions and laws might recognise fisheries as a regional power, but if policy is made by the states and Commission, that power is at best one of implementation. The result is that we should assume, in the absence of other evidence, that the EU tends to remove powers from regions, abstracting competencies to a forum dominated by states and a supranational executive and court. This is certainly the experience of other countries (Brugué et al, 1997; Hooghe and Marks, 2001; Börzel, 2002; Jeffery, 2005; Subirats, 2006).

The compensation is that MLG stresses the interdependence and interpenetration of governments. No matter how strong the hierarchical relationship between them, different governments will all turn out to have resources that are required if any policy is to happen or work. Regions, runs the MLG argument, have to be consulted because regional non-compliance could ruin the fisheries policy that the Commission and the states enact. This gives them some bargaining power. It is this bargaining position, rather than their constitutional position, that MLG partisans tend to take as the basis of regional governments' power. The problem is that the ability to cause policy failure (intentionally or unintentionally) is not the same thing as political power. Indeed, there are many cases of policies that fail because subordinate governments were not consulted and could not make them work. Many of them are in the EU.

The upshot is that the EU is not a happy place for regional governments to develop distinctive social models. Globalisation of many different sorts, the reduction of geopolitical pressure and European integration might expand their options and importance, but the EU they face is no Europe of the regions. Insofar as they must submit to its policies – and they must, every bit as much as states – they are obliged to comply with policies made in an arena where they can only lobby and do not enjoy a very privileged position. Indeed, the most important mechanisms might be the effect of increased fiscal and other competition on member states' willingness to strengthen their territorial coherence through regional policies focused on redistribution. Formal redistribution might be harder for states to justify, if nothing else because it involves taking from rich regions competing against other rich regions and spawns angry 'bourgeois regionalist', or at least new regionalist, reactions in those regions (Harvie, 1992). This is difficult to quantify, but regional policy in essentially every EU country has shifted from redistribution between regions to efforts to increase the growth rate of every region. That suggests that regions are not so much making EU policy as they are responding to the competitive demands that European integration places on them. And it means that we must subsume any discussion of the prospects for regional (that is, devolved) distinctiveness in social rights into a discussion of the prospects for social citizenship in the EU. That is what the next section does.

The EU and social citizenship rights

> There are no EU social rights in a traditional national sense.
> (Kolb, 1999, p 177)

A social right is, for Marshall, 'an invasion of contract by status, the subordination of market price to social justice, the replacement of the free bargain by the declaration of rights' (Marshall, 1950 [1992], p 40). That makes a social right an island of equality in a capitalist society that otherwise produces, and depends on, inequality. What is the concrete impact of the EU on the parts of the welfare state that deliver given social rights? This is not a new question or debate. There are three broad images of social rights in the EU: the EU as destroyer of social rights, the EU as avatar of social rights and the EU as a regulatory state with a logic orthogonal to social rights.

The EU as 'capitalisme sauvage'

One image begins with the fact that the EU is basically a free trade zone, albeit one with extensive scope for upwards harmonisation by legislation. This produces a basic argument that we should expect a race to the bottom. The argument is simple and well rehearsed. Social rights cost money. That money has to come from taxes (or, if they are pursued through labour regulations, higher labour costs). This puts firms at a competitive disadvantage against their rivals in lower-cost places. Politicians, finding that the cost of social rights is strangling their economies and tax bases, will eventually abrogate those social rights. EU structural funds, for all their public profile, are far too minimal to defend them. This can be presented positively; the tendentious Gillingham excitedly identifies negative integration as the basis of most of what he likes in EU history (Gillingham, 2003).

There are two reasons that the EU has not, apparently, produced this expected race to the bottom. One is that the structure of the EU itself builds in harmonisation to prevent just that. A huge part of EU legislation is just such harmonisation, intended to keep states from dropping beneath certain regulatory floors. When there is no such harmonisation and the factors of production are mobile, the internal market can trigger races to the bottom. Corporation tax looks like it might be a victim of the right, created by the ECJ, to incorporate many kinds of firms anywhere in the EU, and the decision of member states to avoid EU tax legislation that might stop the competition at the price of reducing their effective ability to decide tax rates.

The other is that race-to-the-bottom effects are nowhere near as pronounced as we might expect from the clarity and simplicity of the argument. Some of the world's most competitive workers are highly taxed Scandinavians. There is an enormous literature on the nature and extent of races to the bottom; the key point is that they are not simple, not always big and are not universal, in the EU or elsewhere (Goodhart, 1998; Oates, 1999; Hansen, 2006; Rom, 2006; Simeon, Richard, 2006b).

The EU as a social model

If the EU is not a free trade zone that undermines social rights, could it instead be a positive force, producing quantitative convergence upward and qualitative convergence on something desirable? For some, the EU is rather the institutional support that enables something called a European social model to survive in a global economy and produce convergence on a more, rather than less, generous set of social rights (for one prominent example, see Giddens et al, 2006; for the history and an analysis of the ideological project see Jepsen and Serrano Pascual, 2006).

If we look at the direct efforts of the EU institutions to produce, or declare, convergence on high levels of social rights, the situation does not look good (Goetschy, 2006). The Presidency of the Nice Summit declared that the European social model, 'characterised by ... systems that offer a high level of social protection, by the importance of social dialogue and by services of general interest covering activities vital for social cohesion, is today based, beyond the diversity of the Member States' social systems, on a common core of values' (Adnett and Hardy, 2005, pp 2-3) As the Commission put it in the accompanying 2000 *Social Agenda*, a document substantially reaffirmed in 2005, a quality social policy involves 'a high level of social protection, good social services available to all the people in Europe, real opportunities for all, and the guarantee of fundamental and social rights' (COM(2000)379, pp 13, 20-3). The problem comes about when we look at the actions suggested to achieve these goals. The actions are to establish a social protection committee,[3] support its work, 'contribute to the reflection on the future of social protection ... by issuing a communication', present an annual report, 'invite the social partners to develop and discuss their contribution to the modernisation and improvement of social protection', and 'develop close cooperation ... to elaborate an agenda of social protection' (Kvist and Saari, 2007, provide a thorough and up-to-date review).

The reason for this is fairly simple. The EU does not have significant positive social policy competencies (especially if we exclude workplace health and safety law, where it is powerful and has articulated a distinctive model, from the scope of social citizenship rights). There has never been much appetite among member states for an EU social policy competency; social policy, taxation and nationality are issues that member states have jealously guarded. We can gauge this by looking at the social policy competencies allocated to the EU in the treaties. That is quick and easy because there are next to none. Social policy is, after all, crucial in politics and morally freighted. 'Nobody should be surprised that there is so little "social Europe"', writes Schmitter. 'If anything, the absence of any substantial commitment by the members of the EU to harmonize, or even to coordinate, their social policies is overdetermined' (Schmitter, 2000, p 43).

But it is never wise to restrict discussions of Europeanisation to the pronouncements and deeds of the EU institutions alone. Perhaps the EU institutions' discussion of a European social model feeds into broader patterns of convergence. Here the concept of a European social model flies in the face of a consensus in the welfare state literature. Esping-Andersen divided welfare state regimes into three types; all three (liberal, conservative and social democratic) can be found within the EU, and the liberal regime type includes, inconveniently, both two EU states and some states that nobody thinks have a European model, such as the US (Esping-Andersen, 1990). Subsequent theorists often added southern European types, giving the EU four different kinds of welfare state regime (Ferrara, 1996), or added new axes. That is without mentioning the 'cavernous gulf in welfare and labour market institutions and histories' between western Europe and the post-Communist accession states (Clift, 2007, p 250). Jens Alber, in the best review of the topic, found essentially no evidence for a European social model – not even compared with the US, which is usually evoked as the very opposite of European approaches to welfare (Alber, 2006). Most of the time he shows that the US fits comfortably within the spectrum of social policy indicators found in the EU.

Given the abundant research identifying, if not any particular set of sub-types, at least very different kinds of welfare states within Europe (Pierson, 2007, p 174), it seems that any European model would have to be abstract if it were not to immediately disqualify at least a few EU members (Scharpf, 2002, p 650; Sapir, 2006, p 370).[4] The political, social and economic costs of convergence on a single model with distinctively European characteristics would be enormous.

Enormous, but prohibitive? There is a flourishing new field of convergence studies that looks at the ways policies converge, one that is blurring with 'Europeanisation' studies as the latter loses its focus on member state adaptation to EU policy (Holzinger and Knill, 2005; Radaelli, 2006; Graziano and Vink, 2007). The problem is that the arguments for convergence rely on the power of ideas. Ideas are, at first glance, far too weak to produce convergent social models. Furthermore, ideas might not travel; policy makers, if they search out ideas, search them out in countries they think are relevant. There is not much evidence that Italian and Dutch policy makers would even consider borrowing ideas from each other on anything more than the most superficial level. The more plausible source of convergence is imposition – rules with which policy makers must comply. The problem is that most of the EU's rules are designed to force compliance with the internal market, not a social model.

Nor is there aggregate evidence for a distinctive EU welfare model developing over time (Castles, 2004, pp 73-93). I have found no study of EU welfare states that suggests they are converging in terms of overall spending, programme structure, or, beyond the most minimal definitions (shared with many other countries), their social rights. In fact, it is quite the opposite (Alber, 2006). So Francis Castles is right that 'the upward harmonization thesis is largely an in-house product of EU institutions' (Castles, 2004, p 75).

If there is not much convergence and it is impossible to make many substantive claims about what comprises a European social model specific to the EU, there still might be the possibility that the EU is a geo-economic defence – a perfect way to create a benign environment for expansive social rights (reviewed in Wincott, 2000). In theory, it does not work as well; it is 'logically inconsistent' to claim that the EU defends a social model that does not exist (Kleinman, 2002, p 58). In practice, EU institutions are not even about defending expansive welfare states. The European Central Bank, a key player, is insulated from politics, focused on preventing inflation and prone to lecture Euro-zone countries about the perils of expansive welfare states (Martin and Ross, 2004). Most EU law relevant to social policy enhances and deepens the single internal market, subjecting increasing areas of European society to regulation and competition from across the EU. That is difficult to present as a victory for an expansive welfare state and labour involvement. Many people in Europe value their expansive social citizenship, and the value they place on it is politically significant, but that does not mean that the EU defends or gives better definition to the already existing models we see across the continent.

The EU as a regulatory state

The EU, in short, has not unleashed downward competitive pressures sufficient to weaken social rights in the UK (or other member states). Nor has it directly or indirectly produced a social model that would strengthen or Europeanise social rights.

What it has done is regulate an increasingly large part of European life, starting with areas distant from social rights but increasingly affecting the nature of the bureaucracies that make social rights concrete. Expanding regulation of provision is at the heart of what the EU does. This breaks down into two issues: what explains the expansion of regulation, and what does the regulation mean?

Competency creep

Accounting for the expansion of EU competencies – which are overwhelmingly regulatory – is tantamount to accounting for the phenomenon of European integration. This sort of question looks dated to many EU scholars; it has been years since a general consensus emerged that the EU poses many interesting problems, of which authority migration is among the least interesting, and that the relevant concepts are more to do with governance and policy making than the process of integration itself (Hix, 2005; Smith, 2006). That reflects the fact that in many areas of politics European integration is a fact, not a process. But in social policy, Europe is still integrating. It is doing this primarily through the efforts of EU institutions themselves (the clearest explanations are still Leibfried and Pierson, 1995; Pierson and Leibfried, 1995).

The approach that focuses on this dynamic is known as neofunctionalism. Its key concept is spillover – the shift of EU competencies into adjacent areas. There are two broad ways to think about spillover, the key concept of 'neofunctionalists'. One is social. It argues that the process of integration creates its own momentum. Free movement of goods means that companies integrate production networks more closely and they begin to chafe under inharmonious transport or communications systems. The example of telecommunications seems to show a case of this kind of broad-based spillover; once the UK had liberalised its telecommunications markets, firms that operated across Europe began to locate their telecommunications networks in the UK to save money. The resulting flight to UK operators began to convert continental incumbents to the virtues of liberalisation – they found themselves unable to compete because of the regulatory mechanisms that had ceased to protect them (Bartle, 2005). This broad, society-driven understanding of neofunctionalism is quite common and often appears to be what authors mean when they mention it. But it is not the necessary emphasis of neofunctionalist theory; European society and policy areas need not integrate for European integration to happen.

Rather, it can happen through political activity, even when there is no demand in society. This is because this second understanding of spillover is quite narrow and precise: it is caused by the activities of supranational political institutions. The father of neofunctionalism, Ernst Haas, seemed to make this argument. Haas explained the pressure for European integration once supranational institutions have been created as a result of the activities of domestic interest groups. Some groups, failing to get their preferred policies at the domestic level, will push for transfer of powers to the supranational organisation. The powers, as used, will then provoke demands for more or less power to be transferred to the supranational organisation. Integration in a policy area starts with interest groups and an EU institution, but once there is a supranational policy it rapidly creates a supranational policy arena around it, with groups organising on the new level (Haas, 1958 [2004], pp xxxii–xxxiii).

What it requires to produce spillover is somebody with motive to request an expansion of EU competencies and, crucially, an EU institution that is willing to press the expansion forward. There are two candidate organisations in the EU. One is the European Commission, and the other is the ECJ (Majone, 1998). The Commission is willing to strategically pump-prime, trying to draw interest groups and demands for EU action; it is rightly called a 'purposive opportunist' for its combination of adaptability and determination to expand the EU's, and its own, role (Cram, 1997). The ECJ has a well-documented habit of enunciating principles that expand the role of EU law, finding EU law (principally internal market law) where there is no EU legislation (Burley and Mattli, 1993; Mattli and Slaughter, 1998; Alter, 2001; Stone Sweet, 2004b). The ECJ 'has positioned itself as the balancer of constitutional rights guaranteed under the EU's constitution against an asserted public interest expressed in member-state policy ... potentially any national legal controversy can be transformed into EU litigation' (Stone Sweet, 2004a, p 52). The best weapons the ECJ and Commission have are the 'four freedoms': the commitment of the EU to expanding the freedom of movement of goods, services, capital and labour. EU institutions do almost nothing as well as this 'market-making' (Warleigh, 2003, p 94; Stone Sweet, 2004a).

The key thing to remember is that spillover can be purely political, partly because political rights to participate in, or restrain, the exercise of EU power are so inadequate. There is comparatively limited social pressure for the incorporation of welfare bureaucracies in the internal market. Rather, it can be driven by EU institutions and produce markets where there were none, in order to make systems compatible with the EU internal market. That is what is happening, and that is why neofunctional arguments explain the development of EU policy towards the welfare state (Greer, 2006b).

Regulation

By and large, EU policies that affect social rights are regulatory ones justified by the internal market – regulations on people who deliver services, such as professionals, and regulations on how governments structure their welfare states. They regulate the provision and finance of social services, obliging it to accord to a greater or lesser extent with the internal market and a few other areas of law.

This regulatory bent is the habitual, indeed necessary, *modus operandi* of the EU. Creating the single internal market means eliminating barriers to movement and trade within the EU. In other words, regulating the regulations – creating opportunities to challenge member state policies and vetting them for possible discriminatory effects – is the most important thing that the EU does and it is by far what it is most able to do (Wincott, 2004, p 94). The focus on regulation as the basic form of the EU began with the work of Giandomenico Majone, who developed the concept of the 'regulatory state' in Europe (Majone, 1994). His basic argument is that states in Europe have shifted from direct control over activities to control through regulation. Rather than incur the costs of directly doing things, they regulate those who do. Regulatory states do not pay as much of the cost of what they do, with negative consequences for both efficiency and democracy. While this is a widespread phenomenon, the EU is clearly the purest example of regulatory politics because it does so little, wields such substantial powers through its rules and bears so few of the administrative, economic or political costs of complying with EU law.

The development of regulatory policy based on the narrow treaty bases of the EU means that regulations are biased towards the development of the internal market rather than any other social goals. This is not to question the goal or obscure the effects of other kinds of EU regulation (such as environmental protection). It is to point out that adopting those principles radically reduces the importance of the trade-offs elected politicians must make about social rights – trade-offs between cost and quality, between timely access and universal access, between health budgets and education budgets, or between services for older people and services for the young. Those concerns, which are the heart not just of arguments about social citizenship but also the practical policy making that concerns governments, are marginal in EU debate but the regulations that EU debate produces reshuffle the costs and benefits of different policies.[5]

Some of the most serious and persuasive scholars extend this to argue that the structure of the EU gives it a structural neoliberal tendency (Scharpf, 1996; Streeck, 1996; Bartolini, 2005; Ferrera, 2005; Smith, 2005). Their argument is that the EU institutions and community method have a built-in tendency to produce deregulation through expansion of the internal market. EU institutions are particularly good at removing member state laws and policies that inhibit the free movement of goods, services, capital and people. These barriers and policies, however, often turn out to have been props of some sort of social right. By contrast, positive integration – the development of policies that preserve or expand social rights at the EU level – requires use of the elaborate, complex and unpredictable EU legislative route and is hampered by the treaties' weak social policy competencies. The collective action problems faced by defenders of social rights, such as trades unions, are consequently almost insurmountable. That, of course, is why they have no better option for shaping policy than the 'soft governance' of committees, norms and the OMC.

Supranational regulation and social rights in the UK

In social policy, therefore, the EU enters as exactly what we should expect: a supranational regulatory machine that subordinates most concerns to the promotion of the four freedoms that are its main constitutional principles. We should not look for the establishment of new EU social rights, because, as Scharpf and others point out, it is extremely difficult to legislate or implement new social rights in the EU (Scharpf, 1999). Instead, the EU's regulatory bent, coupled to its institutional bent to market-making, means that existing systems engaged in satisfying social rights must restructure to comply with the developing internal market.

A health example

Health is surely close to any model of social citizenship. Universal healthcare touches people at any stage of their lives, is a hard-won victory even in the least egalitarian systems, and in the form of the National Health Service (NHS) systems has a prominent place in UK society and politics. And it is a highly plausible component of any European model, given that it is one thing the US emphatically lacks. So European member states have had no trouble declaring that they all seek to have sustainable, high-quality healthcare systems with access for all (Hunter, 2007; Greer and Vanhercke, 2008). But such declarations are based on weak treaty powers for the EU. As ever, internal market law matters, and it is pressing down from many sides.

The issue of patient mobility is a particularly clear case of what can happen to the government bodies that make social rights concrete when they interact with the EU (for an overall view, see Mossialos et al, 2008; Newdick, 2008). There have long been EU-wide arrangements for posted workers and tourists to receive care, but non-emergency care outside the member state of residence required pre-authorisation. The challenge to this regime, which left financial and clinical discretion with the member states, began with a pair of cases, *Kohll* and *Decker*.[6] Starting with them, the ECJ ruled that publicly financed systems could not discriminate against providers in other EU member states. This automatically required an administrative transition, but it was mostly restricted to reimbursement-based systems. It also dealt with small numbers; there are simply not that many cases of cross-border patient mobility.

The decision that applies it to the UK is the *Watts* decision.[7] This is the case of a woman from Bedfordshire who went to France for a hip replacement and then attempted to bill her local primary care trust (PCT). The PCT declined to pay on the basis that it had given her an appointment for the hip replacement. Mrs Watts decided to appeal to the EU basis of her citizenship, rather than her UK citizenship, and argued that the PCT's decision interfered with her rights as a European. There are two issues in the case: the extent to which the decisions on mobility apply to the NHS (that is, the extent to which it is a business, rather than a public service), and the extent to which the NHS systems' core form of rationing, the waiting list, is compliant with EU law. The ECJ ruled that the NHS systems did indeed act in a market, and so should be able to price their services even if they did not choose to do it internally. It also ruled that waiting lists based on financial exigencies are illegitimate – waiting lists must be clinical, not financial, and adapted to the individual needs of the patient.

What this means is unclear but threatening to the NHS systems for two reasons. The logic of the decision comes not from an explicit value judgement on the merits of the waiting list as a form of healthcare rationing, but rather as a consequence of the logic of Europeans' freedom of movement.[8] Putting her on a waiting list for a hospital in Bedfordshire did not deliver quick care but it let the PCT try to avoid funding quicker care at a faster provider elsewhere in the EU. Its justification – limited funds – was thrown out (the ECJ has reliably said it could permit restrictions on the internal market in health in order to preserve the financial stability of systems, but has equally reliably refused to accept anything under that provision). Instead, waiting must be clinical and based on patient needs. Waiting is, of course, a form of rationing rather than a clinically advisable or patient-friendly thing to do. The result is far more legal uncertainty – and a direct attack on the basic rationing mechanism that makes possible other, desirable, attributes of the NHS. By contrast, co-payments and insurance-based systems have not opted for this principle, and do not suffer as much. So the social right to equal healthcare as it exists in the UK is undermined by elimination of the principle of rationing that underpins it.

The second reason it is a threat is that patient mobility is part of a larger thread of decisions that are progressively narrowing the scope states have to argue that their public services are exempt from the internal market. The *Watts* decision obliges the NHS to price services in order to establish a basis on which providers located elsewhere in the EU can compete. The effects will to some extent be territorially differentiated; the English NHS is being restructured into a market (albeit a tightly managed creation of Whitehall that does not comply with EU internal market law). Scotland and Wales are doing nothing of the sort (Greer, 2004, 2007). It is therefore possible that the UK government will have fewer problems of principle and possibly lower transition costs as it integrates its NHS into internal market law than Scotland and Wales. It is more likely, however, that the increasingly marketised English NHS is likely to fall afoul of EU law some day. Either way, it is still dangerous. The efficiency and (by international standards) low administrative costs of the NHS have been based on its ability to plan in ways that are difficult in a market.

Patient mobility is not the only issue. There is an interesting clash between different aspects of the social model in the application of the Working Time Directive to health. By making junior doctors work shorter and shift-based hours, it makes health services less financially sustainable but is a victory for labour (Greer, 2006b). The tensions are obvious and echo debates in broad literature about welfare – are the social consequences of EU citizenship to be welfare services or labour protection?

A less attractive prospect is that health and other services will be forced to comply with EU competition and public procurement law. This is a large and complicated area of law (Prosser, 2005), but its thrust is clear. States must not discriminate in favour of their own providers, including ones that they own. This limits, for example, their ability to bail out failing airlines, banks or other businesses; the argument is that a bailout to a country's flag airline is a distortion of competition by other European providers. Applied to, for example, the 'mimic market' that governs the English NHS (Klein, 2006), this would mean that NHS commissioners could not discriminate in favour of NHS providers by putting only a few services out to tender or controlling the participation of the public sector. Scholars had been saying this for some time, but it was still a novelty when the former director of the Department of Health's Commercial Directorate (responsible for extending the use of the private sector by the NHS) agreed, telling the *Financial Times* in January 2007: 'My personal conviction is that once you open up NHS services to competition, the ability to shut that down or call it back passes out of your hands.... At some point European law will take over and prevail.... In my opinion, we are at that stage now' (Timmins, 2007).

The consequences for the ability of the NHS to plan or allocate resources internally, as well as the sheer costs of transition, are worrisome. Once an area is opened to competition, the 'ratchet effect' is such that it would be difficult for government to draw back from a market if it did not like the consequences. It also suggests that the EU will create unintended consequences for the UK government's idea of a choice-driven English NHS with some private sector spice.

Social rights in an integrating Europe

'What's amazing to lawyers is not that the Court did this. It's that it took so long for it to do it', remarked a Brussels health policy analyst in a September 2005 interview. Naturally, however, the other dynamic part of the EU, the Commission, has responded. There are many health-related activities in the Commission, as its purposeful opportunists in different Directorates-General look for opportunities to pursue their purpose of competency expansion (or policy activities that presuppose and entail it) (Greer, 2008). The ECJ led the competency expansion, but the Commission is eager to capture health for its various purposes – purposes as distinct as the enhancement of a European social model and the development of competition free from 'state aid' to, for example, the NHS.

The lessons from health are that the development of the EU institutions, which as neofunctionalists point out is difficult to stop, takes the form of regulations that constrain and change the environment for policy and for the delivery of social rights. By subordinating much provision to the internal market, the EU regulatory regime subordinates other goals and changes the terms of trade-offs. It makes arguments from solidarity difficult (Giubboni, 2006, p 153). It makes arguments from the administrative needs of welfare states impossible – the implicit assumption of EU law is that any desirable public end can be achieved through mechanisms that are compliant with EU law. This assumption is dangerous and unrealistic.

Even if the assumption holds, compliance can produce transition costs as well as gains or losses in efficiency – and if an organisation charged with delivering the substantive content of a social right suffers a loss in efficiency due to the regulation, the regulation has undermined the social right. There are mechanisms that might produce better policy than the ECJ and the more right-wing parts of the Commission. They are legislation and networks. Both are more realistic, and respect subsidiarity more, because the member states and often civil society or elected representatives are involved. The problem is that the member states are reluctant to create treaty bases that would allow for more

EU social policy law, and soft law of networks can be cut by the hard law of the internal market.

A second lesson is that compliance with internal markets can require the creation of markets – the ECJ does not just eliminate discrimination in markets; it also relabels non-market activities as market activities in order to better regulate them in the name of the internal market. Political spillover can then lead to regulatory demands to restructure the public sector in order to make it compatible with the internal market.

A third lesson is that the effects of EU regulation, like any other form of regulation, can be difficult to gauge – it is only with hindsight that we can necessarily identify whether they required large or small transition costs, efficiency gains or losses or compromises of social rights. To a large extent, figuring out the consequences of EU law is guesswork even for those in the NHS and health departments who are most intimately involved. It would be difficult to predict the consequences of the development of the EU for other parts of the public sector that deliver the substantive content of social rights. This is because the devil is in the detail. It is also because while we can confidently predict that the EU will increasingly shape social rights through internal market-based regulation driven by political spillover, we cannot predict much about the concrete development of policies dealing with such detailed areas as harmonisation of qualifications, trade in services, the concept of a 'service of general interest' or pension and tax jurisprudence. This might eventually produce social spillover, adding lobbies to the mix as fleet-footed young Europeans shop for care and engage in reimbursement arbitrage, their parents learn how to retire to sunnier countries and providers adapt to lobby for EU laws that benefit them.

The fourth lesson is that Europeanisation changes priorities. The demand for compliance is essentially a demand that fitting with the new EU regulatory framework be a priority. Compliance becomes a new goal, and fulfilling it diverts resources and attention from other goals. Scarce resources, including time, thought and effort as well as money, must go to compliance. The policy might be good or bad, and its effects might turn out to be good or bad, but it is a change, and that involves opportunity costs and compliance costs. While there is a case that EU mechanisms such as the OMC will lead to convergence, it seems that they will only do it by constraining EU systems differently, and perhaps in a way that is more compatible with the priorities of those who care about social citizenship.

Conclusion

Crudely, devolution is about shifting power downwards from London, to Belfast, Cardiff and Edinburgh, while Europeanisation shifts power upwards from London and devolved capitals to Brussels and Luxembourg. Devolution, as chapters in this book (most forcefully Chapter Six by Michael Keating) argue, creates an opportunity to create a Scottish, Welsh or even Northern Irish social citizenship that is distinctive from that of England. But, as other contributors point out, the ability of devolved or any government to develop distinctive policies depends on the regulatory and financial constraints that they face (anybody can develop a distinctive discourse; making it stick is much easier if there are distinctive policies to match).

This creates the problem. Europeanisation can overpower devolution. If all UK health systems, for example, must comply with EU law on professional mobility, patient waiting times, private health insurance, public procurement, state aids and a variety of other internal market rules, their ability to set their own priorities or even maintain existing ones is limited. A distinctive social citizenship is hard to operate when it conflicts with EU regulation on government, and regions' ability to create positive policy that would enable it is even more limited than that of member states. In a Europe that is not of the regions, regional governments that would construct a distinctive social citizenship face a regulator that increasingly matters to their social policies but that they have a hard time affecting.

The effect of the EU is, above all, to throw tremendous force behind one particular civil right: the right to freedom of movement within the Union. The price is an institutional infrastructure that erodes political rights and a long series of increasingly important policy puzzles for those who must give substance to social rights. A Europeanised politics of social policy and social rights is clearly coming. It is not coming because the EU unleashed a race to the bottom. Nor is it coming because there is enough concrete EU policy that creates convergence on a qualitatively distinct and quantitatively improved level of social rights that might constitute a social model. Nor is it coming because there are obvious arguments that it is a good thing (on the contrary, see Weale, 2006). And it is certainly not coming because of any affective loyalty to the EU or demand for a social policy.

This is a concrete, political process of spillover. Governments have made it clear at every step that they do not want an EU social policy, and few have done so more strenuously than the UK. Insofar as that is changing, and it is changing, that is because the ECJ has created so much instability that more EU law will be required to stabilise the situation. The further result, of course, is to constrain the devolved administrations yet further. Their recently won scope to increase and alter social citizenship rights is now constrained by the EU's campaign to expand civil rights.

The tangible consequences of EU policy are the ones we would expect from reading any of the many empirical studies and theoretical essays on Europeanisation: high transition costs and a set of changes that are basically patternless from a policy or social rights perspective but are required to comply with the logic of expansion of the EU regulatory state. In the case of health, this presages either an assault on the basic egalitarianism of the NHS model – the extent to which it is an 'invasion of contract by status' – or a health budget that, no longer underpinned by its traditional rationing mechanisms, spirals out of control. In other cases, it is likely to be less serious, and simply force the bureaucracies that implement social rights to use their resources to pay transition costs. Some of these will be one-offs; others will be lasting.

The market-led neofunctionalism that has created much EU social policy also explains why those who worry about social policy divergence will not find useful EU standards. EU formal citizenship is a poor thing, a few institutional additions to the rights that come with citizenship in a member state (Shaw, 2007; Commission of the European Communities, 2008). EU institutions have weak competencies to establish positive standards, and the level would be low if it were not to be irrelevant to its poorer countries. If there is to be a shared, high level of social citizenship across the UK, the governments of the UK will have to create it. EU standards will never be high enough, binding enough or sufficiently entrenched in popular consciousness to make up for a lack of social citizenship in a given place.

Likewise, if there is to be divergence, the governments of the UK will need to work to protect it. The UK, with devolution, established a 'fragile divergence machine', likely and able to produce great policy divergence, but also institutionally unstable and dependent on weak assumptions (Greer, 2007b). Among those weak assumptions of stability lay this important one: that the EU would not upset the balance of devolved powers. That reliance on the EU's respect for subsidiarity in social policy was one of the reasons the divergence machine was always fragile. The EU has established a social policy often against the wishes of member states; regions' freedom is hardly a match for the EU.

The development of citizenship in the EU has made clear the aspect that Daniel Wincott's chapter (Chapter Three, this volume) noted in Marshall's work: civil, political and social rights are 'interacting elements' rather than stages. Superficially, it looks like the EU is following Marshall's stages. The right to go to work where you like was won within England, according to Marshall, in the 18th century (Marshall, 1950 [1992], p 10). It has been developing within the EU since the creation of the common market. Then came political rights for Marshall. The right to participate in EU politics directly, as against through member state governments, emerged with direct election of the European Parliament. It should not be surprising that there is consequent pressure now to create social rights; insofar as the EU is the community to which people belong (regardless of whether they feel that they belong), the EU is where they would logically look to exercise their civil and political rights in pursuit of social ones. In its most flattering light, we could say that the EU's main effect has been to develop the civil right of movement at some cost to political and social rights. Perhaps that development will produce a broad regulatory and social reaction and EU-level social rights, just as Marshall (and Polanyi, 1957[1944]) suggest.[9]

But the problem with applying such a sequence is that EU institutions and voting procedures do not work like that and it is difficult to see how they could be changed to do so. Increased attention to 'civil society' is a poor substitute for the equal right to participate in the exercise of political power, but so long as member states and public indifference hobble the European Parliament, it is difficult to see how to restore equal political rights. In the areas of policy that actually produce the basket of services that constitutes social rights, the EU is likely to continue to regulate – disrupt – those who deliver the services rather than create new rights. Member states, hobbled by their decision not to create direct EU competencies, find themselves in a catch-22: if they create a treaty base to legislate, they give up control to the EU, but if they do not, political spillover incorporates those areas into the internal market and they lose control anyway.

The most we can hope for is that the civil right to move is worth it, that innovation improves political rights and that the process of market-making improves social rights. Given the poor connection between the EU's processes of political spillover and the issues at stake in policy making for social rights, that would probably be happenstance.

Notes

[1] I would like to thank the other authors for their comments, as well as attendees at the Political Studies Association British and Comparative Territorial Politics Specialist Group at its Edinburgh conference in January 2008, Colleen Grogan, and participants in the University of Chicago's School of Social Administration workshop series, in October 2007.

[2] It is also worth noting that a significant critique of the MLG perspective points out that it initially developed out of the study of structural funds – an area designed specifically to empower sub-state, particularly regional, actors – and therefore can be accused of overstating the necessary integration of regional governments (Tarrow, 2004).

[3] This is part of the open method of coordination (OMC), a system of peer review in social policy. See Greer and Vanhercke (2008); Wincott (2003); Zeitlin and Pochet (2005) and Zeitlin (2005).

[4] Martin and Ross, in their excellent book (2004), simply expel the UK (and Ireland?) from the 'European social model' and are still unable to define said model by much more than a more expansive welfare state and stronger labour regulation than is found in the 'Anglo-American' systems.

[5] Writes Perry Anderson (2006): 'Just those issues that voters usually feel most strongly about – jobs, taxes and social services – fall squarely under the guillotines of the Bank and the Commission. The history of the past years has shown that this is not an academic matter. It was pressure from Brussels to cut public spending which led Juppé's government to introduce the fiscal package that detonated the great French strike-wave of the winter of 1995, and brought him down. It was the corset of the Stability Pact that forced Portugal into slashing social benefits and plunging the country into a steep recession in 2003. The government in Lisbon did not survive either. The notion that today's EU comprises little more than a set of innocuous technical rules, as value-neutral as traffic lights, is a fatuity.'

[6] C-158/96, Judgment of the Court of 28 April 1998, *Raymond Kohll v Union des caisses de maladie*, ECR 1998 I-01931, 28 April 1998. And C-120/95, *Nicolas Decker v Caisse de maladie des employés privés*, ECR 1998 I-01831.

[7] Case C-372/05 *Watts*, 16 May 2006.

[8] This is one of many cases in which the ECJ turned member state value judgments into (automatically suspect) derogations from the internal market. It did it in *Grogan* with the Republic of Ireland's constitutional ban on abortion, and more recently in undermining the Swedish state alcohol monopoly (Phelan, 1992; Eurohealth, 2007; also Kurzer, 2001).

[9] Even though Marshall's timeline for the sequence – centuries – invites despair.

ELEVEN

Conclusion

Scott L. Greer

It would not be much of an overstatement to say that citizenship should be and is the key term for understanding the relationship of individuals and modern democratic states. It combines belonging, solidarity, rights and responsibilities into something powerful, normatively freighted and often very diffuse. For all its complexities and fuzzy borders, citizenship is a powerful tool to understand the normative and political issues at work in the UK's territorial politics.

Devolution shapes citizenship in the UK, but going beyond platitudes demands looking into some areas of policy, such as intergovernmental finance and European Union (EU) policy making, that are not always associated with citizenship theory. Citizenship theory is often inattentive to the concrete mechanisms that underpin rights. But a formal right to something depends on implementation, and implementation depends on the kinds of legal and administrative issues that the authors discussed in Part II to this volume. And so normative social theory leads directly into the thickets of empirical social policy.

In those thickets we find scholars of devolution, territorial politics and policy making. Despite the rising number of citations to Marshall, and the developing interest in the territorial politics of welfare states, most devolution scholarship focuses on formal institutions and politics – the causes and consequences of specific devolved institutions. In the same way, studies of policy divergence typically focus on the fact of policy divergence and on what it tells us about the policy-making systems. They are less likely to stand back and consider the overall stakes, and the trends that emerge when we stand back from the examination of individual policy decisions.

The limitation of a focus only on the politics and policy making, about small decisions and lessons about institutions, is that it can obscure the larger stakes. Those stakes are high. They are people's rights – the social rights that underpin a measure of equality amidst the larger inequality of society. Public education and health are not just corrections for market failure; they are also social components of citizenship itself. Just as citizens are equal in the privacy of the voting booth, they should enjoy equal access to schools and health facilities.

But recognising the importance of citizenship and the equality it demands only opens up new questions – the ones phrased by Martin Powell in Chapter Two as 'who' enjoys the status of citizen, 'what' exactly that equality means and 'which' governments are responsible for delivering the services. The answers to those questions radically change the nature and meaning of social citizenship by questioning both its reality and its future. The authors, in their various ways, have explored the questions and their answers, sometimes with different conclusions. But almost all undermine, or completely collapse, some myths that underpin much debate about citizenship, social policy and devolution.

Beyond the myths of centralism and localism

The theory and practice of citizenship rights in the devolved UK matters partly because discussions of social citizenship and discussions of territorial politics will make less sense without attention to their interaction. Territorial politics are suffused with citizenship debates as governments compete for citizens. Social citizenship as citizens experience it varies with territory and is shaped by the politics and intergovernmental relations of the devolved and UK governments. But the reasons to pay attention do not stop there. First of all, looking through the perspective of social citizenship and territorial politics makes it clear how wrong, and pernicious, some of the myths of UK governance can be. Second, it highlights some problems that politicians and students of social policy would be well advised not to ignore.

The first myth to go, one that almost every chapter undermines, is that there is one social citizenship for the UK. This is a close cousin to all arguments that confuse the UK government's policies with policy in the UK or that confuse England with the UK. There is no single, equal, UK social citizenship. We know that because the decision makers and their practical politics are different; because their policies differ; because their interaction with citizens differs, above all with gender (Chapter Four); and because the mechanisms that connect them, such as the intergovernmental relations and finance discussed in Chapters Seven and Eight, would not matter if there were a single UK standard of social citizenship. A single, shared, social citizenship for the UK is today a contested political goal if it is not purely a myth. It might be worth creating one, and there are raw materials to do it, but it cannot be assumed.

The second myth is that there ever was such a single social citizenship. The history of actual policy shows that, as discussed by Daniel Wincott and Martin Powell, and it should be no surprise, given the organisational challenges Powell discusses in Chapter Nine. It is, furthermore, a conceptual error to assume that the welfare state of Beveridge is the social citizenship of Marshall; even if the social policy of 1965 were as egalitarian as its aspirations, it would not necessarily be Marshall's citizenship (as Martin Powell argues in Chapter Two). So, harking back to a pre-devolution era of unity and shared Britishness is empirically wrong for the whole UK, and of course spectacularly wrong for Northern Ireland.

The third is that the EU supplies standards that can replace those of the UK. As Chapter Ten argues, the EU is well adapted to creating civil rights to movement, but its political and social rights are much weaker. Not only is it hard to imagine effective standards that cover Belgium and Bulgaria, it is also not in the character of the EU institutions to produce, extend and defend a social model. It is in their character to regulate in the interests of a shared European market. And even when they try, most or all of the chapters in this book show how difficult it is to create and sustain a meaningfully egalitarian social citizenship right. The EU, in short, counts more as a threat to shared UK standards than a replacement.

The fourth myth is that the variation between systems is like variation within systems. As Chapter Nine explains, there is variation in background conditions and available services., their quality and their appropriateness within England, Scotland, Northern Ireland and Wales But as Chapter Seven should make clear, local divergence matters much less for UK politics than devolved divergence. Local government is too weak to intentionally create divergence in social citizenship rights in the way that devolved and UK politicians can. Nor are the stakes in local politics so high. Local government, or school, or NHS disparities do not involve nations or national identities, and the arguments are not conducted by first-rank politicians in the full glare of the cameras. Perhaps there should be major public debates about the the social policy performance of different councils, or about inequality between English regions (see Chapter Eight), but there is not – and there would be a constitutional cataclysm if London sought to oversee Scotland in the way it oversees Salford.

The fifth myth is that UK social citizenship does not matter. It does, greatly. It does for two reasons. First, there is not a lot of evidence that any population of the UK wants distinctive social citizenship, or distinctive education, health and welfare benefits (see Chapter Five).

Divergence might reflect revealed public preferences, or be purely a creation of distinctive political systems, but it is not a result of expressed public wishes to be different. Second, the UK government is expressly appealing to shared social citizenship (especially 'the' NHS) as a basis for its own legitimacy and as a sorely needed counterweight to nationalists. This is partly the political strategy of Gordon Brown, but it is unlikely to leave office with him because it is a key part of any central government's bid for legitimacy. The social contract of citizenship is underpinned by social rights, and no state that wants to keep citizens' loyalty will thinkingly cede responsibility for social rights to a different government. Indeed, the sheer extent of autonomy that the devolved governments enjoy in social policy is a striking sign that the Blair governments were not thinking through the consequences of devolution (Trench, 2008a). Thinking Unionists would not have ceded some of the most important social rights so completely to governments that might be led by nationalists. And it is a bit late to recoup them.

Devolution politics and social citizenship

The structure of devolution, in fact, almost guarantees that political divergence will affect social rights. The areas where divergence is most possible, and where elites are most capable of political differentiation, are precisely the areas that immediately affect most of the rights of social citizenship: education and health above all, but also a variety of more complicated areas including the Legal Aid that Marshall viewed as the capstone of social citizenship. If the Northern Ireland Assembly, Scottish Parliament and National Assembly for Wales are to matter at all, they are likely to matter in reshaping those social rights.

That sets the UK government and any but the most Unionist devolved governments on a collision course. A measure of policy divergence is natural and to be expected in any multilevel system. It happens because different media markets, party competition, personalities and problems drive different agendas and mean that even the same policies are often adopted at different times and in different contexts, with different consequences. For a policy scholar, the question is not whether there is divergence; it is whether the divergence is basically noise or the development of distinctive policy trajectory or style (Greer, 2006d; Greer and Jarman, 2008). Given what Charlie Jeffery calls the progressive 'segmentation' of public opinion (Chapter Five), divergence in policy making is also likely over time to produce more public support for policies that are divergent, or divergence per se. So insofar as the UK government depends on UK social citizenship for its legitimacy, any change is a potential problem for it, and change is guaranteed.

Change in the social contract we call citizenship is often driven by political elites trying to differentiate themselves from each other and from their local partisan rivals. This is a key message from Charlie Jeffery, especially when read in conjunction with Michael Keating's argument. As Jeffery interprets the public opinion data, 'diversity of social rights and equity of social rights appear reconcilable from the perspective of citizens around the UK'. It is almost by definition an elite task to construct the distinctive Scottish political narrative of which Keating speaks. The result is elite-led divergence that is neither unexpected nor bad.

Beyond the sort of divergence that comes from the normal operations of politics in each jurisdiction, there is latent competition among governments for citizens' loyalties that takes place whenever governments need to justify their existence and roles. Under Gordon Brown, this has meant a set of unsupported assertions about shared British institutions – while talking about 'the' NHS as a guarantor of Britishness has some public resonance, it makes little or no legal and technical sense. Legally, it is clear that the field is open to the devolved governments to develop their distinctiveness. But it is possible to imagine a variety of UK government strategies to capture citizens' loyalties. And of the best and most obvious ways to do it (war, economic success, symbolism and social rights), taking on responsibility as the guardian of social citizenship is relatively easy and practical.

But fulfilling the guarantee depends on the institutional structures of the state. This does not just mean the basic facts about devolution, such as its asymmetry or its potential to create competing social citizenships. It also means that particular questions of social citizenship depend heavily on the associated institutions. Consider intergovernmental finance, discussed in Chapter Eight. As the authors, Iain McLean, Guy Lodge and Katie Schmuecker, make clear, the current distribution of spending in the UK is difficult to justify on grounds of equal social citizenship; the distribution of spending is a combination of intentional and unintentional mechanisms that produce territorial inequality. Getting out of this situation, in which the territorial distribution of funds is bad for UK territorial equity, probably requires a new formula for distributing funds. That is not a perfect fit with the policy autonomy of the devolved governments, because money given to ensure social rights might be spent 'worse' or badly. Matching political rights to social rights by devolving taxation authority would be good for both democratic accountability and devolved autonomy, but would require a form of equalisation if it were not to further interfere with the social citizenship of the UK. Most decentralised and federal countries use earmarked funds to deal with these mismatches, with the central state funding other governments while holding them to a set of standards it sets. Without the money, such standards tend to have no force. But while combining standards and money to recoup UK social citizenship is a logical Unionist strategy, it would require a degree of foresight, tactical skill and luck that UK governments might not possess.

Talk about shared social citizenship when the UK government has no way to create it is just hot air (benefits matter more to real citizens' experiences than to devolution debates, oddly). Shared standards underpinned by law alone would require reopening the devolution settlement. Shared standards underpinned by money could only come out of a UK government with a good strategy for the use of its resources and an opportunity to comprehensively reshape the funding system for devolution. Weirdly, it is Scotland and Wales that are best able to develop distinctive new social citizenships, but their ability to do that relies on fragile contracts between the UK state and the devolved governments.

This means that the likeliest outcome for the UK is tense intergovernmental relations combined with an increasingly divergent set of social citizenship standards – both territorial inequalities in services, ratified by democracy, and territorial differences in the extent to which social citizenship counteracts economic inequality. Allowing that to happen was in many ways the point of devolution, and devolution as constructed does indeed protect Northern Ireland, Scotland and Wales against many English policy innovations. The price is that the political rights of devolved electors are mostly constrained to rearranging their social rights. So it is precisely at the core of social citizenship where we find the greatest structural divergence.

Mesmerised by the bloody birth of the modern state, and by the heroism that suffrage campaigns require, students of the state often forget how important the positive side of citizenship is in creating loyalty. States that depend on blood and valour for loyalty are no longer the norm; economic success, political participation and social citizenship all matter. That means that a state, such as the UK, that has war, foreign policy and economic management for its key attributes is necessarily a weak one in domestic politics (although it also suggests that UK governments, if they do not wish to radically change the devolution settlement, should play to those strengths, and nationalist parties should criticise those policies).

The US diplomat Dean Acheson said in 1962 that 'Great Britain has lost an empire and not yet found a role'.[1] His comment, much noted in international relations, also stands for domestic policy. Once the map was no longer red, what would 'British' mean? One obvious role for the post-imperial UK was as the creator and defender of a shared British social citizenship, and that was indeed the direction of politics and policy in the immediate postwar decades. But such a role as guarantor of shared citizenship does not just demand trust in the government that was severely dented in the 1980s and 1990s. It also depends on institutional prerequisites that are simply not there, or not strong enough to overcome the pressures for territorial differentiation in social citizenship. With the design of devolution, the UK unwittingly gave away much of the role that states as distinct as Canada, Spain and Germany have found for themselves, as guardians of social citizenship. Thatcherism undermined its credibility in that role, but the devolution laws undermined its ability to play it at all, as suggested by Gordon Brown's near-exclusive reliance on rhetoric to promote citizenship.

Neither the law nor the current politics of devolution suggest that the role of the UK state is to be the protector of its citizens' social rights. It is the policy maker for the English, but that is irrelevant – or perhaps detrimental – to its role as the UK state. As a consequence, either devolution will have to change substantially, and in a way that will look centralising to most, or the social contract between the citizens of the UK and the UK state will have to be struck on a different basis. There have long been arguments, most associated with Tom Nairn, that the UK is obsolescent. The 'break-up' of Britain, for him, would come because the empire and shared elite goals that sustained it no longer existed (Nairn, 1981). The answer to Nairn's claim was for a long time that the UK had shifted – once based on shared imperial ambition, it came to be based on shared social citizenship. Much of postwar policy was a story of governments, in pursuit of electoral legitimacy, becoming steadily more involved in the operation of social policy. This carried its own political and organisational costs, and it is no surprise that Westminster was happy to disengage from the minutia of Scottish and Welsh public policy in 1998 (Bulpitt, 1983). Even when it re-engages, via EU policy, that kind of policy making is largely free from interaction with or knowledge of devolved circumstances.

But that disengagement came at a price. The price was reducing the number of ways in which the UK state has a direct social contract with its citizens – reducing its most important functions down to foreign affairs and defence; economic management; and taxes and benefits. Of these, only taxes and benefits directly contribute to shared social citizenship, and tax policy's contribution to equality can be minimal. If there is to be a 'break-up of Britain', it will not come because of some abstract macro-historical obsolescence. It will be because the UK centre failed to renegotiate a stable social contract with its individual citizens, and waited too long to negotiate a political contract with its various peoples. Nationalists in Northern Ireland, Scotland and Wales are not the only ones to point out that drawing back from a guarantee of social citizenship ought to put any state's legitimacy in question.

Note

[1]   See www.whosaidwhat.co.uk/quotes/favourite/dean_acheson

References

Adams, J. and Schmuecker, K. (eds) (2005) *Devolution in practice 2006: Public policy differences within the UK*, London: IPPR.

Adnett, N. and Hardy, S. (2005) *The European social model: Modernisation or evolution?*, Cheltenham: Edward Elgar.

Agranoff, R. (2004) 'Autonomy, devolution and intergovernmental relations', *Regional and Federal Studies*, vol 14, no 1, pp 26-65.

Alber, J. (1995) 'A framework for the comparative study of social services', *Journal of European Social Policy*, vol 5, no 2, pp 131-49.

Alber, J. (2006) 'The European Social Model and the United States', *European Union Politics*, vol 7, pp 393-419.

Alexander, W. (2007) 'A new agenda for Scotland', Speech at Edinburgh University, 30 November (www.scottishlabour.org.uk/a_new_agenda_for_scotland).

Alter, K.J. (2001) *Establishing the supremacy of European Law*, Oxford: Oxford University Press.

Amenta, E. (2006) *When movements matter: The Townsend Plan and the rise of social security*, Princeton, NJ: Princeton University Press.

Anderson, P. (2006) 'Depicting Europe', *London Review of Books*, 20 September.

Ashcroft, B., McGregor, P. and Swales, K. (2005) 'Devolution and the economy: a Scottish perspective', in J. Adams and K. Schmuecker (eds) *Devolution in practice 2006. Public policy differences within the UK*, London: IPPR, pp 160-71.

Bache, I. and Flinders, M. (eds) (2004) *Multi-level governance*, Oxford: Oxford University Press.

Banting, K.G. (2005a) 'Community, federalism, and fiscal arrangements in Canada', in H. Lazar (ed) *Canadian fiscal arrangements: What works, what might work better*, Kingston, Ontario: Institute of Intergovernmental Relations, Queens University, pp 37-50.

Banting, K.G. (2005b) 'Canada – nation-building in a federal welfare state', in H. Obinger, S. Leibfried and F.G. Castles (eds) *Federalism and the welfare state: New world and European experiences*, Cambridge: Cambridge University Press, pp 89-137.

Banting, K.G. (2006) 'Social citizenship and federalism: is a federal welfare state a contradiction in terms?', in S. Greer (ed) *Territory, justice and democracy, regionalism and federalism*, London: Palgrave, pp 44-66.

Banting, K.G. (1999) 'Social citizenship and the multicultural welfare state', in A.C. Cairns, J.C. Courtney, P. MacKinnon, H.J. Michelmann and D.E. Smith (eds) *Citizenship, diversity and pluralism: Canadian and comparative perspectives*, Montreal/Kingston: McGill-Queens University Press, pp 108-36.

Banting, K.G. and Kymlicka, W. (eds) (2006) 'Introduction: multiculturalism and the welfare state: setting the context', in K.G. Banting and W. Kymlicka, *Multiculturalism and the welfare state: Recognition and redistribution in contemporary democracies*, Oxford: Oxford University Press, pp 1-47.

Banting, K.G. and Simeon, R. (1985) 'Introduction: the politics of constitutional change', in K.G. Banting and R. Simeon (eds) *Redesigning the state. The politics of constitutional change in industrial nations*, Toronto: University of Toronto Press, pp 1-29.

Barbalet, J. (1988) *Citizenship*, Milton Keynes: Open University Press.

Barr, N. (2004) *The economics of the welfare state* (4th edn), Oxford: Oxford University Press.

Bartle, I. (2005) *Globalisation and EU policymaking: The neo-liberal transformation of telecommunications and electricity*, Manchester: Manchester University Press.

Bartolini, S. (2005) *Restructuring Europe: Centre formation, system building and political structuring between the nation state and the European Union*, Oxford: Oxford University Press.

Beck, U. (2000) *What is globalization?*, Cambridge: Polity Press.

Becker, G. (1981) *A treatise on the family*, Cambridge, MA: Harvard University Press.

Béland, D. and Lecours, A. (2008) *Nationalism and social policy: The politics of territorial solidarity*, Oxford: Oxford University Press.

Bendix, R. (1964) *Citizenship and nation-building: Studies of our changing social order*, New York: John Wiley and Sons.

Bhavnani, K.K. (2001) *Feminism and 'race'*, Oxford: Oxford University Press.

Blau, F.D., Ferber, M.A. and Winkler, A.E. (2002) *The economics of women, men and work* (4th edn), Upper Saddle River, NJ: Prentice Hall.

Blondel, J. (1974) *Voters, parties and leaders*, Harmondsworth: Penguin.

Blunkett, D. and Jackson, K. (1987) *Democracy in crisis*, London: Hogarth Press.

Bogdanor, V. (1987) 'Review: constitutional law and politics', *Oxford Journal of Legal Studies*, vol 7, no 3, pp 454-64.

Bogdanor, V. (2001) 'Constitutional reform' in A. Seldon (ed) *The Blair effect; The Blair government 1997–2001*, London: Little Brown, pp 139-59.

Bogdanor, V. (2002) *Memorandum to House of Lords Select Committee on the Constitution*, February (http://publications.parliament.uk/pa/Id200102/Idselect/Idconst/147/202202.htm).

Bogdanor, V. (2003) 'The elements of a codified British constitution', *Financial Times*, 8 December.

Bogdanor, V. (2006) 'The new localism', Lecture at Gresham College, 12 December (http://Gresham.ac.uk/printtranscipt.asp?EventId=531).

Bonoli, G. (2005) 'The politics of the new social policies. Providing coverage against new social risks in mature welfare states', *Policy & Politics*, vol 33, no 3, pp 431-49.

Bonoli, G. (2007) 'Time matters: postindustrialization, new social risks, and welfare state adaptation in advanced industrial democracies', *Comparative Political Studies*, vol 40, pp 495-520.

Börzel, T. (2002) *States and regions in the European Union: Institutional adaptation in Germany and Spain*, Cambridge: Cambridge University Press.

Bottomore, T. (1992) 'Citizenship and social class: forty years on', in T. Marshall and T. Bottomore, *Citizenship and social class*, London: Pluto Press, pp 55-93.

Boyne, G. and Powell, M. (1991) 'Territorial justice: a review of theory and evidence', *Political Geography Quarterly*, vol 10, pp 263-81.

Boyne, G. and Powell, M. (1993) 'Territorial justice and Thatcherism', *Environment and Planning C*, vol 11, pp 35-53.

Boyne, G., Farrell, C., Law, J., Powell, M. and Walker, N. (2003) *Evaluating public management reforms*, Buckingham: Open University Press.

Brazier, M. (1993) 'Rights and health care', in R. Blackburn (ed) *Rights of citizenship* (1993 edn), London: Mansell, pp 56-74.

Breiner, P. (2006) 'Is social citizenship really outdated? T.H. Marshall revisited', Paper presented at the Annual Meeting of the Western Political Science Association, Albuquerque, NM, 17-19 March.

Bromley, C., Curtice, J., McCrone, D. and Park, A. (2003) *Devolution – Scottish answers to Scottish questions?*, Edinburgh: Edinburgh University Press.

Bromley, C., Curtice, J., McCrone, D. and Park, A. (2006) 'Conclusion', in C. Bromley, Curtice, J., McCrone, D. and Park, A. (eds) *Has devolution delivered?*, Edinburgh: Edinburgh University Press, pp 187-91.

Brown, G. (1999) Speech at the Smith Institute, 15 April.

Brubaker, R. (1992) *Citizenship and nationhood in France and Germany*, Cambridge, MA: Harvard University Press.

Brugué, Q., Gomà, R. and Subirats, J. (1997) 'Multilevel governance and Europeanization: the case of Catalonia', in K. Featherstone and G. Kazamias (eds) *Europeanization and the southern periphery*, Portland, OR: Frank Cass, pp 95–118.

Brundage, A. (2002) *The English Poor Laws, 1700–1930*, Basingstoke: Palgrave.

Bulmer, M. and Rees, A. (1996) 'Conclusion: citizenship in the twenty-first century', in M. Bulmer and A. Rees (eds) *Citizenship today. The contemporary relevance of T.H. Marshall*, London: UCL Press, pp 269-83.

Bulpitt, J. (1983) *Territory and power in the United Kingdom*, Manchester: Manchester University Press.

Bungay, H. (2005) 'Cancer and health policy: the postcode lottery of care', *Social Policy and Administration*, vol 39, no 1, pp 35–48.

Burley, A.M. and Mattli, W. (1993) 'Europe before the court: a political theory of legal integration', *International Organization*, vol 47, pp 41-76.

Cairns, D. (2008) 'How Holyrood and Westminster make devolution work', *The Herald* (Glasgow), 11 January.

Campbell, J. (1987) *Nye Bevan and the mirage of British socialism*, London: Weidenfeld and Nicolson.

Carabine, J. (2004) *Sexualities: Personal lives and social policy*, Bristol: The Policy Press.

Castles, F.G. (2004) *The future of the welfare state: Crisis myths and crisis realities*, Oxford: Oxford University Press.

Christie, A., McLachlan, H. and Swales, J. (2007) *Scotland, devolution and justice*, Discussion paper 15, Glasgow: Centre for Public Policy for Regions, University of Strathclyde.

Christie, S., Morgan, G., Heaven, M., Sandifer, Q. and van Woerden, H. (2005) 'Analysis of renal service provision in south and mid Wales', *Public Health*, vol 119, pp 738-42.

Clift, B. (2007) 'Europeanizing social models?', *Journal of European Integration*, vol 29, pp 249-54.

Commission of the European Communities (2008) *Fifth report on citizenship of the Union (1 May 2004–30 June 2007) (SEC(2008)197)*, Brussels: Commission of the European Communities.

Committee for Finance and Personnel, Northern Ireland Assembly (2007) *Report on the Executive's Draft Budget 2008–2011* (www.niassembly.gov.uk/finance/2007mandate/execreport.htm).

Connell, R.W. (2001) 'The social organisation of masculinity' in S. Whitehead and F. Barrett (eds) *The masculinities reader*, Cambridge: Polity.

Cram, L. (1997) *Policy-making in the European Union: Conceptual lenses and the integration process*, London: Routledge.

Crepaz, M. (1998) 'Inclusion versus exclusion: political institutions and welfare expenditures', *Comparative Politics*, vol 31, pp 61-80.

Crompton, R. (ed) (1999) *Restructuring gender relationships and employment: The decline of the male breadwinner*, Oxford: Oxford University Press.

Crompton, R. and Harris, F. (1998) 'Explaining women's employment patterns: orientations to work revisited', *British Journal of Sociology*, vol 49, no 1, pp 118-36.

Crosland, C.A.R. (1964) *The future of socialism*, London: Cape.

Crossman, V. (2006) *Politics, pauperism and power in late nineteenth century Ireland*, Manchester: Manchester University Press.

Crouch, C. (2003) *Commercialisation or citizenship. Education policy and the future of public services*, London: Fabian Society.

Crowley, J. (1998) 'The national dimension of citizenship in T.H. Marshall', *Citizenship Studies*, vol 2, no 2, pp 165-78.

Curtice, J. (2007) *Where stands the Union now? Lessons from the 2007 Scottish Parliament election*, London: Institute for Public Policy Research.

Curtice, J. (2008) 'Public attitudes and elections', in C. Jeffery (ed) *Scotland devolution monitoring report January 2008* (www.ucl.ac.uk/constitution-unit/research/devolution/MonReps/Scotland_Jan08.pdf), pp 39-60.

Dahrendorf, R. (1996) 'Citizenship and social class', in M. Bulmer and A. Rees (eds) *Citizenship today. The contemporary relevance of T.H. Marshall*, London: UCL Press, pp 25-48.

Daly, M. (1992) 'Europe's poor women: gender in research on poverty', *European Sociological Review*, vol 8, pp 1-12.

Daly, M. and Rake, K. (2003) *Gender and the welfare state*, Bristol: The Policy Press.

Davidoff, L., Doolittle, M., Fink, J. and Holden, K. (1999) *The family story: Blood, contract and intimacy, 1830–1960*, London: Longman.

Davies, B. (1968) *Social needs and resources in local services*, London: Michael Joseph.

Davis, J. (2000) 'Central government and the towns', in M. Daunton (ed) *The Cambridge urban history of Britain. Volume III 1840–1950*, Cambridge: Cambridge University Press, pp 261-86.

DCA (Department for Constitutional Affairs) (2001) *Memorandum of understanding and supplementary agreements between the United Kingdom Government, Scottish Ministers, the Cabinet of the National Assembly for Wales and the Northern Ireland Executive Committee*, Cm 5240, London: The Stationery Office.

De Tocqueville, A. (1998) *De la démocratie en Amérique*, Paris: Flammarion.

Deacon, A. (2002) *Perspectives on welfare*, Buckingham: Open University Press.

Dean, H. (1999) 'Citizenship', in M. Powell (ed) *New Labour, new welfare state? The 'third way' in British social policy*, Bristol: The Policy Press, pp 213-33.

Dean, H. (2002) *Welfare rights and social policy*, Harlow: Pearson Education.

Denver, D., Johns, R., Mitchell, J. and Pattie, C. (2007) 'The Holyrood elections 2007: explaining the results' (www.scottishelectionstudy.org.uk/paperspubs.htm).

DH (Department of Health) (1997) *The new NHS*, London: The Stationery Office.

DH (2000) *The NHS plan*, London: The Stationery Office.

DH (2007a) *Report on the national patient choice survey – March 2007 England*, London: DH.

DH (2007b) 'Health Secretary unveils new drive to improve access to GP services', Press Release, 24 July.

DTI (Department of Trade and Industry) (2001) *Work and families: Choice and flexibility: A consultation document*, London: DTI.

Dwyer, P. (2000) *Welfare rights and responsibilities*, Bristol: The Policy Press.

Dwyer, P. (2004) *Understanding social citizenship*, Bristol: The Policy Press.

Esping-Andersen, G. (1990) *The three worlds of welfare capitalism*, Cambridge: Polity Press.

Eurohealth (2007) 'ECJ rules against Swedish alcohol restrictions', *Eurohealth*, vol 13, pp 37-8.

Ewing, K. (1999) 'Social rights and constitutional law', *Public Law*, pp 104-23.

Ewing, K. (2000) 'The politics of the British constitution', *Public Law*, pp 405-37.

Faulks, K. (2000) *Citizenship*, London: Routledge.

Ferrara, M. (1996) 'The "southern model" of welfare in social Europe', *Journal of European Social Policy*, vol 6, pp 17-37.

Ferrera, M. (2004) 'Social citizenship in the European Union: toward a spatial reconfiguration?', in C. Ansell and G. dePalma (eds) *Restructuring territoriality: Europe and the United States compared*, Cambridge: Cambridge University Press.

Ferrera, M. (2005) *The boundaries of welfare: European integration and the new spatial politics of social protection*, Oxford: Oxford University Press.

Finch, J. and Groves, D. (eds) (1983) *A labour of love: Women, work and caring*, London: Routledge.

Finer, S. (1974) *Comparative politics*, Harmondsworth: Penguin.

Fink, J. (2004) *Care: Personal lives and social policy*, Bristol: The Policy Press.

Finlayson, G. (1994) *Citizen, state and social welfare in Britain, 1830–1990*, Oxford: Clarendon Press.

Flora, P. and Alber, J. (1981) 'Modernisation, democratisation and the development of welfare states in Europe', in P. Flora and A.J. Heidenheimer (eds) *The development of welfare states in Europe and America*, Edison, NJ: Transaction Publishers.

Flora, P. and A.J. Heidenheimer (eds) (1981) *The development of welfare states in Europe and America*, Edison, NJ: Transaction Publishers.

Flora, P., Kuhnle, S. and Urwin, D. (eds) (1999) *State formation, nation-building and mass politics in Europe. The theory of Stein Rokkan*, Oxford: Oxford University Press.

Folbre, N. and Nelson, J.A. (2000) 'For love, money or both', *Journal of Economic Perspectives*, vol 14, no 4, pp 123-40.

Foster, C., Jackman, R. and Perlman, M. (1980) *Local government finance in a unitary state*, London: Allen & Unwin.

Fraser, D. (2003) *The evolution of the British welfare state* (3rd edn), Basingstoke: Macmillan.

Fraser, N. (1997) 'After the family wage: a postindustrial thought experiment', in N. Fraser (ed) *Justice interruptus: Critical reflections on the postindustrial condition*, London: Routledge.

Galligan, B., Hughes, O. and Walsh, C. (1991) *Intergovernmental relations and public policy*, Sydney: Allen & Unwin.

Gamble, A. (2003) *Between Europe and America*, London: Palgrave.

Gamble, A. (2006) 'The constitutional revolution in the United Kingdom', *Publius. The Journal of Federalism*, vol 36, no 1, pp 19-36.

Gambles, R., Lewis, S. and Rapoport, R. (2006) *The myth of work–life balance: The challenge of our time for men, women and societies*, Chichester: Wiley.

Gambles, R., Lewis, S. and Rapoport, R. (2007) 'Evolutions and approaches to equitable divisions of paid work and care in three European countries: a multi-level challenge', in R. Crompton, S. Lewis and C. Lyonette (eds) *Women, men, work and family in Europe*, Basingstoke: Palgrave Macmillan, pp 17-34.

Gerber, E.R. and Kollman, K. (2004) 'Introduction: authority migration: defining an emerging research agenda', *PS: Political Science and Politics*, vol 37, pp 397-400.

Giddens, A., Diamond, P. and Liddle, R. (2006) *Global Europe, social Europe*, Cambridge: Polity Press.

Gillingham, J. (ed) (2003) *European integration, 1950–2003: Superstate or new market economy?*, Cambridge: Cambridge University Press.

Ginn, J., Street, D. and Arber, S. (2001) *Women, work and pensions: International issues and prospects*, Buckingham: Open University Press.

Giubboni, S. (2006) *Social rights and market freedom in the European constitution: A labour law perspective*, Cambridge: Cambridge University Press.

Glennerster, H. (1995) *British social policy since 1945*, Oxford: Blackwell Publishers.

Goetschy, J. (2006) 'Taking stock of social Europe: is there such a thing as a community social model?', in M. Jepsen and A. Serrano Pascual (eds) *Unwrapping the European social model*, Bristol: The Policy Press, pp 47-72.

Goldsmith, M. (2003) 'Variable geometry, multilevel governance: European integration and subnational government in the new millennium', in K. Featherstone and C. Radaelli (eds) *The politics of Europeanization*, Oxford: Oxford University Press, pp 112-33.

Goode, J., Callender, C. and Lister, R. (1998) *Purse or wallet? Gender inequalities and income distribution within families on benefits*, London: Policy Studies Institute (for summary of key findings see www.jrf. org.uk/knowledge/findings/socialpolicy/pdf/spr468.pdf).

Goodhart, D. (1998) 'Social dumping within the EU', in D. Hine and H. Kassim (eds) *Beyond the market: The EU and national social policy*, London: Routledge, pp 79-90.

Gornick, J. and Meyers, M. (2003) *Families that work: Policies for reconciling parenthood and employment*, New York: Russell Sage Foundation.

Graziano, P. and Vink, M.P. (eds) (2007) *Europeanization: New research agendas*, Basingstoke: Palgrave Macmillan.

Greer, S.L. (2004) *Territorial politics and health policy: UK health policy in comparative perspective*, Manchester: Manchester University Press.

Greer, S.L. (2006a) 'The politics of health policy divergence', in J. Adams and K. Schmuecker (eds) *Devolution in practice 2006: Public policy differences within the UK*, London: IPPR, pp 98-120.

Greer, S.L. (2006b) 'Uninvited Europeanization: neofunctionalism and the EU in health policy', *Journal of European Public Policy*, vol 13, pp 134-52.

Greer, S.L. (ed) (2006c) *Territory, democracy and justice: Regionalism and federalism in western democracies*, Basingstoke: Palgrave Macmillan.

Greer, S.L. (2006d) 'The politics of policy divergence', in S.L. Greer (ed) *Territory, democracy, and justice*, Basingstoke: Palgrave Macmillan.

Greer, S.L. (2007a) *Nationalism and self-government: The politics of autonomy in Scotland and Catalonia*, Albany, NY: State University of New York Press.

Greer, S.L. (2007b) 'The fragile divergence machine: citizenship, policy divergence, and intergovernmental relations', in A. Trench (ed) *Devolution and power in the United Kingdom*, Manchester: Manchester University Press, pp 136-59.

Greer, S.L. (2008) *Power struggle: The politics and policy consequences of patient mobility in Europe*, Brussels: OSE.

Greer, S.L. and Jarman, H. (2008) 'Devolution and policy styles', in A. Trench (ed) *State of the nations 2009*, Exeter: Imprint Academic, pp 167-96.

Greer, S.L. and Vanhercke, B. (2008, forthcoming) 'New forms of EU governance applicable to healthcare', in E. Mossialos, G. Permanand, R. Baeten, and T.K. Hervey (eds) (2008) *Health systems governance in Europe: The role of EU law and policy.* Brussels: European Observatory on Health Systems and Policies/Cambridge: Cambridge University Press

Griffiths, D. (1995) *Thatcherism and territorial politics: A Welsh case study*, Aldershot: Avebury.

Haas, E.B. (1958 [2004]) *The uniting of Europe: Political, social, and economic forces, 1950–1957*, Notre Dame: University of Notre Dame Press.

Hacker, J.S. (1998) 'The historical logic of national health insurance: structure and sequence in the development of British, Canadian, and US medical policy', *Studies in American Political Development*, vol 12, pp 57-130.

Hakim, C. (1996) *Key issues in women's work: Female heterogeneity and the polarization of women's employment*, London: The Athlone Press.

Hakim, C. (2000) *Work–lifestyle choices in the 21st century: Preference theory*, Oxford: Oxford University Press.

Hall, P. and Taylor, R. (1996) 'Political science and the three new institutionalisms', *Political Studies*, vol 44, no 5, pp 936-57.

Hansen, S.B. (2006) *Globalization and the politics of pay*, Washington, DC: Georgetown University Press.

Harris, D. (1987) *Justifying state welfare*, Oxford: Basil Blackwell.

Harris, J. (1996) 'Contract and citizenship', in D. Marquand and A. Seldon (eds) *The ideas that shaped post-war Britain*, London: Fontana, pp 122-38.

Harris, J. (2004) 'Nationality, rights and virtue: some approaches to citizenship in Great Britain', in R. Bellamy, D. Castiglione and E. Santaro (eds) *Lineages of European citizenship. Rights, belonging and participation in eleven nation-states*, Basingstoke: Palgrave Macmillan, pp 73-91.

Harvie, C. (1992) 'In the time of the breaking of nations', *Scottish Affairs*, pp 78-87.

Hay, C. (1996) *Re-stating social and political change*, Buckingham: Open University Press.

Hazell, R. and O'Leary, B. (1999) 'A rolling programme of devolution: slippery slope or safeguard of the Union?', in R. Hazell (ed) *Constitutional futures. A history of the next ten years*, Oxford: Oxford University Press, pp 21-46.

Heald, D. and McLeod, A. (2002a) 'Fiscal autonomy under devolution: introduction to symposium', *Scottish Affairs*, vol 41, pp 5-26.

Heald, D. and Macleod, A. (2002b) 'Beyond Barnett? Funding devolution', in J. Adams and P. Robinson (eds) *Devolution in practice: Public policy differences within the UK*, London: Institute for Public Policy Research.

Heald, D. and Macleod, A. (2005) 'Embeddedness of UK devolution finance within the public expenditure system', *Regional Studies*, vol 39, no 4, pp 495-518.

Healthcare Commission (2006) 'Annual health check', Press release: 'Quality of services in detail', 12 October.

Hearn, J. (1998) 'The welfare of men', in J. Popay, J. Hearn and J. Edwards (eds) *Men, gender divisions and welfare*, London: Routledge.

Hearn, J. (2000) *Claiming Scotland. National identity and liberal culture*, Edinburgh: Polygon.

Heater, D. (1990) *Citizenship: The civic ideal in world history, politics and education*, Harlow: Longman.

Heath, A. (2005) 'Is a sense of British identity in decline?', Devolution Briefings No 36, ESRC Devolution and Constitutional Change Programme (www.devolution.ac.uk/Briefing_papers.htm).

Heclo, H. and Wildavsky, A. *The private government of public money* (2nd edn), London: Macmillan.

HES (Hospital Episode Statistics) (2007) *SHA of residence table 2005–06* (www.hesonline.nhs.uk).

Hewitt, P. (1993) *About time: The revolution in work and family life*, London: IPPR/Rivers Oram.

Hewitt, M. and Powell, M. (1998) 'A different "back to Beveridge?"', in E. Brunsdon, Dean, H. and Woods, R. (eds) *Social Policy Review 10*, London: Social Policy Association, pp 85-104.

Hicks, A. (1999) *Social democracy and welfare capitalism: A century of income security politics*, Ithaca, NY: Cornell University Press.

Himsworth, C. (2001) 'Rights versus devolution', in T. Campbell, K.D. Ewing and A. Tomkins (eds) *Sceptical essays on human rights*, Oxford: Oxford University Press, pp 145-62.

Hix, S. (2005) *The political system of the European Union*, New York: Palgrave Macmillan.

HM Treasury (1979) *Needs assessment – Report*, London: HMSO.

HM Treasury (2002) Press notice 90/02, 18 September, 'Joint Ministerial Committee on Poverty' (www.hm-treasury.gov.uk/newsroom_and_speeches/press/2002/press_90_02.cfm).

HM Treasury (2007a) *A statement of funding policy*, London: The Stationery Office.

HM Treasury (2007b) *Funding the Scottish Parliament, National Assembly for Wales and Northern Ireland Assembly: Statement of funding policy* (5th edn), London: The Stationery Office.

Hobson, B. (1990) 'No exit, no voice: women's economic dependency and the welfare state', *Acta Sociologica*, vol 33, pp 235-50.

Hochschild, A. (1989) *The second shift: The revolution at home*, London: Piatkus.

Hochschild, A. (1997) *The time bind*, New York: Henry Holt.

Hoffman, J. (2004) *Citizenship beyond the state*, London: Sage Publications.

Holzinger, K. and Knill, C. (2005) 'Cases and conditions of cross-national policy convergence', *Journal of European Public Policy*, vol 12, pp 775-96.

Hooghe, L. (1996) *Cohesion policy and European integration: Building multi-level governance*, Oxford: Oxford University Press.

Hooghe, L. and Marks, G. (2001) *Multi-level governance and European integration*, Lanham: Rowman and Littlefield.

Hough, D. and Jeffery, C. (eds) (2006) *Devolution and electoral politics*, Manchester: Manchester University Press.

House of Commons Treasury Committee (1998) *The Barnett formula, Second Report of Session 1997–98*, London: The Stationery Office.

House of Lords (2003) *Devolution: Inter-institutional relations in the United Kingdom*, Select Committee on the Constitution Session 2002–03 Second Report, HL Paper 28, London: The Stationery Office.

Huber, E., Ragin, C. and Stephens, J.D. (1993) 'Social democracy, Christian Democracy, constitutional structure, and the welfare state', *American Journal of Sociology*, vol 99, pp 711-49.

Hunter, D.J. (2007) 'Values and health policy in the European Union', in S.L. Greer and D. Rowland (eds) *Devolving policy, diverging values? The values of the United Kingdom's national health services*, London: The Nuffield Trust, pp 69-86.

Hunter, D.J. and Wistow, G. (1987) 'The paradox of policy diversity in a unitary state: community care in Britain', *Public Administration*, vol 65, no 1, pp 3-24.

Immergut, E.M. (1992) 'The rules of the game: the logic of health policy-making in France, Switzerland, and Sweden', in S. Steinmo, K. Thelen and F. Longstreth (eds) *Structuring politics: Historical institutionalism in comparative analysis*, Cambridge: Cambridge University Press, pp 57-89.

Isin, E. and Turner, B. (eds) (2002) *Handbook of citizenship studies*, London: Sage Publications.

James, S. (1992) 'The good-enough citizen: citizenship and independence', in G. Bock and S. James (eds) *Beyond equality and difference: Citizenship, feminist politics and female subjectivity*, London: Routledge.

Janoski, T. (1998) *Citizenship and civil society. A framework of rights and obligations in liberal, traditional and social democratic regimes*, Cambridge: Cambridge University Press.

Janoski, T. and Gran, B. (2002) 'Political citizenship and foundations of rights', in E. Isin and B. Turner (eds) *Handbook of citizenship studies*, London: Sage.

Janowitz, M. (1980) 'Observations on the sociology of citizenship: obligations and rights', *Social Forces*, vol 59, no 1, pp 1-24.

Jeffery, C. (ed) (1997) *The regional dimension of the European Union: Towards a third level in Europe?*, Portland, OR: Frank Cass.

Jeffery, C. (ed) (1999) *Recasting German federalism: The legacies of unification*, London: Pinter.

Jeffery, C. (2005) 'Regions and the European Union: letting them in, and leaving them alone', in S. Weatherill (ed) *The role of regions and sub-national actors in Europe*, Oxford: Hart Publishing, pp 33-46.

Jeffery, C. (2006a) 'Devolution and social citizenship: which society, whose citizenship?', in S.L. Greer (ed) *Territory, democracy, and justice*, Basingstoke: Palgrave Macmillan, pp 67-91.

Jeffery, C. (2006b) 'Devolution and divergence: public attitudes and institutional logics', in J. Adams and K. Schmuecker (eds) *Devolution in practice 2006: Public policy differences within the UK*, London: IPPR, pp 10-28.

Jeffery, C. (2008) 'The dynamics of devolution', in A. Gamble and M. Flinders (eds) *The Oxford handbook of British politics*, Oxford: Oxford University Press.

Jeffery C. and Palmer R. (2007) 'The European Union, devolution, and power', in A. Trench (ed) *Devolution and power in the United Kingdom*, Manchester: Manchester University Press, pp 218-38.

Jenkins, S. (1996) *Accountable to none: The Tory nationalization of Britain*, Harmondsworth: Penguin.

Jepsen, M. and Serrano Pascual, A. (2006) 'The concept of the ESM and supranational legitimacy-building', in M. Jepsen and A. Serrano Pascual (eds) *Unwrapping the European social model*, Bristol: The Policy Press, pp 25-46.

Johnson, P. (1996) 'Risk, redistribution and social welfare from the Poor Law to Beveridge', in M. Daunton (ed) *Charity, self-interest and welfare in the English past*, London: UCL Press.

Jones, B. and Keating, M. (1995) *The European Union and the regions*, Oxford: Oxford University Press.

Kalecki, M. (1943) 'Political aspects of full employment', *Political Quarterly*, vol 14, no 4, pp 322-31.

Kaus, M. (1992) *The end of equality*, New York: Basic Books.

Keating, M. (1975) 'The role of the Scottish MP', PhD thesis, Glasgow College of Technology and Council for National Academic Awards (CNAA).

Keating, M. (2002) 'Devolution and public policy in the United Kingdom: convergence or divergence?', in J. Adams and P. Robinson (eds) *Devolution in practice. Public policy differences within the UK*, London: Institute for Public Policy Research, pp 3-21.

Keating, M. (2003) 'Social inclusion, devolution and policy divergence', *Political Quarterly*, vol 77, no 4, pp 429-38.

Keating, M. (2005a) *The government of Scotland. Public policy making after devolution*, Edinburgh: Edinburgh University Press.

Keating, M. (2005b) 'Higher education policy in Scotland and England after devolution', *Regional and Federal Studies*, vol 14, no 4, pp 423-35.

Keating, M. (2007) 'Public services: renewal and reform', in M. Keating (ed) *Scottish social democracy*, Brussels: Presses interuniversitaires européennes.

Keating, M., Loughlin, J. and Deschouwer, K. (2003a) *Culture, institutions and economic development. A study of eight European regions*, Aldershot: Edward Elgar.

Keating, M., Cairney, P. and Hepburn, E. (forthcoming) 'Territorial policy, communities and devolution in the United Kingdom', *Cambridge Journal of Regions, Economy and Society*.

Communities and Devolution in the United Kingdom[1], Cambridge Journal of

Regions, Economy and Society (in press)

Keating, M., Stevenson, L., Cairney, P. and Taylor, K. (2003b) 'Does devolution make a difference? Legislative output and policy divergence in Scotland', *Journal of Legislative Studies*, vol 9, no 3, pp 110-39.

King, D. (1987) *The new right*, London: Macmillan.

King, D. and Waldron, J. (1988) 'Citizenship, social citizenship and the defence of welfare provision', *British Journal of Political Science*, vol 18, no 4, pp 415-43.

King, D. and Wickham-Jones, M. (1999) 'Bridging the Atlantic: the Democratic (Party) origins of welfare to work', in M. Powell (ed) *New Labour, new welfare state?*, Bristol: The Policy Press, pp 257-80.

King, S. (2000) *Poverty and welfare in England, 1780–1850: A regional perspective*, Manchester: Manchester University Press.

Klausen, J. (1995) 'Social rights advocacy and state building: T.H. Marshall in the hands of social reformers', *World Politics*, vol 47, no 2, pp 244-67.

Klein, R. (1988) 'Acceptable inequalities?', in D. Green (ed) *Acceptable inequalities*, London: IEA, pp 3-20.

Klein, R. (2006) *The new politics of the NHS* (5th edn), Oxford: Radcliffe Publishing.

Kleinman, M. (2002) *A European welfare state? European Union social policy in context*, Basingstoke: Palgrave.

Knijn, T. (2000) 'The rationalized marginalization of care: time is money, isn't it?', in B. Hobson (ed) *Gender and citizenship in transition*, Basingstoke: Macmillan, pp 201-20.

Kohler-Koch, B. (2000) 'Beyond Amsterdam: regional integration as a social process', in A. Wiener and K. Neunreither (eds) *European integration after Amsterdam: Institutional dynamics and prospects for democracy*, Oxford: Oxford University Press, pp 68-91.

Kolb, A.K. (1999) 'European social rights towards national welfare states: additional, substitute, illusory?', in J. Bussemaker (ed) *Citizenship and welfare state reform in Europe*, London: Routledge, pp 167-82.

Kuhnle, S. and Rokkan, S. (1979) 'Marshall, T.H.', in D. Sills (ed) *International encyclopedia of the social sciences, Vol 18 biographical supplement*, New York: Free Press.

Kurzer, P. (2001) *Markets and moral regulation: Cultural change in the European Union*, Cambridge: Cambridge University Press.

Kvist, J. and Saari, J. (eds) (2007) *The Europeanisation of social protection*, Bristol: The Policy Press.

Le Grand, J. (1982) *The strategy of equality*, London: George Allen & Unwin.

Le Grand, J. (2003) *Motivation, agency and public policy: Of knights and knaves, pawns and queens*, Oxford: Oxford University Press.

Le Grand, J., Propper, C. and Robinson, R. (1992) *The economics of social problems* (3rd edn), Basingstoke: Macmillan.

Lees, L.H. (1998) *The solidarities of strangers: The English Poor Laws and the people, 1700–1948*, New York: Cambridge University Press.

Leibfried, S. and Pierson, P. (1995) 'Semisovereign welfare states: social policy in a multitiered Europe', in S. Leibfried and P. Pierson (eds) *European social policy: Between fragmentation and integration*, Washington, DC: Brookings, pp 43-77.

Lewis, G. (2003) 'Difference and social policy', in N. Ellison and C. Pierson (eds) *Developments in British social policy 2*, Basingstoke: Palgrave Macmillan, pp 90-106.

Lewis, G. (ed) (2004) *Citizenship*, Bristol: The Policy Press.

Lewis, J. (1991) *Women and social action in Victorian and Edwardian England*, Aldershot: Edward Elgar.

Lewis, J. (1992) 'Gender and the development of welfare regimes', *Journal of European Social Policy*, vol 2, no 3, pp 159-73.

Lewis, J. (2002) 'Gender and welfare state change', *European Societies*, vol 4, no 4, pp 351-7.

Lewis, S. (2001) 'Restructuring workplace cultures: the ultimate work-family challenge?', *Women in Management Review*, vol 16, no 1, pp 21-9.

Lipsky, M. (1980) *Street-level bureaucracy*, New York: Russell Sage Foundation.

Lister, M. (2005) '"Marshall-ing" social and political citizenship: towards a unified conception of citizenship', *Government and Opposition*, vol 40, no 4, pp 471-91.

Lister, R. (1990) *The exclusive society. Citizenship and the poor*, London: CPAG.

Lister, R. (1994) '"She has other duties" – women, citizenship and social security', in S. Baldwin and J. Falkingham (eds) *Social security and social change*, London: Harvester Wheatsheaf.

Lister, R. (2003) *Citizenship. Feminist perspectives* (2nd edn), Basingstoke: Palgrave Macmillan.

Lohde, L.A. (2005) 'Child poverty and devolution', in J. Adams and K. Schmuecker (eds) *Devolution in practice 2006: Public policy differences within the UK*, London: IPPR.

Low, S. (1904) *The governance of England*, London: T Fisher Unwin.

Lowi, T. (1972) 'Four systems of policy politics and choice', *Public Administration Review*, vol 32, pp 298-310.

Lundberg, S., Pollak, R.A. and Wales, T.J. (1997) 'Do husbands and wives pool their resources?', *Journal of Human Resources*, vol 32, pp 463-80.

McAra, L. (2007) 'Welfarism in crisis. Crime control and penal practice in post-devolution Scotland', in M. Keating (ed) *Scottish social democracy*, Brussels: Presses interuniversitaires européennes.

McCrone, D. and Keating, M. (2007) 'Social democracy and Scotland', in M. Keating (ed) *Scottish social democracy*, Brussels: Presses interuniversitaires européennes.

McEwen, N. (2002) 'State welfare nationalism: the territorial impact of welfare state development in Scotland', *Regional and Federal Studies*, vol 12, pp 66-90.

McEwen, N. (2006) 'Does the recognition of national minorities undermine the welfare state?', in K.G. Banting and W. Kymlicka (eds) *Multiculturalism and the welfare state: Recognition and redistribution in contemporary democracies*, Oxford: Oxford University Press, pp 247-71.

McEwen, N. and Moreno, L. (eds) (2005) *The territorial politics of welfare*, London: Routledge.

McEwen, N. and Parry, R. (2005) 'Devolution and the UK welfare state', in N. McEwen and L. Moreno (eds) *The territorial politics of welfare*, London: Routledge, pp 41-61.

McLean, I. (2005) *The fiscal crisis of the United Kingdom*, Basingstoke: Palgrave.

McLean, I. (2005) 'The national question', in A. Seldon and D. Kavanagh (eds) *The Blair effect: 2001-05*, Cambridge: Cambridge University Press, pp 339-61.

McLean, I. and McMillan, A. (2003) 'The distribution of public expenditure across the UK regions', *Fiscal Studies*, vol 24, no 1, pp 45-71.

McLean, I., Lodge, G. and Schmuecker, K. (2008) *Fair shares? Barnett and the politics of public expenditure*, London: IPPR.

McLeish, H. (2004) *Scotland first. Truth and consequences*, Edinburgh: Mainstream.

Mac Ginty, R. (2006) 'Public attitudes to constitutional options in the context of devolution', in P. Carmichael, C. Knox and R. Osborne (eds) *Devolution and constitutional change in Northern Ireland*, Manchester: Manchester University Press, pp 31-46.

Majone, G. (1994) 'The rise of the regulatory state in Europe', *West European Politics*, vol 17, pp 77-102.

Majone, G. (1998) 'Understanding regulatory growth in the European Community', in D. Hine and H. Kassim (eds) *Beyond the market: The EU and national social policy*, London: Routledge, pp 14-35.

Marks, G., Hooghe, L. and Blank, K. (1996) 'European integration from the 1980s: state-centric v multi-level governance', *Journal of Common Market Studies*, vol 34, pp 341-78.

Marks, G., Hooghe, L. and Schakel, A. (eds) (2008) 'Regional authority in 42 countries, 1950-2006. A measure and five hypotheses', special issue of *Regional and Federal Studies*, vol 18, no 2-3.

Marquand, D. (1988) *The unprincipled society*, London: Jonathan Cape.

Marquand, D. (1992) *The progressive dilemma*, London: Heinemann.

Marquand, D. (2004) *Decline of the public. The hollowing-out of citizenship*, Cambridge: Polity Press.

Marshall, T.H. (1950 [1992]) *Citizenship and social class*, London: Pluto.

Marshall, T.H. (1963) *Sociology at the crossroads*, London: Heinemann.

Marshall, T.H. (1970) *Social policy*, London: Hutchinson.

Marshall, T.H. (1981) *The right to welfare*, London: Heinemann.

Martin, A. and Ross, G. (eds) (2004) *Euros and Europeans: Monetary integration and the European model of society*, Cambridge: Cambridge University Press.

Martins, H. (1974) 'Time and theory in sociology', in J. Rex (ed) *Approaches to sociology*, London: Routledge & Kegan Paul.

Mattli, W. and Slaughter, A.M. (1998) 'Revisiting the European Court of Justice', *International Organization*, vol 52, pp 177-209.

Mätzke, M. (2006) 'Institutional choices about inequality between programmatic intentions and practical decisions: welfare reforms in Germany since WWII', in R. Beatty Riedl, S. Aksartova and K. Michell (eds) *Bridging disciplines, spanning the world. Approaches to inequality, identity, and institutions*, Princeton, NJ: Princeton Institute for International and Regional Studies, pp 50-82.

Midwinter, A., Keating, M. and Mitchell, J. (1991) *Politics and public policy in Scotland*, London: Macmillan.

Ministry of Justice (2007) *The governance of Britain*, Cm 7170, London: The Stationery Office.

Mitchell, J. (2004) 'Scotland: expectations, policy types and devolution', in A. Trench (ed) *Has devolution made a difference? State of the nations 2004*, Exeter: Imprint Academic.

Mitchell, J. (2006) 'Evolution and devolution: citizenship, institutions and public policy', *Publius*, vol 36, no 1, pp 153-68.

Mooney, G. (2004) *Work: Personal lives and social policy*, Bristol: The Policy Press.

Mooney, G., Scott, G. and Williams, C. (2006) 'Introduction: rethinking social policy through devolution', *Critical Social Policy*, vol 26, no 3, pp 483-97.

Moran, M. (1991) 'The frontiers of social citizenship: the case of health care entitlements', in U. Vogel and M. Moran (eds) *The frontiers of citizenship*, Basingstoke: Macmillan, pp 32-57.

Moran, M. (2003) *The British regulatory state: High modernisation and hyper-innovation*, Oxford: Oxford University Press.

Morgan, K. (2001) 'The new territorial politics: rivalry and justice in post-devolution Britain', *Regional Studies*, vol 35, no 4, pp 343-8.

Mossialos, E., Permanand, G., Baeten, R. and Hervey, T.K. (eds) (2008) *Health systems governance in Europe: The role of EU law and policy*. Brussels: European Observatory on Health Systems and Policies/Cambridge: Cambridge University Press.

Mulgan, G. (2005) Responses to questions at the conference 'Que reste-t'il de Cool Britannia?' Le Royaume-uni après huit ans de gouvernement Blair', 4 May (www.cerium.montreal.ca/video/coolbrit_mulgan_questions.wmv).

Nairn, T. (1981) *The break-up of Britain* (2nd edn), London: New Left Books.

Newdick, C. (2008, forthcoming) 'The ECJ, trans-national health care and social citizenship: the accidental death of a concept?', *Wisconsin International Law Journal*.

Noël, A. (1999) 'Is decentralization Conservative?', in R. Young (ed) *Stretching the federation. The art of the state in Canada*, Kingston: Institute of Intergovernmental Relations, Queen's University, pp 195-218.

Oates, W.E. (1999) 'An essay on fiscal federalism', *Journal of Economic Literature*, vol 37, pp 1120-49.

Obinger, H., Leibfried, S. and Castles, F. (2005) *Federalism and the welfare state*, Cambridge: Cambridge University Press.

Ong, A. (2005) '(Re)articulations of citizenship', *PSOnline*, vol 38, pp 697-9.

Orloff, A. (1993) 'Gender and the social rights of citizenship. State policies and gender relations in comparative perspective', *American Sociological Review*, vol 58, no 3, pp 303-28.

Ormston, R. and Curtice, J. (2007) 'Attitudes towards a "British institution": comparing public views of the NHS in England and Scotland', *Scottish Affairs*, no 61, autumn, pp 50-73.

Osborne, D. and Gaebler, T. (1992) *Reinventing government: How the entrepreneurial spirit is transforming the public sector*, Reading, MA: Addison-Wesley.

Pahl, J. (1989) *Money and marriage*, Basingstoke: Macmillan.

Parry, R. (2004) 'The Civil Service and intergovernmental relations', *Public Policy and Administration*, vol 19, no 2, pp 50–63.

Pascall, G. (1986) *Social policy: A new feminist analysis*, Tavistock: London.

Pateman, C. (1988) *The disorder of women*, Cambridge: Polity Press.

Pateman, C. (1992) 'Equality, difference, subordination: the politics of motherhood and women's citizenship', in G. Bock and S. James (eds) *Beyond equality and difference: Citizenship, feminist politics and female subjectivity*, London: Routledge, pp 14-27.

Pateman, C. (1988 [2000]) 'The patriarchal welfare state', reprinted in C. Pierson and F. Castles, *The welfare state reader*, Oxford: Oxford University Press, pp 134-52.

Perrons, D. (2003) 'The new economy and the work life balance. A case study of the new media sector in Brighton and Hove', *Gender, Work and Organisation*, vol 10, no 1, pp 65-93.

Phelan, D.R. (1992) 'Right to life of the unborn v promotion of trade in services: the European Court of Justice and the normative shaping of the European Union', *Modern Law Review*, vol 55, pp 670-89.

Pierson, C. (1998) *Beyond the welfare state?* (2nd edn), Cambridge: Polity Press.

Pierson, C. (2001) *Hard choices*, Cambridge: Polity Press.

Pierson, C. (2007) *Beyond the welfare state? The new political economy of welfare*, Cambridge: Polity Press.

Pierson, P. (1994) *Dismantling the welfare state? Reagan, Thatcher and the politics of retrenchment*, Cambridge: Cambridge University Press.

Pierson, P. and Leibfried, S. (1995) 'The dynamics of social policy integration', in S. Leibfried and P. Pierson (eds) *European social policy: Between fragmentation and integration*, Washington, DC: Brookings, pp 423-65.

Pinker, R. (1971) *Social theory and social policy*, London: Heinemann.

Plant, R. (1991) 'Social rights and the reconstruction of welfare', in G. Andrews (ed) *Citizenship*, London: Lawrence and Wishart, pp 50-64.

Plummer, K. 'The square of intimate citizenship: some preliminary proposals', *Citizenship Studies*, vol 5, no 3, pp 237–53.

Polanyi, K. (1957 [1944]) *The great transformation: The political and economic origins of our times*, Boston: Beacon.

Powell, M. (1995a) 'The strategy of equality revisited', *Journal of Social Policy*, vol 24, pp 163-85.

Powell, M. (1995b) 'Did politics matter? Municipal public health expenditure in the 1930s', *Urban History*, vol 22, pp 360-79.

Powell, M. (1995c) 'On the outside looking in', *Health and Place*, vol 1, no 1, pp 41-50.

Powell, M. (1997) *Evaluating the NHS*, Buckingham: Open University Press.

Powell, M. (1998) 'In what sense a *national* health service?', *Public Policy and Administration,* vol 13, no 3, pp 56–98.

Powell, M. (ed) (1999) *New Labour, new welfare state? The 'third way' in British social policy*, Bristol: The Policy Press.

Powell, M. (2002) 'The hidden history of social citizenship', *Citizenship Studies*, vol 6, no 3, pp 229-44.

Powell, M. and Boyne, G. (2001) 'The spatial strategy of equality and the spatial division of welfare', *Social Policy and Administration*, vol 35, no 2, pp 163-94.

Powell, M. and Exworthy, M. (2003) 'Equal access to health care and the British National Health Service', *Policy Studies*, vol 24, no 1, pp 51-64.

Powell, M. and Hewitt, M. (1998) 'The end of the welfare state?', *Social Policy and Administration*, vol 32, no 1, pp 1-13.

Powell, M. and Hewitt, M. (2002) *Welfare state and welfare change*, Buckingham: Open University Press.

Prowse, M. (2000) 'Mind the gap', *Prospect*, January.

Prosser, T. (2005) *The limits of competition law: Markets and public services*, Oxford: Oxford University Press.

Radaelli, C. (2006) 'Europeanization: solution or problem?', in M. Cini and M.K. Bourne (eds) *Palgrave advances in European Union studies*, Basingstoke: Palgrave Macmillan, pp 56-76.

Raffe, D. (2005) 'Devolution and divergence in education policy', in J. Adams and K. Schmuecker (eds) *Devolution in practice 2006: Public policy differences within the UK*, London: IPPR, pp 52-69.

Rake, K. (1999) 'Accumulated disadvantage? Welfare state provision and the incomes of older women and men in Britain, France and Germany', in J. Clasen (ed) *Comparative social policy: Concepts, theories and methods*, Oxford: Blackwell.

Rapoport, R., Bailyn, L., Fletcher, J. and Pruitt, B. (2002) *Beyond work–family balance: Advancing gender equality and work performance*, London: Wiley.

Rees, A.M. (1995) 'The other T.H. Marshall', *Journal of Social Policy*, vol 24, pp 341-62.

Rees, A.M. (1996) 'T.H. Marshall and the progress of citizenship', in M. Bulmer and A.M. Rees (eds) *Citizenship today: The contemporary relevance of T.H. Marshall*, London: UCL Press, pp 1-24.

Rhodes, R.A.W. (1988) *Beyond Westminster and Whitehall: The sub-central governments of Britain*, London: Unwin Hyman.

Rieger, E. (1992) 'T.H. Marshall: Soziologie, gesellschaftliche Entwicklung und die moralische Ökonomie des Wohlfahrtsstaates', in T.H. Marshall, *Bürgerrechte und soziale Klassen. Zur Soziologie des Wohlfahrtsstaates*, Frankfurt am Main: Campus, pp 7-32.

Robson, W.A. (1953) 'Labour and local government', *Political Quarterly*, vol 24, pp 39-53.

Roche, M. (1992) *Rethinking citizenship: Welfare, ideology and change in modern society*, Cambridge: Polity Press.

Roche, M. (2002) 'Social citizenship: grounds of social change', in E. Isin and B. Turner (eds) *Handbook of citizenship studies*, London: Sage, pp 69-86.

Rom, M.C. (2006) 'Policy races in the American states', in K. Harrison (ed) *Racing to the bottom? Provincial interdependence in the Canadian Federation*, Vancouver: UBC Press, pp 229-56.

Rose, R. (1982) *Understanding the United Kingdom: The territorial dimension in government*, Harlow: Longman.

Rose, R. (1987) *Ministers and ministries: A functional analysis*, Oxford: Clarendon Press.

Sacks, J. (2000) *The politics of hope*, London: Vintage.

Sandford, M. and Hetherington, P. (2005) 'The regions at the crossroads: the future for sub-national government in England', in A. Trench (ed) *The dynamics of devolution: State of the nations 2005*, Exeter: Imprint Academic.

Sapir, A. (2006) 'Globalization and the reform of European social models', *Journal of Common Market Studies*, vol 44, pp 369-90.

Scharpf, F.W. (1996) 'Negative and positive integration in the political economy of European welfare states', in G. Marks, F. Scharpf, P.C. Schmitter and W. Streeck (eds) *Governance in the European Union*, London: Sage Publications, pp 15-39.

Scharpf, F.W. (1999) *Governing in Europe: Effective and democratic?*, Oxford: Oxford University Press.

Scharpf, F.W. (2002) 'The European social model: coping with the challenges of diversity', *Journal of Common Market Studies*, vol 40, pp 645-70.

Schmitter, P.C. (2000) *How to democratize the European Union, and why bother?*, Lanham, MD: Rowman and Littlefield.

Schmuecker, K. and Adams, J. (2005) 'Divergence in priorities, perceived policy failure and pressure for convergence', in J. Adams and K. Schmuecker (eds) *Devolution in practice 2006: Public policy differences within the UK*, London: IPPR, pp 29-51.

Scottish Constitutional Convention (1995) *Scotland's Parliament. Scotland's right*, Edinburgh: Scottish Constitutional Convention.

Scottish Government (2007) *Choosing Scotland's future: A national conversation*, Edinburgh: Scottish Executive.

Seedhouse, D. (1994) *Fortress NHS*, Chichester: John Wiley and Sons.

Segall, S. (2007) 'How devolution upsets redistributive justice', *Journal of Moral Philosophy*, vol 4, no 2, pp 257-72.

Sharpe, L.J. (1982) 'The Labour Party and the geography of inequality: a puzzle' in D. Kavanagh (ed), *The politics of the Labour Party*, London: George Allen and Unwin, pp 135-70.

Sharpe, L.J. (1993) 'The European meso: an appraisal', in L.J. Sharpe (ed) *The rise of meso government in Europe*, London: Sage Publications.

Shaw, J. (2007) *The transformation of citizenship in the European Union*, Cambridge: Cambridge University Press.

Simeon, Rachel (2003) 'The long-term care decision: social rights and democratic diversity', in R. Hazell (ed) *The state and the nations: The third year of devolution in the United Kingdom*, Exeter: Imprint Academic, pp 215-32.

Simeon, Richard (2006a) *Federal-provincial diplomacy: The making of recent policy in Canada* (2nd edn), Toronto: University of Toronto Press.

Simeon, Richard (2006b) 'Federalism and social justice: thinking through the tangle', in S.L. Greer (ed) *Territory, democracy, and justice*, Basingstoke: Palgrave Macmillan, pp 18-43.

Smith, A. (1995) *L'Europe politique au miroir du local: Les fonds structurels et les zones rurales en France, en Espagne, et au Royaume-Uni*, Paris: L'Harmattan.

Smith, A. (2006) 'The government of the European Union and a changing France', in P.D. Culpepper, P.A. Hall and B. Paler (eds) *Changing France: The politics that markets make*, Basingstoke: Palgrave Macmillan, pp 179-97.

Smith, M.P. (2005) *States of liberalization: Redefining the public sector in integrated Europe*, Albany, NY: SUNY.

Somers, M.R. (2005) 'Citizenship troubles: genealogies of struggle for the soul of the social', in J. Adams, E.S. Clemens and A.S. Orloff (eds) *Remaking modernity: Politics, history, and sociology*, Durham, NC: Duke University Press, pp 438-69.

Somers, M.R. (2008) *Genealogies of citizenship: Markets, statelessness and the right to have rights*, Cambridge: Cambridge University Press.

Stevenson, G. (2005) *Unfulfilled union: Canadian federalism and national unity* (4th edn), Montreal and Kingston: McGill–Queen's University Press.

Stewart, J. (1999) *The battle for health. A political history of the Socialist Medical Association, 1930–51*, Aldershot: Ashgate.

Stewart, J. (2004) *Taking stock: Scottish social welfare after devolution*, Bristol: The Policy Press.

Stone Sweet, A. (2004a) 'The constitutionalization of the EU: steps towards a supranational polity', in S. Fabbrini (ed) *Democracy and federalism in the European Union and the United States*, New York: Routledge, pp 55–146.

Stone Sweet, A. (2004b) *The judicial construction of Europe*, Oxford: Oxford University Press.

Streeck, W. (1996) 'Neo-voluntarism: a new European social policy regime?', in G. Marks, F. Scharpf, P.C. Schmitter and W. Streeck (eds) *Governance in the European Union*, London: Sage Publications, pp 64–94.

Subirats, J. (2006) 'The triumph and troubles of the Spanish model', in S.L. Greer (ed) *Territory, justice, and democracy*, Basingstoke: Palgrave Macmillan, pp 175–200.

Swank, D. (2001) 'Institutions and welfare state restructuring: the impact of institutions on social policy change', in P. Pierson (ed) *Developed democracies. In the new politics of the welfare state*, Oxford: Oxford University Press, pp 197–236.

Tarrow, S. (2004) 'Center-periphery alignments and political contention in late-modern Europe', in C.K. Ansell and G. DiPalma (eds) *Restructuring territoriality: Europe and the United States compared*, Cambridge: Cambridge University Press, pp 45–65.

Tilly, C. (1995) 'Citizenship, identity and social history' in C. Tilly (ed) *Citizenship, identity and social history*, International Review of Social History supplement, Cambridge, Cambridge University Press, pp 1–19.

Tilly, C. (1998) 'Where do rights come from?', in T Skocpol (ed) *Democracy, revolution, and history*, Ithaca, NY: Cornell University Press, pp 55–72.

Tilly, C. (1999) 'Conclusion: why worry about citizenship', in M. Hanagan and C. Tilly (eds) *Extending citizenship, reconfiguring states*, Lanham, MD: Rowmand and Littlefield, pp 247–59.

Timmins, N. (2001) *The five giants: A biography of the welfare state* (revised and updated), London: HarperCollins.

Timmins, N. (2007) 'European law looms over NHS contracts', *Financial Times*, 16 January, p 3.

Titmuss, R. (1968) *Commitment to welfare*, London: Allen & Unwin.

Titmuss, R. (1974) *Social policy*, London: George Allen & Unwin.

Tosh, J. (1999) *A man's place: Masculinity and the middle class home in Victorian England*, Bath: Bath Press.

Trench, A. (2005) 'Whitehall and the process of legislation after devolution', in R. Hazell and R. Rawlings (eds) *Devolution, law-making and the constitution*, Exeter: Imprint Academic.

Trench, A. (2006a) 'Intergovernmental relations: in search of a theory', in S.L. Greer (ed) *Territory, democracy and justice*, Basingstoke: Palgrave Macmillan.

Trench, A. (2006b) 'The Government of Wales Act 2006: the next steps in devolution for Wales', *Public Law*, pp 687-96.

Trench, A. (ed) (2007) *Devolution and power in the United Kingdom*, Manchester: Manchester University Press.

Trench, A. (2008a, forthcoming) 'Devolution in Scotland and Wales: muddled thinking and unintended results', in Unlock Democracy (ed) *Unlocking democracy: Twenty years of Charter 88,* London: Politico's.

Trench, A. (2008b) *Higher education and devolution: A report for Universities UK*, London: Universities UK.

Turner, B.S. (1993) 'Contemporary problems in the theory of citizenship', in B.S. Turner (ed) *Citizenship and social theory*, London: Sage Publications, pp 1-18.

Twine, F. (1994) *Citizenship and social rights. The interdependence of self and society*, London: Sage Publications.

van Parijs, P. (ed) (1992) *Arguing for basic income*, London: Verso.

Vogel, U. (1991) 'Is citizenship gender specific?', in U. Vogel and M. Moran (eds) *The frontiers of citizenship*, London: Macmillan Press, pp 58-85.

Vogel, U. (1994) 'Marriage and the boundaries of citizenship', in B. van Steenbergen (ed) *The condition of citizenship*, London: Sage Publications, pp 76-90.

Warleigh, A. (2003) *Democracy in the European Union*, London: Sage Publications.

Watts, R. (1989) *Executive federalism: A comparative analysis*, Kingston: Institute of Intergovernmental Relations, Queen's University.

Weale, A. (2006) *Democratic citizenship and the European Union*, Manchester: Manchester University Press.

Weatherill, S. and Bernitz, U. (eds) (2005) *The role of regions and sub-national actors in Europe*, Oxford: Hart.

White, J. (2004) *From Herbert Morrison to command and control: The decline of local democracy* (www.historyandpolicy.org).

References

White, S. (2000) 'Review article: Social rights and the social contract – political theory and the new welfare politics', *British Journal of Political Science*, vol 30, pp 507-32.

White, S. (2003) *The civic minimum*, Oxford: Oxford University Press.

Williams, F. (2001) 'In and beyond New Labour: towards a new political ethic of care', *Critical Social Policy*, vol 21, no 4, pp 467-93.

Williams, F. (2004) *Rethinking families*, London: Calouste Gulbenkian Foundation.

Williamson, A. and Room, G. (eds) (1983) *Health and welfare states of Britain*, London: Heinemann.

Wincott, D. (2000) 'Globalization and European integration', in C. Hay and D. Marsh (eds) *Demystifying globalization*, Basingstoke: Macmillan, pp 168-90.

Wincott, D. (2003) 'Beyond Social Regulation? New instruments and/ or a new agenda for social policy at Lisbon?', *Public Administration*, vol 81, pp 533-53.

Wincott, D. (2004) 'Rights and regulations in (the) Europe(an Union): after national democracy?', in L. Trägårdh (ed) *After national democracy: Rights, law and power in America and the New Europe*, Oxford: Hart, pp 79-102.

Wincott, D. (2006) 'Social policy and social citizenship: Britain's welfare states', *Publius*, vol 36, no 1, pp 169-88.

Wollstonecraft, M. (1792 [1978]) *A vindication of the rights of women: With strictures on political and moral subjects*, Harmondsworth: Penguin Books.

Woodhouse, D. (1998) 'The judiciary in the 1990s: guardians of the welfare state?', *Policy & Politics*, vol 26, no 4, pp 457-70.

Wyn Jones, R. and Scully, R. (2006) 'Devolution and electoral politics in Wales and Scotland', *Publius: The Journal of Federalism*, vol 36, no 1, pp 115-34.

Wyn Jones, R. and Scully, R. (2008) *Wales devolution monitoring report January 2008* (www.ucl.ac.uk/constitution-unit/research/devolution/ MonReps/Wales_Jan08.pdf).

Young, L. (1994) 'Paupers, poverty and place: a geographical analysis of the English, Irish and Scottish Poor Laws in the mid nineteenth century', *Environment and Planning D: Society and Space*, vol 12, no 3, pp 325-40.

Zeitlin, J. (2005) 'Introduction: the open method of co-ordination in question', in J. Zeitlin and P. Pochet (eds) *The open method of co-ordination in action: The European Employment and Social Inclusion Strategies*, Brussels: Peter Lang Publishing Group, pp 19-35.

Zeitlin, J. and Pochet, P. (eds) (2005) *The open method of co-ordination in action: The European Employment and Social Inclusion Strategies*, Brussels: Peter Lang Publishing Group.

Index

Note: Page references for notes are followed by *n*.

political and social rights 8, 84, 85-6
poverty 155, 156, 157
public services 103-7
public spending 136*n*, 141, 145-8
public support for devolution 81,
    83, 84
social citizenship 111, 112-14, 132
trust in government 86
voting behaviour 91
wealth 151, 152, 153, 154
Wallace, Jim 108
Watts 189-90
wealth 149, 150-4, 159
Webb, Sidney 165
welfare state 49
  continuum 33-4
  and decentralisation 9-10, 11
  and devolution 102
  elite consensus 9-10
  local 164-5
  and Marshallian citizenship 23-4
  see also Beveridge welfare state
    (BWS); Marshall welfare state
    (MWS)
welfare state regimes 182-3
West Lothian Question 80, 92, 93, 95
White, J. 166-7, 169
Wickham-Jones, M. 31
Williamson, A. 163-4
Wilson, Harold 143
Wincott, D. 75
Wistow, G. 163
Wollstonecraft, Mary 64
women
  exclusion and inclusion from
    citizenship 61-5
  Marshall 4, 53
  political rights 25
  social rights 57, 58-61
  universal caregiver model 66-7
Working Time Directive 190
  Wyn Jones, R. 91